THE CONFESSIONS OF A
BEACHCOMBER

"The Beachcomber" and his dog, 1922. *Photo: A. W. Pearse*

THE CONFESSIONS OF A
BEACHCOMBER

Scenes and Incidents in the Career of an Unprofessional
Beachcomber in Tropical Queensland

E. J. BANFIELD

Introductions
ALEC H. CHISHOLM

*If a man does not keep pace with his companions
perhaps it is because he hears a different drummer.
Let him step to the music which he hears.*—THOREAU.

Eden

EDEN PAPERBACKS
an imprint of Angus & Robertson Publishers

Unit 4, Eden Park, 31 Waterloo Road,
North Ryde, NSW, Australia 2113;
94 Newton Road, Auckland 1,
New Zealand; and
16 Golden Square, London W1R 4BN,
United Kingdom

First published by Unwin, London 1908
Reissued 1910, 1913, 1923 and 1924
First Australian edition by Angus & Robertson 1933
Australian Pocket Library edition by
A'sian Publishing Co. 1945
Revised Australian edition by Angus & Robertson 1968
A&R Paperback edition 1974
A&R Non-fiction Classics edition 1977
Arkon paperback edition 1980
Reprinted 1982, 1985
This Eden paperback edition 1987
Reprinted in 1989

ISBN 0 207 15864 9

Printed in Australia by Australian Print Group

INTRODUCTION TO THE FIRST AUSTRALIAN EDITION

RATHER more than twenty years ago, as a bush-fond youth who watched the pageant of the seasons in a quiet district of southern Australia, I somehow acquired a book called *The Confessions of a Beachcomber*, then recently published. How well I remember the glow imparted by those pages! Robinson Crusoe's isle was veiled in the mists of romance. Melville's Marquesas were scarcely less vague. But Dunk Island, albeit never heard of before, had been proclaimed in such forthright fashion, and was relatively so close home, that it became at once definitely tangible—a *real* tropic island. E. J. Banfield had given to airy nothing a local habitation and a name. Here, on a little isle off the coast of northern Queensland, Romance and Reality met and were blended.

Is not one entitled, therefore, to rejoice at having discovered recently—when conning *The Confessions* in the interests of this, the first Australian edition—that the old colour is still present, that it was no mere creation of youthful imaginings? I think now, as I thought long ago, that much of the sunlight and fragrance of tropical Australia is contained in this book. Indeed, I find still a tropic allurement in the very title, and not only the English one, but (in a modified degree) that of the Dutch edition, *Bekentenissen van een Strandvonder*.

This reminiscence of the early appeal of Banfield's first book is not offered merely as a personal tribute, but rather because the particular case had a general application—thousands of readers were similarly captivated. The author was a man who, falling desperately ill through overwork, had retreated to a tropic Isle, where, on regaining strength, he had discovered a new interest in life; and there he and his wife had carved for themselves a home in the wilderness; there they had made friends with aborigines; and, above all, together they had placated the Spirit of the Isle, so that as the years passed they became more and more attached to their insular kingdom and had no desire to return to the haunts of men.

Much of the Beachcomber's warm affection for the Isle—for the untrammelled life which it afforded, and for its novelty, beauty and interest—welled out in his *Confessions*, and at once the imagination of a considerable audience was captured. Jaded book reviewers, stirred by the freshness of the story and the vividness of the telling, cried out that they longed to go a-Dunking. Restless spirits in various corners of the earth wrote to Banfield and begged to be permitted to share his life. One, zestful and determined, came from England unannounced, dropped off a little steamer in Brammo Bay, and imposed upon the hospitality of the Isle for several weeks. Years later, when my own vague dream of a visit to Dunk had become reality, the Beachcomber and I stood on a neighbouring island and regarded silently the ruins of that bold Englishman's cabin in the jungle. Doubtless Banfield reflected then, as I did, that the tropic battle is not always to the physically strong—that temperamental fitness is at least one essential for life on a small island.

The lure of Dunk Island abated somewhat as the initial interest in *The Confessions* eased, but it became potent again with the appearance of other Banfieldian books, and especially so when the Beachcomber's death was proclaimed in the newspapers of the world. It was, indeed, a striking manifestation of the fair fame of the Isle and its overlord that people in every continent wrote to Mrs Banfield, most by way of condolence and some desiring to take up where the Beachcomber left off. A group of prisoners in an American penitentiary (who probably had fallen upon *The Confessions* under a pardonable misapprehension) solicited a copy of one of the later books. At the opposite end of the social scale, a small girl in Wales wrote of her interest in Dunk Island, which, she suggested, would doubtless be "a fine place to play Indians!" That child was wiser than many adults who yearned for cloistered happiness.

The idyll of Dunk Island, extending over twenty-five years, closed on 2nd June 1923, when Banfield was seventy-one years of age. How he died, how his widow kept lonely vigil for three days, and how the crew of a passing steamer came to the rescue—these and kindred matters have been discussed in an Introduction to the posthumous book, *Last Leaves from Dunk Island*. There, too, some account has been given of Banfield himself—his surprising energy, his mercurial temperament, and his jealous regard for the welfare of his neighbours and brother beachcombers. Let it be repeated, however, that Banfield was no mere lotus-eater, and moreover, for all his desertion of the crowded places called civilization, neighbourly feeling amounted almost to a passion with him. I shall never forget the fever of excitement aroused in the master of Dunk Island when we searched for a mainland settler who had disappeared; and I recall also how agitated he became when, through official indifference, he failed to obtain a licence for a Finnish oyster-seeker who worked among the islands. The securing of that licence was a simple task for a journalist within reach of the central authority in Brisbane, but to Banfield the little matter had assumed such importance that he shouted with joy at the outcome, and thereupon sent me a book bearing the scribbled inscription, "To my friend the Dictator—he nods, and even bower-birds twitter!" (That, clearly, was an accolade of sorts, the point being that bower-birds, though highly accomplished, are not given to twittering.)

I have sometimes wondered whether it was because or in spite of his vivid temperament that Banfield was able to remain enthralled by a small island for a quarter-century. Perhaps it was largely a matter of mental balance. He lived as he wrote, with a fine gusto, and yet he was sufficiently disciplined to be content to loiter at the proper time—to watch the play of wild life about him, and to acquire a knowledge of natural history remarkable in a man who lacked the first-hand assistance available in cities. Moreover he retained at all times a lively sense of humour, a fact to which his sketches of the aborigines bear witness.

For all his zest, however, and for all his "inordinate passion for freedom and fresh air", Banfield could scarcely have carried on— certainly he would not have been the clean-living, clear-brained Beachcomber of four books—without the companionship of his cheerful and refined little wife. The former Bertha Golding (English-born like her husband) was no less vital a factor than the Isle itself in the life of her "Teddy". She made as light of her deafness as he did of the loss of an eye, and in stimulating him she put away all thoughts of loneliness in isolation.

Knowing from experience on the Isle something of the ties of affection which bound this childless couple, I sorrowed at the knowledge that Mrs Banfield had been left alone with her dead husband, and this is what she wrote in reply: "I had no idea that

vii

Death could come so peacefully. Indeed, to me at the time it was beautiful, and my chief feeling was one of intense thankfulness that he could suffer no more. As to my being alone, I had not the least fear. What was there to fear in being with the one I have loved best in the world?"

Leaving the Isle rather more than a year later (in August of 1924) Mrs Banfield lived variously in Queensland, New South Wales and Victoria, excusing such belated adventuring with the remark that she was entitled to "a walk-about" after "sitting down" on an island for a quarter-century. But wherever she went, and whatever she did, her thoughts never wandered far from Dunk Island. Nor did any consideration of self intrude on her loyalty to "the master". "Is it necessary," she asked, when the posthumous book was being prepared, "that any portrait of me should be published? I cannot think it is, and somehow feel that I want the book to be just all him." Again, there came this simple note: "You know that my life was for him, and beyond that there is nothing to be said."

Mrs Banfield survived her husband by ten years. She died in August of 1933, and her ashes were deposited beneath the cairn that marks the resting-place of the Beachcomber on Dunk Island. That cairn is, and must always be, a significant Australian memorial. But a greater monument has been created by the four books that were born upon the Isle, and especially by the first and freshest of them, *The Confessions of a Beachcomber*. It is fitting that this book should be issued in an Australian edition—slightly abridged in order to make it more freely available—twenty-five years after its first publication and ten years after the death of its author. It is a book of perennial charm, a distinctive contribution to the romance, literature, and natural history of Australia and the world.

Melbourne, 1933   ALEC H. CHISHOLM

INTRODUCTION TO THE PRESENT EDITION

THIS Introduction is supplementary in a double sense. It succeeds a discussion of "The Beachcomber" and his activities which I wrote when assembling the posthumous book of 1925, *Last Leaves from Dunk Island*, and, more directly, it is a sequel to the Introduction published in the present work when it was first issued in an Australian edition in 1933 and when it was re-issued as a Guild Press paperback in 1945.

At this stage, however, it seems desirable to give those notes of 1933 yet another airing—as is here done, with slight amendments —the point being that both *The Confessions* and *Last Leaves* (and the other two Banfield books as well) have long been out of print, and therefore many people of today, potentially interested, may know little of the novel and picturesque story that centres upon the "fairest and best" of Australia's tropic islands.

Otherwise, my chief concern is to make certain comments regarding developments on Dunk Island in the post-Banfield period.

Personally, I had remained out of direct contact with the Isle for forty-six years. That is to say, after residing there as guest of Ted and Bertha Banfield in 1921 I had refrained (chiefly to avoid a possible shattering of memories) from returning to the spot until 1967; and then, as matters fell out, two visits were made in the one year, the first in April for the unveiling of a portrait of The Beachcomber and the second six months later in connection with the selecting of a site for a museum of Banfieldiana.

It impressed me on these later occasions, when we flew from Sydney to the Isle in one day, to reflect that in 1921 my shorter journey to Dunk, from Brisbane, through the medium of a train, two ships, and a row-boat, had occupied almost a week. By the same token, however—while reflecting on the march of progress —I was disturbed by the thought that "development" may have grievously affected the once-tranquil island. Possession of the freehold portion had, according to report, changed hands several times since Banfield's day, and as the Isle as a whole had become a tourist attraction, complete with aircraft facilities, certain forebodings seemed to be justified.

How refreshing it was, therefore, to discover that commonsense and discretion had obtained, at least latterly, in relation to the claims of that assertive influence, "Development".

True, the Banfield bungalow and workshop had vanished— their site, indeed, was now lost amid the impetuous re-growth of rain-forest—but otherwise I found little reason for lamentation. No trace remained of the military installations established on the Isle during World War II. The "new" buildings, consisting of numbers of cabins, together with a small hotel and restaurant that included parts of the old bungalow, were neatly placed among the palms and other tropical plants beside Brammo Bay. No less gratifying, two runways for aircraft had been constructed without damage to anything more than a relative trifle of scrub. And, of course, the ridgy backbone of the Isle, most of it reserved as a National Park, featuring rich vegetation and aboriginal art, remained, as of yore, a haunt of ancient peace.

In brief, then, it was distinctly uplifting to find (as in fact a visiting American professor had assured me would be the case) that Dunk Island was still a most endearing spot. Whatever clearances had been effected in the immediate post-Banfield period, and they may really have been slight, the present owners of the private portion, the Avis Air Charter Company, together with the Queensland Forest Service, had co-operated with Nature to heal the scars and to create and maintain that all-too-rare condition, an amiable balance between the "wild" and the "tame". (Actually, the reserved portion greatly predominates, consisting as it does of 6000 acres as opposed to 360 acres in private control.)

It soon became apparent, too, that my own relief gained from this state of affairs was shared by those original inhabitants of the Isle, the tropical birds. Here at once I saw the beautiful little sun-birds feasting among the blossoms of hibiscus, as their predecessors did in the Banfield garden. Here also, fairly among the trees surrounding the cabins, varied honeyeaters were chortling melodiously and numbers of the curious fish-tailed drongos (Banfield's "black detectives") flitted into view. And, a little later, in the tall and thick vegetation that has upsurged on the site of the former homestead, I heard the mound-building jungle-fowl uttering his odd cackling, together with the dulcet voice of the island thrush which the aborigines used to term "Moor-goody".

Those particular bird-contacts were not unexpected. Surprisingly, however, as dusk descended each day there arose from trees near Brammo Bay the singular calls of the large-tailed nightjar— the measured "tock-tock-tock" that has caused this nocturnal roamer to be known as the "carpenter-bird" and "axe-bird". I had not heard calls of the kind when dwelling on the Isle long ago, and thus it was agreeable to find such a notable bird adapting itself to the changed conditions.

On the whole, then, when standing in the secluded grove where a cairn surmounts the grave of Edmund James and Bertha Banfield, I felt almost disposed to offer them both a measure of assurance—to tell them that their cherished Isle was still in good shape, and to inform Bertha, in particular, that the descendants of "Jacky", her pet visiting honeybird, and other kinds which she esteemed, were keeping the flag flying.

Possibly The Beachcomber sometimes cogitated concerning the fate of his little kingdom in the years ahead. If so, doubtless he guessed that the flora of the Isle, having remarkably recuperative powers, would hold its own if given a reasonable chance. Possibly, too, he did sometimes think (on the basis of his own worrying experiences with indiscreet callers) that the spot might eventually become popular. What he certainly did not envisage, however, was that he himself would become something in the nature of a national figure. Essentially a modest fellow, one who had to be coaxed into submitting to even a casual photograph, he would, I imagine, have been staggered by a vision of himself as the subject of two portraits (in one year) and as the focusing-point of a distinctive museum on his tropic isle.

For my own part, when thinking back to those springtime nights of 1921, as we sat talking and arguing about books and birds in the peace of the island bungalow, a peace not unduly disturbed by our own voices or the "clickety-clacking" of jungle-fowl in the adjacent scrub—when meditating on those occasions I find difficulty in imagining what thoughts fore-knowledge would have aroused. It is, indeed, a nice problem as to which of us would have been the more astonished if informed that in time—almost half a century later—I would unveil those two portraits of E.J.B., the one (by J. Louttit) on the Isle itself, and the other (by Clifton

Pugh) at History House in Sydney. Mark the oddities that arise through the operations of the whirligig of Time!

The fact that one of the unveilings took place in Sydney makes it desirable to add that although the reputation of Banfield is indelibly associated with the tropics, his Australian experience began in Victoria and New South Wales. Born in Liverpool, on 4th September 1852, he left England in care of his mother, along with two sisters and a brother (aged from eight to four), in November 1854. Their ship, the *Indian Queen*, a vessel of 1050 tons carrying 367 passengers, reached Melbourne in February '55.

The father, Jabez W. Banfield, with his brother James, had migrated earlier, and after joining in several rushes to goldfields, varied by employment in Melbourne at his English trade, printing, had gone to central Victoria and joined in founding the *Maryborough and Dunolly Advertiser*. (This newspaper, which still continues, was incidentally the one on which I made my own journalistic beginning in 1911.) Then, in 1857, J. W. Banfield took his wife and family to Ararat where he launched another *Advertiser*, one upon which he remained and which is in the control of his descendants to this day.

Ararat was the scene of two governing developments in Ted Banfield's career. It was there that he began his journalistic experience, and there too (as certain volumes now in my possession make clear) that he founded a life-long devotion to Shakespeare.

Newspaper work lured him to Sydney later, and in 1882 he took what was a daring step at the time by transferring to far-off Townsville. There, intensive work on the *Daily Bulletin* was broken by a visit to England in 1884—an excursion that, happily, resulted in Bertha Golding migrating to Australia and marrying him in 1886. But, as recorded earlier, nervous exhaustion put an end to newspaper employment in time; and thus in 1897 there began, more or less as a matter of desperation, the insular life that was, unexpectedly, to transform an average, diligent journalist into a notable figure and to give the world what is now known as the Idyll of Dunk Island.

Various factors sustained Banfield in his early years on the Isle, and indeed during the whole of his quarter-century of life there. Most importantly, he was stimulated by the companionship of his intelligent and cheery little wife. Between whiles too he served as counsellor to fishermen and other casual workers in the region, and at intervals he came into friendly contact with the few settlers on the mainland opposite, notably three well-informed pioneers, the Cutten brothers of Clump Point. Moreover, in the nature of his semi-isolated case The Beachcomber was faced with a wide range of workaday tasks—did he not confess to being a slave to his own wheelbarrow?—and, in a broader aspect, his active mind became engrossed from an early stage in both the human history and the natural history of his domain.

Although a sound reader, he had only a sketchy knowledge of Australian history before settling on the Isle. But he knew the basic story of the days of discovery, at least on the east coast, and it was largely his appreciation of a great navigator that caused him to join officialdom in retaining the Cook-given name of Dunk rather than the native term, Coonanglebah.

Most of the names bestowed on features of the locality by Cook commemorated English notabilities. They included Rockingham Bay, after the Marquis of Rockingham (sometime Prime Minister), Hinchinbrook Island, which he supposed to be part of the mainland and named (as a mount) in recognition of a Montagu family seat, and Halifax Bay, Cape Sandwich, and Dunk Isle, all having reference to either John or George Montagu, the one Earl of Sandwich and the other Earl of Halifax whose family name was Dunk. Incidentally, when on 8th June (1770) Cook was recording "a tolerable high Island known in the Chart by the name of Dunk Isle", he commented that it lay "so close to the shore as not to be distinguished from it unless you are well in with the land". That implies, of course, that the *Endeavour* party gained a fair view of the little island, and one imagines that Joseph Banks gazed with longing at it; certainly he would have profited by even a few hours among its rich plant-life.

Cook left some other names in the area. He and his colleagues had been much impressed by the multitude of isles thereabouts, and (as does not appear to be generally known) they went ashore twice on the adjacent mainland. The first stop, a brief one on 7th June at a point slightly below Rockingham Bay, revealed somewhat barren country (though Banks "made a shift to gather 14 or 15 new plants" there); and the second landing, on 9th June, was at the inlet now known as Mission Bay, in the vicinity of the present city of Cairns. In the latter case, Cook had thoughts of staying at least a day, the intention being "to have looked into the

Country had we met with fresh water convenient or any other refreshment", but as the water was "difficult to get at" they decided to push on—and on the next night the gallant little ship crashed on to Endeavour Reef.

Building upon knowledge of Cook's contact with the region, Banfield became keenly interested in two other historical figures, namely Edmund B. Kennedy and John MacGillivray. It was from Tam o' Shanter Point, immediately opposite the Isle, that Kennedy began his tragic overland expedition to Cape York in 1848, and in the same year MacGillivray, a very competent naturalist attached to the exploratory vessel H.M.S. *Rattlesnake*, worked on Dunk Island, where his discoveries included the first specimen of a dainty little bird now known as the white-eared flycatcher. Almost inevitably, therefore, The Beachcomber's peeps into the past, linking with growth of attachment to his new environment, caused him to become a district historian of merit and a naturalist who revealed many curious facts, hitherto unknown, concerning wildlife of the tropics.

Given less mental resilience, the former busy city-dweller might have found, in time, that even such engaging surroundings were not proof against the pressure of isolation. Certainly that would have been the case with many others, mainly armchair adventurers, who yearned to follow his example. It was The Beachcomber's good fortune that he was able to look upon his Isle as a happy haven, that his loyalty to tropical Australia and its people remained strong, and, above all, that he never allowed familiarity to dim his sense of wonder.

It is, I think, the persisting sense of wonder, no less than information, that illumines the Banfield books and gives them broad and permanent appeal. And if, as seems probable, little Dunk Island itself is to retain and extend that appeal, we may fairly hope that it will not be looked upon simply as a "tourist attraction", but will promote among visitors the appreciation of scenic beauty, and the response to the wonders of tropical flora and fauna, that so enriched the lives of Edmund and Bertha Banfield.

Sydney, 1968.   ALEC H. CHISHOLM

FOREWORD

DOES the fact that a weak mortal sought an unprofaned sanctuary —an island removed from the haunts of men—and there dwelt in tranquillity, happiness and security, represent any just occasion for the relation of his experiences—experiences necessarily out of the common? To this proposition it will be for these pages to find answer.

We cannot always trust in ourselves and in the boldest of our illusions. There must be trial. Then, if success be achieved and the illusion becomes real and transcendental, and other things and conditions merely "innutritious phantoms", were it not wise, indeed essential, to tell of it all, so that mayhap the illusions of others may be put to the test?

Not that it is good or becoming that many should attempt the part of the beachcomber. All cannot play it who would. Few can be indifferent to that which men commonly prize. All are not free to test touchy problems with the acid of experience. Besides, there are not enough thoughtful islands to go round. Only for the few are there ideal or even convenient scenes for those who, while perceiving some of the charms of solitude, are at the same time compelled by circumstances ever and anon to administer to their favourite theories resounding smacks, making them jump to the practical necessities of the case.

Here then I come to a point at which frankness is necessary. In these pages there will be an endeavour to refrain from egotism; and yet, how may one who lives a lonesome life on an island and who presumes to write its history evade that duty? My chief desire is to set down in plain language the sobrieties of everyday occurrences—the unpretentious homilies of an unpretentious man— one whose mental bent enabled him to take but a superficial view of most of the large, heavy and important aspects of life, but who has found light in things and subjects homely, slight and casual; who perhaps has queer views on the pursuit of happiness, and who above all has an inordinate passion for freedom and fresh air.

Moreover, these chronicles really have to do with the lives of two people—not youthful enthusiasts, but beings who had arrived at an age when many of the minor romances are of the past. Whosoever looks for the relation of sensational adventures, exciting situations, or even humorous predicaments, will assuredly be disappointed. Possibly there may be something to interest those who wish to learn a few of the details of the foundation of a home in tropical Australia; and to understand the conditions of life here, not as they affect the man of independence who seeks to enlarge his fortune, nor the settler who in the sweat of his face has to eat bread, but as they affect one to whom has been given neither poverty nor riches, and who has proved (to his own satisfaction at least) the wisdom of the sage who wrote—"If you wish to increase a man's happiness seek not to increase his possessions, but to decrease his desires." Success will have been achieved if these pages reveal candour and truthfulness, and if thereby proof is given that in North Queensland one "can draw nearer to nature, and though the advantages of civilization remain unforfeited, to the happy condition of the simple, uncomplicated man".

Brammo Bay,   E. J. BANFIELD.
  Dunk Island.

CONTENTS

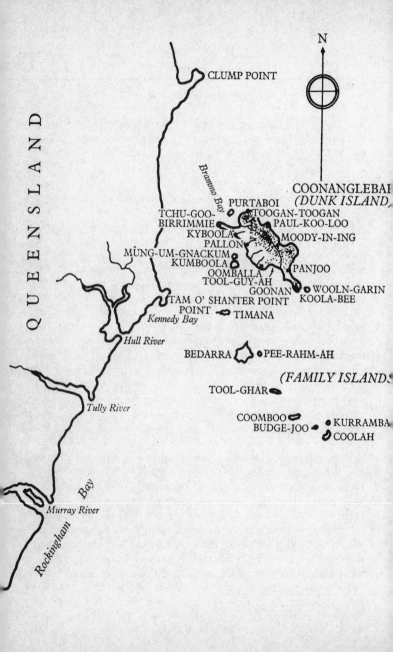

CHAPTER I

Two and a half miles off the north-eastern coast of Australia—midway, roughly speaking, between the southern and the northern limits of the Great Barrier Reef, that low rampart of coral which is one of the wonders of the world—is an island bearing the old English name of Dunk.

Other islands and islets are in close proximity, a dozen or so within a radius of as many miles, but this Dunk Island is the chief of its group, the largest in area, the highest in altitude, the nearest the mainland, the fairest, the best. It possesses a well-sheltered haven (herein to be known as Brammo Bay), and three perennially running creeks mark a further splendid distinction. It has a superficial area of over three square miles. Its topography is diversified—hill and valley, forest and jungle, grassy combes and bare rocky shoulders, gloomy pockets and hollows, cliffs and precipices, bold promontories and bluffs, sandy beaches, quiet coves and mangrove flats. A long V-shaped valley opens to the south-east between steep spurs of a double-peaked range. Four satellites stand in attendance, enhancing charms superior to their own.

This island is our home. He who would see the most picturesque portions of the whole of the two thousand miles of the east coast of Australia must pass within a few yards of our domain.

In years gone by, Dunk Island, "Coonanglebah" of the blacks, had an evil repute. Fertile and fruitful, set in the shining sea abounding with dugong, turtle and all manner of fish; girt with rocks rough-cast with oysters; teeming with bird-life, and but little more than half an hour's canoe trip from the mainland, it carried dusky denizens who were fat, proud, high-spirited, resentful, treacherous, and far from friendly or polite to strangers. One sea-captain was maimed for life in our quiet little bay during a misunderstanding with a hasty black possessed of a new bright tomahawk, a rare prize in those days. This was the most trivial of the many incidents by which the natives expressed their character. Inhospitable acts were common when the white folks first

3

began to pay the island visits, for they found the blacks hostile and daring. Why invoke those long-silent spectres, white as well as black, when all active boorishness is of the past? Civilization has almost fulfilled its inexorable law; only four out of a considerable population remain, and they remember naught of the bad old times when the humanizing processes, or rather the results of them, began to be felt. They must have been a fine race—fine for Australian aboriginals at least—judging by the stamp of two of those who survive; and perhaps that is why they resented interference, and consequently soon began to give way before the irresistible pressure of the whites. Possibly, had they been more docile and placid, the remnants would have been more numerous though less flattering representatives of the race. You shall judge of the type by what is related of some of the habits and customs of the semi-civilized survivors.

Dunk Island is well within the tropical zone, its true bearings being 146 deg. 11 min. 20 sec. E. long., and 17 deg. 55 min. 25 sec. S. lat. It is but thirty miles south of the port of Innisfail, the wettest place in Australia, as well as the centre of the chief sugar-producing district of the State of Queensland. There the rainfall averages about 140 inches per annum. Innisfail has in its immediate background two of the highest mountains in Australia (5400 feet), and on these the monsoons buffet and break their moisture-laden clouds, affording the district much meteorological fame. Again, twenty miles to the south lies Hinchinbrook Island, twenty-eight miles long, twelve miles broad, and mountainous from end to end: there also the rain-clouds revel. The long and picturesque channel which divides Hinchinbrook from the mainland, and the complicated ranges of mountains away to the west, participate in phenomenal rain.

Opposite Dunk Island the coastal range recedes and is of much lower elevation, and to these facts perhaps is to be attributed our modified rainfall compared with the plethora of the immediate north; but we get our share, and when people deplore the droughts which devastate Australia, let it be remembered that Australia is huge, and the most rigorous of Australian droughts merely partial.

Within the tropics heat is inevitable, but our island enjoys several climatic advantages. The temperature is equable. Blow the wind whithersoever it listeth, and it comes to us cooled by contact with the sea. Here may we drink oft and deep at the never-

4

failing font of pure, soft, beneficent air. We have all the advantages which residence at the happy mean from the equator bestows, and few of the drawbacks. By its fruits ye shall know the fertility of the soil.

Birds are numerous, from the "scrub fowl" which dwells in the dim jungle and constructs of decaying leaves and wood and light loam the most trustworthy of incubators, and wastes no valuable time in the dead-and-alive duty of sitting, to the tiny sun-bird of yellow and purple, which flits all day among scarlet hibiscus blooms, sips nectar from the flame-tree, and rifles the dull red studs of the umbrella-tree of their sweetness.

The stalled ox is not here, nor the fatted calf, nor any of the mere advantages of the table; but there is the varied harvest of the sea, and all the freshness of an isle clean and green. The heat, the clatter, the stuffy odours, the toilsomeness, the fatigue of town life are abandoned; the careless quiet, the calm, the refreshment of the whole air, the tonic of the wide sea are gained. From the moment the sun illumines our hills and isles with glowing yellow until it drops in fiery splendour suddenly out of sight, leaving a band of gleaming red above the purple western range, and a rippling red path across to Australia, the whole realm of nature seems ours to command.

OFFICIAL LANDING

Dunk Island was not selected haphazard as an abiding place. By camping-out expeditions and the cautious gleaning of facts from those who had the repute of knowing the country, useful information had been acquired unobtrusively. We were determined to have the best obtainable isle. More than one locality was favourably considered ere good fortune decided to send us hither to spy out the land. A camp-out on the shore of then unnamed Brammo Bay—a holiday-making party—and the result of the first day's exploration decided a revolutionary change in the lives of two seriously-minded persons. A year after, a lease of the best portion of the island having been obtained in the meanwhile, we came for good.

Wholly uninhabited, entirely free from traces of the mauling paws of humanity, lovely in its mantle of varied foliage, what better sphere for the exercise of benign autocracy could be desired? Here was virgin country, twenty miles from the nearest port—sad and neglected Cardwell cut off from the mainland by more than two miles of estranging ocean, and yet lying in the track of small coastal steamers—here all our pet theories might develop serenely.

But it was an inauspicious landing. With September begin the north-east winds, and we had an average experience that afternoon. Was it not a farce—a great deal more than a farce: a saucy, flippant imposition on the tender mercies of providence—for an individual who could not endure a few hours of tossing on the bosom of the ocean without becoming deadly sick, to imagine that he possessed the hardihood to establish a home even in this lovely wilderness? We had tents and equipment and a boat of our own, a workman to help us at the start, and two faithful black servants.

The year before, we had made the acquaintance of one of the few survivors of the native population of the island—stalwart Tom. Although our project and preparations had been kept fairly secret, he had overhead a casual reference to them; had made a canoe, and paddling from island to island with his gin, an infant and mother-in-law, had preceded our advent by a week. His duties began with the discharging of the first boatload of portable property. He comes and goes now after the lapse of years.

They spread out tents and rugs for the weak mortal who had greatly dared, but who, thus early, was ready to faint from weariness and sickness. They made comforting and soothing drinks, and spoke of cheery things in cheery tones; but the sick man refused to be comforted. He wished himself back, a participator in the conflicts of civilization, and was fain to cover his face—there was no wall to which to turn—and fancy that the most dismal sound in the universe was the surly monotone the north-easter harped on the beach. We reposed that night among the camp equipment, the sick man caring for naught in his physical collapse and disconsolation.

But the first morning of the new life! A perfect combination of invigorating elements. The cloudless sky, the clear air, the shining sea, the green folded slopes of Tam o' Shanter Point opposite, the cleanliness of the sand, the sweet odours from the eucalypts and the dew-laden grass, the luminous purple of the islands to the south-east; the range of mountains to the west and north-west, and our own fair tract—awaiting and inviting, and all the mystery of petted illusions about to be solved! Physic was never so eagerly

6

swallowed nor wrought a speedier or surer cure.

Feebleness and dismay vanished with the first plunge into the still sleepy sea, and alertness and vigour returned, as the incense of the first morning's sacrifice went straight as a column to the sky.

Over half a century before, Edmund B. Kennedy, the explorer, landed on the opposite shore, on his ill-fated expedition up Cape York, to find the country inland from Tam o' Shanter Point altogether different from any previously-examined part of Australia. We gave no thought to the gallant explorer, near as we were to the scenes of his desperate struggle in the entanglements of the jungle.

The bustle of the transport of goods and chattels to the site in the thick forest invisible from the sea began at once. Before sunset, tents were pitched among the trees, and a few yards of bush surrounding them cleared, and we were at home.

Prior to departing from civilization we had arranged for the construction of a hut of cedar, so contrived with nicely adjusting parts and bolts, and all its members numbered, that a mere amateur could put it together. If at the end of six months' trial the life was found to be unendurable, or serious object not dreamt of in our salad philosophy became apparent, then our dwelling could be packed up again. All would not be lost.

The clearing of a sufficient space for the accommodation of the hut was no light task for unaccustomed hands, for the bloodwood trees were mighty and tough, and the dubious work of burning up the trunks and branches while yet green, in our eagerness for free air and tidiness, was undertaken. It was also accomplished.

For several weeks there was little done save to build a kitchen and shed and widen the clearing in the forest. Inspection of the details of our domain was reserved as a sort of reward for present task and toil. According to the formula neatly printed in official journals, the building of a slab hut is absurdly easy—quite a pastime for the settler eager to get a roof of bark or thatch over his head. The frame, of course, goes up without assistance, and then the principal item is the slabs for walls. When you have fallen your tree and sawn off a block of the required length, you have only to split off the slab. Ah! but suppose the timber does not split freely, and your heavy maul does; and the wedges instead of entering have the habit of bouncing out as if they were fitted with internal springs; and your maul needs renewal several times, until

7

you find that the timber prescribed is of no account for such tools; and at best your slabs run off to nothing at half length; and several trees have to be cut down before you get a single decent slab, and everybody is peevish with weariness and disappointment—then the rudest house in the bush will be a long time in the building.

"Experience is a hard mistress, yet she teacheth as none other." We came to be more indebted to the hard mistress—she gave us blistering palms and aching muscles—than to all the directions and prescriptions of men who claim to have climbed to the top of the tree in the profession of the "bush". A "bush" carpenter is a very admirable person, when he is not also a bush lawyer. Mere amateurs would be wise if they held their enthusiasm in check when they read the recipe—pat as the recipe for the making of a rice-pudding—for the construction of even a bark hut. It is so very easy to write it all down; but if you have had no actual experience in bark-cutting, and your trees are not in the right condition, you will put your elation to a shockingly severe test, harden the epidermis of your hands, and the whole of your heart, and go to bed many nights sadly ere you get one decent sheet for your roof.

We do not all belong to the ancient and honourable family of the Swiss Robinsons, who performed a series of unassuming miracles on their island. There was no practical dispensation of providential favours on our behalf. Trees that had the reputation of providing splendid splitting timber defiantly slandered themselves, and others that should have almost flayed themselves at the first tap of the tomahawk had not the slightest regard for the reputation vouched for in serious publications.

But why "burden our remembrance with a heaviness that's gone"? Why recall the memory of those acheful days, when all the pleasant and restful features of the island are uncatalogued? Before the rains began we had comfortable if circumscribed shelter. Does not that suffice? Our dwelling consisted of one room and a kitchen. Perforce the greater part of our time was spent out of doors. Isolation kept us moderately free from visitors. Those who did violate our seclusion had to put up with the consequences. We had purchased liberty. Large liberties are the birthright of the English. We had acquired most of the small liberties, and the ransom paid was the abandonment of many things hitherto deemed to form an integral part of existence.

Had we not cast aside all traditions, revolting from the uniformity of life, from the rules of the bush as well as from the conventionalities of society? Here we were to indulge our caprices, work out our own salvation, live in accordance with our own primitive notions, and, if possible, find Pleasure in haunts which it is not popularly supposed to frequent.

Others may point to higher ideals and tell of exciting experiences, of success achieved, and glory and honour won. Ours not to envy superior qualifications and victories which call for strife and struggle, but to submit ourselves joyfully to the charms of the "simple life".

OUR ISLAND

Awake, O North Wind, and come thou South,
Bow upon my garden, that the spices thereof may flow out.

Our island! What was it when we came into possession? From the sea, merely a range displaying the varied leafage of jungle and forest. A steep headland springing from a ledge of rock on the north, and a broad, embayed-based flat converging into an obtruding sand-spit to the west, enclose a bay scarcely half a mile from one horn to the other, the sheet of water almost a perfect crescent, with the rocky islet of Purtaboi, plumed with trees, to indicate the circumference of a circle. Trees come to the water's edge from the abutment of the bold eminence. Dome-shaped shrubs of glossy green (native cabbage—*Scaevola Koenigii*), with groups of pandanus palms bearing massive orange-coloured fruits; and here and there graceful umbrella-trees, with deep-red decorations, hibiscus bushes hung with yellow funnels, and a thin line of ever-sighing beech oaks (*Casuarina*) fringe the clean untrodden sand. Behind is the vistaless forest of the flat.

Run the boat on the sand at high-water, and the first step is planted in primitive bush—fragrant, clean and undefiled. An empty jam tin or a broken bottle, spoors of the rude hoofs of civilization, you might search for in vain. As difficult as would it be to find either as a fellow to the nugget of gold which legend tells was used by a naked black as a sinker when he fished with hook of pearl-shell out there on the edge of the coral reef.

One superficial feature of our domain is distinct and peculiar, giving to it an admirable character. From the landing-place—rather more up towards the north-east cusp than the exact middle

9

of the crescent bay—extends a flat of black sand on which grows a dense bush of wattles, cockatoo apple-trees, pandanus palms, Moreton Bay ash and other eucalypts, and the shapely melaleuca. This flat, here about one hundred and fifty yards in breadth, ends abruptly at a steep bank which gives access to a plateau sixty feet above sea-level. The regularity of the outline of this bank is remarkable. Running in a more or less correct curve for a mile and a half, it indicates a clear-cut difference between the flat and the plateau. The toe of the bank rests upon sand, while the plateau is of chocolate-coloured soil intermixed on the surface with flakes of slate; and from this sure foundation springs the backbone of the island. On the flat, the plateau, and the hillside the forest consists of similar trees—alike in age and character for all the difference in soil—the one tree that does not leave the flat being the tea-tree or melaleuca. In some places the jungle comes down to the water's edge, the long antennae of the lawyer-vine toying with the rod-like aerial roots of the mangrove.

The plateau is the park of the island, half a mile broad, and a mile and more long. Upon it grows the best of the bloodwoods (*Eucalyptus corymbosa*), the red stringybark (*E. robusta*), Moreton Bay ash (*E. tessalaris*), various wattles, and the gin-gee of the blacks (*Diplanthera tetraphylla*). *Pandanus aquaticus* marks the courses and curves of some of the gullies. A creek, hidden in a broad ribbon of jungle and running from a ravine in the range to the sea, divides our park in fairly equal portions.

Most of the range is heavily draped with jungle—that is, on the western aspect. Just above the splash of the Pacific surges on the weather or eastern side, low-growing scrub and restricted areas of forest, with expansive patches of jungle, plentifully intermixed with palms and bananas, creep up the precipitous ascent to the summit of the range—eight hundred and seventy feet above the sea. So steep is the Pacific slope that, standing on the top of the ridge and looking down, you catch mosaic gleams of the sea among the brown and grey tree-trunks. But for the prodigality of the vegetation, one slide might take you from the cool mountain-top to the cooler sea. The highest peak, which presents a buttressed face to the north, and overlooks our peaceful bay, is crowned with a forest of bloodwoods, upon which the jungle steadily encroaches. The swaying fronds of aspiring palms, adorned in due season with masses of straw-coloured inflorescence, to be succeeded by loose bunches of red, bead-like berries, shoot out from the pall of leafage. In the gloomy gullies are slender-shafted palms and tree-ferns, while ferns and mosses cover the soil with living tapestry, and strange, snake-like epiphytes cling in sinuous curves to the larger trees. The trail of the lawyer-vine (*Calamus*), with its leaf sheath and long tentacles bristling with incurved hooks, is over it all. Huge cables of vines trail from tree to tree, hanging in loops and knots and festoons, the largest (*Entada scandens*) bearing pods four feet long and four inches broad, containing a dozen or so brown hard beans which are sometimes used for match-boxes. Along the edge of the jungle, the climbing fern (*Lygodium*) grows in tangled masses sending its slender wire-like lengths up among the trees— the most attractive of all the ferns, and glorified by some with the title of "the Fern of God", so surpassing are its grace and beauty.

September is the prime month of the year in tropical Queensland. Many of the trees and most of the orchids are then in blossom. Nocturnal showers occur fairly regularly in normal seasons, and every sort of vegetable is rampant with the lust of life. It was September when our isolation began. And what a plenteous realization it all was that the artificial emotions of the town had been, haply, abandoned! The blood tingled with keen appreciation of the crispness, the cleanliness, of the air. We had won disregard of the bother and contradictions, the vanities and absurdities of the toilful, wayward, human world, and had acquired a glorious sense of irresponsibleness and independence.

This was our very own life we were beginning to live; not life hampered and restricted by the wills, wishes and whims of others, but life unencumbered by the domineering wisdom, unembarrassed by the formal courtesies of the crowd.

September and the gin-gee! The quaint, grey-barked, soft-wooded tree with broad, rough, sage-green leaves, and florets massed in clumps to resemble sunflowers, was in all its pride, attracting relays of honey-imbibing birds during the day, and at night dozens of squeaking flying-foxes. Within a few yards of high-water stands a flame-tree (*Erythina indica*), the "bingum" of the blacks. Devoid of leaves in this leafy month, the bingum arrays itself in a robe of royal red. All manner of birds, and butterflies and bees and beetles which have regard for colour and sweetness come hither to feast. Sulphur-crested cockatoos sail down upon the red raiment of the tree, and tear from it shreds until all the grass is ruddy with refuse, and their snowy breasts stained as though their feast was of blood instead of colourless nectar. For many days here is a scene of a perpetual banquet—a noisy, cheerful, frolicsome revel. Cockatoos scream with excitement and gladness; honey-eaters whistle and call; drongos chatter and scold the rest of the banqueters; the tiny sun-bird twitters feeble protests; bees and beetles maintain a murmurous soothful sound, a drowsy blending of hum and buzz from the rising of the sun until the going down thereof.

The dark compactness of the jungle, the steadfast but disorderly array of the forest, the blotches of verdant grass, the fringe of yellow-flowered hibiscus and the sapful native cabbage, give way in turn to the greys and yellows of the sand in alternate bands. The slowly-heaving sea trailing the narrowest flounce of lace on the beach, the dainty form of Purtaboi, and the varying tones of great Australia beyond combine to complete the scene, and to confirm the thought that here is the ideal spot, the freest spot, the spot where dreams may harden into realities, where unvexed peace may smile.

You may follow up the creeks until they become miniature ravines, or broaden out into pockets with precipitous sides, where twilight reigns perpetually, and where sweet soft gases are generated by innumerable plants, and distilled from the warm moist soil. How grateful and revivifying!

Past the rocky horn of Brammo Bay, another crescent indents the base of the hill. Exposed to the north-east breeze, the turmoil of innumerable gales has torn tons upon tons of coral from the out-lying reef and cast up the debris with tinkling chips and fragments of shells on the sand for the sun and the tepid rains to bleach into dazzling whiteness. The coral drift has swept up among the dull grey rocks and made a ridge beneath the pendant branches of the trees, as if to establish a contrast between the sombre tints of the jungle and the blueness of the sea. Midway along the curve of vegetation a bingum flaunts its mantle—a single daub of demonstrative colouring. Away to the north stand out the Barnard Islands, and the island-like headland of Double-Point.

Rocky walls and ledges intersected by narrow clefts in which the sea boils, gigantic masses of detached granite split and weathered into strange shapes and corniced and bridged at high water-mark by oysters, bold escarpments and medleys of huge boulders, extend along the weather side. No landing, except in the calmest weather, is possible. To gain a sandy beach, the south-east end of the island, passing through a deep channel separating the rocky islet of Wooln-garin, must be turned. Although there are no great cliffs, no awesome precipices on the weather side, the bluff rocks present many grotesque features, and the foliage is for the most part wildly luxuriant.

From what has been already said, it may be gleaned that in the opinion of the most interested person the island is gilt-edged. So it is, in fact, when certain natural conditions consequent on the presence of coral are fulfilled. A phenomenally high tide deposited upon the rocks a slimy, fragile organism of the sea, in incomprehensible myriads which, drying, adhered smoothly in true alignment. With the sun at the proper angle there appeared, as far as the irregularity of the coast-line permitted, a shining band, broken only where the face of the rock was uneven and detached—a zone of gold bestowed upon the island by the amorous sea. But on the beach the slime which transformed the grey and brown rocks was nothing but an inconsistent, dirty, grey-green, crisp, ill-smelling streak, that haply vanished in a couple of days. As I see less of the weather side than I do of the beach, I tell myself that it is nearer perfection to be minus a streak of dirt than plus a golden edge.

At no season of the year is the island without fragrance. The prevailing perception may be of lush grasses mingled with the soft odour of their frail flowers; or the resin and honey of blossoming bloodwoods; or the essence from myriads of other eucalyptus leaves massaged by the winds. The incomparable beach-loving calophyllums yield a profuse but tender fragrance reminiscent of English meadow-sweet, and the flowers of a vigorous trailer (*Canavila obtusifolia*), for ever exploring the bare sand at high-water mark, resemble the sweet-pea in form and perfume. The white cedar (*Melia composita*) is a welcome and not unworthy substitute in appearance and perfume for English lilac. The aromatic pandanus and many varieties of acacia, each has its appointed time and season; while at odd intervals the air is saturated with the rich and far-spreading incense of the melaleuca, and for many weeks together with the honeyed excellence of the swamp mahogany (*Tristania suaveolens*) and the over-rich cloyness of the cockatoo apple (*Careya australis*). Strong and spicy are the odours of the plants and trees that gather on the edge of and crowd in the jungle, the so-called native ginger, nutmeg, quandong, milkwood, bean-tree, the kirri-cue of the blacks (*Eupomatia laurina*), koie-yan (*Faradaya splendida*), with its great white flowers and snowy fruit, and many others. Hoya, heavy and indolent, trails across and dangles from the rocks; the river mangrove dispenses its sweetness in an unexpected locality; and from the heart of the jungle come wafts of warm breath, which, mingling with exhalation from foliage and flower, is diffused broadcast. The odour of the jungle is definite—earthy somewhat, but of earth clean, wholesome and moist—the smell of moss, fern and fungus blended with balsam, spice and sweetness.

Many a time, home-returning at night—when the black contours of the island loomed up in the distance against the pure tropic sky tremulous with myriads of unsullied stars—has its tepid fragrance drifted across the water as a salutation and a greeting. It has long been a fancy of mine that the island has a distinctive odour, soft and pliant, rich and vigorous. Other mixtures of forest and jungle may smell as strong, but none has the rare blend which I recognize and gloat over whensoever, after infrequent absences for a day or two, I return to accept of it in grateful sniffs. In such a fervid and encouraging clime distillation is continuous and prodigious. Heat and moisture and a plethora of raw material, leaves, flowers, soft, sappy and fragrant woods, growing grass and moist earth, these are the essential elements for the manufacture of ethereal and soul-soothing odours—suggestive of tangible flavours.

I know of but one particular plant that is absolutely repellent. Its large flowers are of vivid gold, pure and refined; the unmixed odour is obscene. A creeper of the jungle bears small yellow flowers (slightly resembling those of the mango, save that they are produced in frail loose cymes instead of on vigorous panicles), the excessive sweetness of which approaches nauseousness. But its essence mingles with the rest, and the compound is singularly rich and acceptable.

On sandy stretches and along the deltas of the creeks are fragrant, gigantic "spider lilies" (*Crinum*). I do not pretend to catalogue botanically all the plants that contribute to the specific odour of the island. I cannot address them individually in scientific phraseology, though with all I am on terms of easy familiarity, the outcome of seasoned admiration. They please by the form and

14

colour of their blossoms, and ring ever-recurring and timeful changes, so that month by month we enjoy the progress of the perfumes—the blending of some, the individual excellence of others. In endeavouring to convey to the unelect an impression of their variety and acceptableness, am I not but discharging a debt of gratitude?

As far as I am aware, but four or five epiphytal orchids add to the scents of the island; and as they have not Christian names, their pagan titles must suffice—*cymbidium suave, Eria fitzalani, Bulbophyllum baileyi, Dendrobium teretifolium* and *D. undulatum*. The last-named is not commonly credited with perfume; but when it grows in great unmolested masses its contribution is pleasant, if not very decided. A pretty terrestrial orchid (*Cyrtostylis reniformis*) is delicately fragrant, but the great showy *Phaius grandifolius* (the tropical foxglove) and the meek *Geodorum pictum* (Queensland's lily of the valley) are denied the gift.

The forest, the jungle, the grassy spots, the hot rocks (with hoya and orchids), and even the sands, with the native sweet-pea, are fragrant. A lowly creeping plant (*Vitex trifolia*), with small spikes of lavender-coloured flowers and grey-green silvery leaves, mingles with the coarse grasses of the sandy flats, and usurping broad areas forms an aromatic carpet from which every footstep expresses a homely pungency as of marjoram and sage. The odour of the island may be specific, and therefore to be prized, yet it gladdens also because it awakens happy and all too fleeting reminiscences. English fields and hedges cannot be forgotten when one of our trees diffuses the scent of meadow-sweet, and one of the orchids that of hawthorn. "Scent and silence" is the phrase which expresses the individuality of our island, and better "scented silence" than all the noisy odours of the town.

EARLY HISTORY

To that grand old mariner, Captain Cook, belongs the honour of the discovery of the island. The names that he bestowed—judicious and expressive—are among the most precious historic possessions of Australia. They remind us that Cook formed the official bond between Britain and this great southern land, and bear witness to the splendid feats of quiet heroism that he performed, the privations that he and his ship's company endured, and the patience and perseverance with which difficulties were faced and overcome.

In his journal, on 8 June 1770, Cook writes: "At noon we were by observation in the lat. of 17° 59′ and abreast of the N. point of Rockingham Bay which bore from us N. two miles. This boundary of the bay is formed by a tolerable high island known in the chart by the name of Dunk Isle; it lay so near the shore as not to be distinguished from it unless you are well in with the land. . . . At this time we were in the long. of 213° 57′, Cape Sandwich bore S. by E. ½ E. distant 19 miles, and the northernmost land in sight N. ½ W. Our depth of water in the course of this one day's sail was not more than 17 nor less than 16 fathoms."

In those history-making days the first Lord of the Admiralty was George Montagu Dunk, First Earl of Sandwich, Second Baron and First Earl of Halifax, and Captain Cook took several opportunities of preserving his patron's name.* Halifax Bay (immediately to the north of Cleveland Bay) perpetuates the title; "Mount" Hinchinbrook (from his course Cook could not see the channel, and did not realize that he was bestowing a name upon an island) commemorates the family seat of the Montagus; Cape Sandwich (the north-east point of Hinchinbrook) the older title, and Dunk Isle the family name of the distinguished friend of the great discoverer of lands.

From this remote and unheard of spot may, accordingly, be traced association with a contemporary of Robert Walpole, of Pitt and Fox, of Edmund Burke, of John Wilkes (of the *North Briton*), of the author of *The Letters of Junius* and of *John Gilpin*, and many others of credit and renown. The First Earl Sandwich of Hinchinbrook was the "my lord" of the gossiping Pepys. Through him Dunk Island possesses another strand in the bond with the immortals, and is ensured connection with remote posterity. He gambled so passionately that he invented as a means of hasty refreshment the immemorial "sandwich", that the fascination of basset, ombre or quadrille should not be dispelled by the intrusion of a meal. He, too, was the owner of Montagu House, behind which "every morning saw steel glitter and blood flow", for the age was that of the duellist as well as the gambler.

Rockingham Bay was so named in honour of the marquis of that title, the wise Whig premier who held that while the British Parliament had an undoubted right to tax the American colonies,

* For discussion of this point see the Introduction to *Last Leaves from Dunk Island*.

the notorious Stamp Act was unjust and impolitic, "sterile of revenue, and fertile of discontent".

Cook and his day and generation passed, and then for many years history is silent respecting Dunk Island. The original inhabitants remained in undisturbed possession; nor do they seem to have had more than one passing visitor until Lieutenant Jeffereys, on the armed transport *Kangaroo*, on his passage from Sydney to Ceylon in 1815, communicated with the natives on then unnamed Goold Island. Captain (afterwards Rear-Admiral) Phillip P. King, who made in the cutter *Mermaid* a running survey of these coasts between the years 1818 and 1822, and who was the first to indicate that "Mount" Hinchinbrook was probably separated from the mainland, arrived in Rockingham Bay on 19 June 1818. He named and landed on Goold Island, and, sailing north on the 21st, anchored off Timana, where he went ashore. "Dunk Island," he writes, "a little to the northward, is larger and higher, and remarkable for its double-peaked summit."

Those natives who are versed in the ancient history of the island, tell of the time when all were amazed by the appearance of bags of flour, boxes of tobacco, and cases of goods drifting ashore. None at the time knew what flour was; only one boy had previously smoked, and the goods were too mysterious to be tested. Many tried to eat the flour direct from the bag. The individual who had acquired the reputation of a smoker made himself so sick that none other had the courage to imitate him, and the tobacco and goods were thrown about playfully. In after years the inhabitants were fond of relating how they had humbugged themselves.

The next ensuing official reference of particular interest is contained in the narrative of the voyage of H.M.S. *Rattlesnake*, by John Macgillivray, F.R.G.S., naturalist of the expedition. The date is 26 May 1848, and an extract reads: "During the forenoon the ship was moved over to an anchorage under the lee (north-west side) of Dunk Island, where we remained for ten days. The summit of a very small rocky island, near the anchorage, named, by Captain Owen Stanley, Mound Islet [Purtaboi], formed the first station. Dunk Island, eight or nine miles in circumference, is well wooded. It has two conspicuous peaks, one of which (the north-west one) is eight hundred and fifty-seven feet in height. Our excursions were confined to the vicinity of the watering-place and the bay in which it is situated."

Tam o' Shanter Point derives its title from the barque of that name, in which the members of the Kennedy exploring expedition voyaged from Sydney, whence they disembarked on 24 and 25 May 1848. H.M.S. *Rattlesnake* had been commissioned to lend Kennedy assistance, and Macgillivray relates that everything belonging to the party (with the exception of one horse drowned while swimming ashore) was safely landed. The first camp was formed on some open forest-land behind the beach at a small fresh-water creek. On the 27th Mr Carson, the botanist of the party, commenced digging a piece of ground, in which he sowed seeds of cabbages, turnips, leek, pumpkin, rock- and water-melons, pomegranate, peach-stones and apple-pips. No trace of this first venture in gardening in North Queensland is now discernible. No doubt, inquisitive and curious blacks would rummage the freshly-turned soil as soon as the back of the good-natured gardener was turned.

Twenty-five years lapsed, and then another official landing took place. In the meantime, the island had been frequently visited, but there are no records, until 29 September 1873, when the "Queensland North-east Coast Expedition", under the leadership of Mr G. Elphinstone Dalrymple, F.R.G.S., landed. Three members of the party have left pleasing testimonies of their first impressions, and I turn to the remarks of the leader for geological definitions. He says: "The formation of Dunk Island is clay slates and micaceous schist. A level stratum of a soft, greasy, and very red decomposing granitic clay was exposed along the south-west tide-flats, and quartz veins and blue slates were found on the same side of the island further in." The huge granite boulders on the south-east aspect and the granite escarpments on the shoulders of the hills above did not apparently attract attention.

One feature then existent has also disappeared. The explorers referred to the belt of magnificent calophyllum trees along the margin of the south-west beach, and Mr Dalrymple thus describes a vegetable wonder: "Some large fig-trees sent out great lateral roots, large as their own trunks, fifty feet into salt water; an anchor-root extending perpendicularly at the extremity to support them. Thence they have sent up another tree as large as the parent stem, at high-water presenting the peculiarity of twin-trees, on shore and in the sea, connected by a rustic root bridge." These trees have no place or part now.

My chronicles are fated to be tinged with the ashen hue of the commonplace, though the scenes they attempt to depict are all of the sun-blessed tropics.

SATELLITES AND NEIGHBOURS

Consultation of the map will show that Dunk Island has four satellites and seven near relations. Though not formally included in the Family Group it stands as sponsor to all its members, and overlords the islets within a few yards of its superior shores. The official chart has been revised, the original and comely titles of the blacks being substituted for the exotic names of the map-makers.

Brief reference to each of the satellites and neighbours of Dunk Island may not be out of place, if only to preserve distinctions which were current long before the advent of white folks, and to make clear remarks in future pages upon the different features of the domain over which the beachcomber exercises jurisdiction. Not to many men is permitted the privilege of choosing for his day's excursion from among so many beautiful spots, certain in the knowledge that to whichsoever he may elect to flutter his handkerchief is reserved for his delight; certain that the sands will be free from the traces of any other human being; certain that no sound save those of nature will break in upon his musings and meditations.

Purtaboi, the first and the nearest of the satellites, lies three-quarters of a mile from the middle of the sweep of Brammo Bay—always in view through the tracery of the melaleuca trees. Mung-um-gnackum and Kumboola, to the south-west, are linked at low-water spring tides to Dunk Island and to each other; and Wooln-garin, to the south-east, is separated from the rocky cliffs and ledges of the island by three hundred yards of deep and swiftly-flowing water.

Purtaboi—dainty and unique—its hill crowned with low-growing trees and shrubs, a ruddy precipice, groups of pandanus palms, beach lined with casuarinas, banks of snow-white coral debris, ridge of sharp-edged rocks jutting out to the north-western cove and out-lying reef of coral, tangle of orchids and scrub all in miniature—save the orchids—gigantic and gross and profuse of old-gold bloom. In October and November hosts of sea-birds come hither to nest, and so also do nutmeg or Torres Strait pigeons, peaceful doves, honey-eaters, wood-swallows, the blue reef-heron, and occasionally the little black cormorant. The large-billed shore plover deposits her single egg on the sand, merely carelessly whisking aside the casuarina needles for its reception.

Hundreds of terns lay their eggs among the tinkling coral chips, and, discarding all attempts at concealment, practise artistic deception. So perfect is the artifice that the eggs are frequently the least conspicuous of the elements of the banks of drift, broken coral and bleached shells. Not until each square yard is steadfastly inspected can they be detected, though there may be dozens around one's feet, the colours—creamy white with grey and brown and purple spots, and blotches and scribblings—blending perfectly with their environment. The eggs, by the way, are a great delicacy, sweet, nutty, and absolutely devoid of fishy flavour. When the downy young are hatched they, too, are almost invisible. They cunningly lie motionless, though within a few inches of your hand, and remain perfectly passive when lifted. Snoodling beside lumps of coral or beneath weather-beaten drift-wood, they afford startling proof of the effect of sympathetic colouration. When one stoops to pick up a piece of wood, whitened and roughened by the salt of the sea, and finds that more than half its apparent bulk is made up of several infants in soft swaddles, crowded together into a homogeneous mass, the result is pleasing astonishment. Only when individuals of the group move do they become visible to their natural enemies. These tender young birds enjoy no protection nor any of the comfort of a nest, and if they were not endowed from the moment of birth with rare consciousness of their helplessness, the species, no doubt, would speedily become exterminated; for keen-sighted hawks hover about, picking up those which, failing to obey the first law of nature, reveal themselves by movement.

If the wind is tempered to the shorn lamb, what is the provision of nature which enables so tender a thing as a young bird, a mere helpless ball of creamy fluff, to withstand the frizzling heat with which the sun bleaches the broken coral? Many do avail themselves of the meagre shadow of shells and lumps of coral, but the majority are exposed to the direct rays of the sun, which brings the coral to such a heat that even the hardened beachcomber walks thereon with uneasy steps, reminding him of another outcast who used that oft-quoted staff as a support over the "burning marl".

The parents of the white-shafted ternlet, the most sylph-like of birds, with others of the family, ever on the look-out, follow in circling, screaming mobs the disturbance on the surface of the sea caused by small fish vainly endeavouring to elude the crafty bonito and porpoise, and take ample supplies to the ever-hungry young. How is it that the hundreds of pairs recognize among the hundreds of fluffy young identical in size and colour, each their particular care?

On another island within the Barrier Reef several species of sea-birds spontaneously adapted themselves to altered circumstances. They, in consonance with the general habits of the species, were wont to lay their eggs carelessly on the sand or shingle, without pretence of nests. A meat-loving pioneer introduced goats to the island, the continual parading about of which so disturbed the birds, and deprived them of their hope of posterity, that they took to the building of nests on dwarf trees, out of the way of the goats. That birds unaccustomed to the building of nests should acquire the habit, illustrates the depths of nature's promptings for the preservation of species; or is it that the faculty existed as an hereditary trait, was abandoned only when its exercise was unnecessary, and resumed when there was conspicuous occasion for it? On a neighbouring island of the same group, unstocked with goats, no change in the habits of the birds has taken place.

Among the rocks of Purtaboi, in cool dark grottoes, the brown-winged tern rears her young. She often permits herself to be trapped rather than indicate her presence by voluntary flight. One of the most graceful of the sea-swallows, this bird is brown of back and greenish-white on the under surface. It "yaps" as a terrier whenever intruders approach the island during the brooding season; and its puff-ball chicken, crouching in dim recesses, takes the bluish-grey hue of the rock.

The blue reef-heron builds a rough nest of twigs on the ledges of the rocks, sometimes at the roots of the bronze orchid (*Dendrobium undulatum*), and endeavours to scare away intruders by harsh squawks stupidly betraying the presence of pale blue eggs or helpless brood. When the blue heron flies with his long neck stiffly tucked between his shoulders, he is anything but graceful; but under other circumstances he is not an ungainly bird.

Low-lying Mung-um-gnackum, the abode of the varied honey-eater, the tranquil dove, and the brooding-place of the night-jar, and lovely Kumboola, lie to the south-west, a bare half-mile away.

Kumboola's sheltered aspect is thickly clad with jungle; a steep grassy ridge springs from the blue-grey rocks to the south-east; and on the precipitous weather side grow low and open scrub and dwarf casuarina. Here is a natural aviary. Pigeons and doves coo; honey-eaters whistle; sun-birds whisper quaint, quick notes; wood-swallows soar and twitter; metallic starlings seek safe sleeping-places among the mangroves, ere they repair last year's villages, and join excitedly in the chorus; while the great osprey wheels overhead, and the grey falcon sits on a bare branch, still as a sentinel, each waiting for an opportunity to take toll of the nutmeg pigeons. The channel-billed cuckoo shrieks her discordant warning of the approaching wet season; and the scrub fowl utters those far-off imitations of the exclamation of civilized hens. Sundown at Kumboola towards the end of September, when the sea laps and murmurs among the rocks, and great white pigeons gather in thousands on the dark foliage, or "coo-hooing" and flapping, disappear beneath the thick leafy canopy, and all the other birds are saying their good-nights, or asserting their rights, or protesting against crowding or intrusion, is an ever-to-be-remembered experience. Added to the cheerful presence of the noisy birds are the pleasant odours which spring from the jungle as coolness prevails, and the flaming west gives a weird tint of red to the outlines of the trees, and of purple to the drowsy sea.

Of entirely different character is the last of the satellites to be mentioned, Wooln-garin. Lying three hundred yards off the south-western end of Dunk Island, across a swift and deep channel, it is naught but a confused mass of weather-beaten rocks, the loftiest not being more than fifty feet above high-water. A few pandanus palms, hardy shrubs and trailers, and mangroves spring from sheltered crevices, but for the most part the rocks are bare. The incessant assaults of the sea have cut deep but narrow clefts in the granite, worn out sounding hollows, and smoothed away angularities. Here a few terns rear their young, and succeeding generations of sooty oyster-catchers lay their eggs just out of the reach of high-tide. A never-ending procession of fish passes up and down the channel, according as the tide flows and ebbs, though they do not at all times take serious heed of bait. To one who generally fishes for a definite purpose, it is tantalizing to peep down into the clear depths and watch the lazy fish come and go, ignoring the presence of that which at other times is greedily snapped at. Turtle, and occasionally dugong, favour the vicinity of Wooln-garin, which on account of its distinctive character is one of the most frequented of the satellites.

The neighbouring islands include Timana, two and a half miles from the sand-spit of Dunk Island and one and a half miles from Kumboola; Bedarra, a little to the southward; Tool-ghar, three-quarters of a mile from Bedarra; Coomboo, half a mile from Tool-ghar; and the group of three—Bud-joo, Kurrambah and Coolah—still farther to the south-east. These comprise the Family Islands of the chart.

On Timana are gigantic milkwood trees (*Alstonia scholaris*) which need great flying buttresses to support their immense height, their roots being mainly superficial. For many generations two ospreys have had their eyrie in one of these giant trees, fit nursery for imperial birds. With annual additions, the nest has attained immense proportions, and as years pass it will still further increase, for blacks capable of climbing such a tree and disturbing the occupants are few and far between. Great distinction and pride, however, are the lot of the athlete who secures the snowy down of the young birds to stick in tufts on his dirty head with fat, gum and bees-wax, for he will be the admired of all admirers at the corroboree. Vanity impels human beings to extraordinary exertions, trials and risks, and the black who desires to outshine his fellows, and who has the essential of strength and length of limb, will make a loop of lawyer-vine round the tree, and with his body within the loop begin the ascent. Having cut a notch for the left great toe, he inclines his weight against the tree, while he shifts the loop three feet or so upwards. Then he leans backward against the loop, cuts a notch for his right great toe, and so on until the nest is reached. There has been but one ascent of this tree in modern times, and the name of the black, "Spider", is still treasured.

A heavy, slovenly-patched mantle of leafage, impervious to sunlight covers the Isle of Timana, creating a region of perpetual dimness from western beach to eastern precipice, where orchids cling and palms peer on rocks below. All the vegetation is matted and interwoven, only the topmost branches of the milkwood escaping from the clinging, aspiring vines. Tradition asserts that not many years since Timana was much favoured by nutmeg pigeons, now sparsely represented; but the varied honey-eater

23

and a friar-bird possessing a most mellow and fluty note, cockatoos and metallic starlings are plentiful. Although there is no permanent fresh water, the pencil-tailed rat leaves numerous tracks on the sand, and scrub fowls keep the whole surface perpetually raked.

From a mound adjacent to the beach a black boy brought fifteen eggs as we picnicked on the beach, and though some of them were nigh upon hatching, not one was covered with white ants—which, an authority asserts, particularly like crawling over the eggshells, so as to be ready when wanted by the chicks! Nor have I ever seen an instance of this alleged exhibition of self-sacrifice on the part of the white ant. Another boy had eaten his very substantial lunch, but the eggs were tempting and he baked two. One, and that new-laid, is ample for an ordinary mortal. The condition of the first resembled that which the embarrassed curate described as "good in parts"; but Mickie was not nice over a half-hatched egg. Indeed, was it not rather more piquant than otherwise? The second proved to contain a fully developed chicken. Now, the chick emerges from the shell feathered, and this, but for the unfortunate accident of discovery, would have begun to scratch for its living in a day or so. Mickie flicked away the fragments of shell from the steaming dainty and laid it snugly on a leaf. "That's for Paddy"—an Irish terrier, always of the party. It was an affecting act of renunciation. Presently Paddy came along; but Paddy, who, too, had lunched, bestowed merely a sniff and a "No, thank you" wag of the tail. "What, you no want 'em? All right." No second offer was risked, and in a moment, in one mouthful, the chick was being crunched by Mickie, feathers and all. The menu of the Chinese—with its ducks' eggs salted, sharks' fins and tails, stewed pups, fowls' and ducks' tongues, fricasseed cat, rat soup, silkworm grubs, and odds and ends generally despised and rejected—is pitifully unromantic when set against the generous omnivority of Australian blacks.

A mile beyond Timana is Bedarra, with its lovely little bays and coves and fantastically weathered rocks, its forest and jungle and scrub, and its rocky satellite Pee-rahm-ah. Several of the most conspicuous landmarks are associated in the minds of blacks with legends, generally of the simplest and most prosaic nature. About this rough rock Pee-rahm-ah is a story which in the minds of the natives satisfactorily accounts for its presence.

In the far-away past two nice young gins, they say, were left by themselves on Dunk Island, while the others of the tribe went away in canoes to Hinchinbrook. Tiring of their lonesomeness, they made up their minds to regain the company of their relatives by swimming from island to island. Kumboola was easily reached; to Timana it is but a mile and a half, and a mile thence to Bedarra. Leaving the most easterly point of Bedarra, they were quickly caught in the swirl of a strong current and spun about until both became dazed and exhausted. As they disappeared beneath the water they were changed to stone, and the stone rose in fantastic shape, and from that day Pee-rahm-ah has weathered all the storms of the Pacific and formed a feature in the loveliest scene these isles reveal.

The largest of the neighbouring isles, Bedarra, has less than a square mile of superficial area; the smallest but four or five acres. The smaller are made up of confused masses of granite, for the most part so overgrown with fig-trees, plumy palms, milkwoods, umbrella-trees, quandongs, eugenias, hibiscus bushes, bananas and lawyer-vines as to be unexplorable without a scrub-knife; for the soil among the rocks is soft and spongy, the purest of vegetable mould, and encourages luxurious growth. The jungle droops over the grey rocks on the sheltered side. Twisted Moreton Bay ash and wind-crippled scrub spring up among the clefts and crevices on the weather frontage—the south-east—while a narrow strip of sand, the only landing-place, is a general characteristic of the north-west aspect. Birds nest in numbers in peace and security, for the islets are off the general track. Seldom is there any disturbance of the primeval quietude, and in the encompassing sea, if the fish and turtle suffer any excitement, rarely is the cause attributable to man.

The islands immediately to the south-east form the Family Group—triplets, twins and two singles. I like to think approving things of them; to note individual excellences; to familiarize myself with their distinguishing traits; to listen to them in their petulence and anger, and in that sobbing subsidence to even temper; to their complacent gurglings and sleepy murmurs. One —and the most infantile of all—not of the Family, has a distinctive note, a copyright tone which none imitates, and which becomes at times a sonorous swelling boom, a lofty recitative. For even an island has its temper and its moods.

The folly of this island! They say there's but five upon this isle; we are two of them; if the other three be brained like us the State totters!

The scheme for the establishment of our island home comprehended several minor industries. This isle of dreams, of quietude and happiness; this fretless scene; this plot of the Garden of Eden, was not to be left entirely in its primitive state. It was firmly resolved that our interference should be considerate and slight; that there should be no rude and violent upsetting of the old order of things; but just a gentle restraint upon an extravagant expression here and there, a little orderliness, and ever so light a touch of practicability. A certain acreage of land was to be cleared for the cultivation of tropical fruits; of vegetables for everyday use, and of maize and millet for poultry, which we proposed to breed for home consumption. Bees were to be an ultimate source of profit. There are millions of living proofs of direct but vagrant descent from the Italian stock, with which we started, humming all over this and the adjacent islands to-day.

How we went about the practical accomplishment of our plans; in what particulars they failed; what proportion of success was achieved, and the process of education in rural enterprises generally, it were idle to account. Be it understood that we depended almost solely on the aid of the blacks. Means at command did not permit the employment of even a single white workman, save for a brief experimental period. Those who have had experience of aboriginals as labourers understand their erratic disposition; yet with considerate treatment, the exact and prompt fulfilment of obligations and promises, the display of some little sympathy with their foibles, interest in their doings, and ready response to any desire expressed to "walk about", they are not wholly to be set at naught as labourers. Some are intelligent and honest to a degree, and when in the humour will work steadily and consistently. When they are not in the humour, it is well to accept the fact cheerfully.

Here I must have leave to be candid, so that the reader may be under no misapprehension as to the exact circumstances under which the undertaking progressed. Income from the land as the result of agricultural operations was not absolutely necessary. This acknowledgment does not imply the possession of, or any disrespect for, "the cumbersome luggage of riches", nor any affectation; but rather an accommodating and frugal disposition —the capacity to turn to account the excellent moral that poor Mr Micawber lamented his inability to obey. Profit from the sale of produce and poultry would have supplied additional comforts which would have been cordially appreciated; but if no returns came, then there was that state of mind which enabled us to endure the deprivation as the Psalmist suffered fools. And shall not this be accounted unto us for righteousness? Shall we not enjoy the warm comfort of virtue? We were at liberty to reflect with the Vicar of Wakefield—"We have still enough left for happiness, if we are wise; and let us draw upon content for the deficiencies of fortune". Certainly, we were not inclined to risk that which, thriftily employed, provided for all absolute necessaries, on the chance of securing that which might, after all, prove to be superfluous. At least, there remains the consciousness of having lived, and of having wrought no evil, and being able to enjoy the sleep which is said to be that of the just.

Occasionally there are as many as four blacks about the place. They come and go from the mainland, some influenced by the wish for the diet of oysters for a time. "Me want sit down now; me want eat oyster." At rare intervals we are entirely alone for months together, and then cultural operations stand still. Twice, a considerable portion of the plantation was silently overrun by the scouts of the jungle, and had to be re-surveyed in order to locate smothered-up orange-trees. Our staff, domestic and otherwise, usually consists of one boy and his gin, and save for the housework, affairs are not conducted on a serious or systematic plan. The spur necessity not being applied, there is no persistent or sustained effort to make a profit, and, of course, none is earned.

In a few months from the felling of the first strip of jungle and the burning off of the timber and rubbish, however, we grew produce that went towards the maintenance of the establishment. Until we grew fruit, the papaw, the quickest and amongst the best, vegetables were more necessary.

Our plantation, all carved out of the jungle, has an area of four and a half acres. We have orange-trees (two varieties), just coming into bearing, and from which profits are expected; pineapples (two varieties), papaws, coffee (*Arabica*), custard apples, sour sop, Jack fruit, pomegranate, the litchee, and mangoes in plenty. Sweet potatoes are always in successive cultivation, also pumpkins and melons, and an occasional crop of maize. Bananas represent a staple food. We have had fair crops of English potatoes, and have grown strawberries of fine flavour, though of deficient size, among the banana plants. Parsley, mint, and all "the vulgar herbs" grow freely. Readers in less favoured climes may hardly credit the statement that pineapples are so plentiful in the season in North Queensland that they are fed to pigs as well as horses. Twenty good pines for sixpence! Who would cultivate the fruit and market it for such remuneration? Hundreds of tons of mangoes go absolutely to waste every year. The taste for this wholesome and most delicious fruit has not yet become established in the large centres of population of Australia. At one time the same could be said of bananas; but now the trade has become prodigious. The era of the mango has yet to come.

The original cedar hut now forms an annexe to a bungalow designed, in so far as means permitted, as a concession to the dominating characteristics of the clime. Around the house is an acre or so given over to an attempt to keep up appearances.

Poultry are comfortably housed; a small flock of goats provides milk and occasionally fresh meat. There are two horses (one a native of the island) to perform casual heavy work; the boat has a shed into which she is reluctantly hauled by means of a windlass to spend the rowdy months; there is a buoy in the bay to which she is greatly attached when she is not sulking in the shed or coyly submitting to the caresses of the waves.

It may have been anticipated that I would, Thoreau-like, set down in details and in figures the exact character and cost of every designed alteration to this scene; but the idea, as soon as it occurred, was sternly suppressed, for however cheerful a disciple I am of that philosopher, far be it from me to belittle him by parody.

A good portion of the house represents the work of my own unaccustomed hands. I have found how laborious an occupation fencing is, and how very exasperating if barbed wire is used; that the keeping in order of even a small plantation in which ill-bred and riotous plants grow with the rapidity of the prophet's gourd, and which if unattended would lapse in a very brief space of time into the primitive condition of tangled jungle, involves incessant labour of the most sweatful kind. A work on structural botany tells me that "the average rate of perspiration in plants has been estimated as equal to that of seventeen times that of man". Only dwellers in the tropics are capable of realizing the profundity of those pregnant words. Nowhere does plant life so thrive and so squander itself. And to toil among all this seething, sweating vegetation! No wonder that the trashing of sugar-cane is not a popular pastime among Britishers.

Given a quiet and contented mind, a banana-grove, a patch of sweet potatoes, orange and mango and papaw trees, a few coffee plants, the sea for fish, the rocks for oysters, the mangrove flats for crabs, and is it not possible to become fat with a minimum of labour? Fewer statements have found wider publicity than that the banana contains more nutriment than meat. I have good reason to have faith in it. Apart from the imposts upon living, moving and having being, what ready money does a man want beyond a few shillings for tea, sugar and other luxuries, and some few articles of essential clothing? But I am attempting to describe a special set of circumstances, and would not have it on my conscience that I indirectly offered encouragement even to a forlorn and shipwrecked brother to abandon hope of becoming the prime minister of the Commonwealth, and to enter upon a life of reckless irresponsibility such as mine.

As soon as test and trial proved in this special case that life on the periphery of the whirl of civilization was not only endurable but "so would we have it", arrangements were made with the government of the State for a change in the tenure upon which the right of possession was upheld.

What has been said of the natural features of Dunk Island is applicable to the coastal tract extending, say, three hundred miles, than which no land is more fertile. A very notable advantage is enjoyed here. Brammo Bay is but three or four minutes' steam from the track of vessels which make weekly trips up and down the coast, and by arrangements with the proprietory of one of the lines we have the boon of a regular weekly mail and of cheap carriage of supplies. Without this connecting link, life on the island would have been very different. The Companies running parallel lines of steamers, one skirting the coast and the other outside the islands in deep water, have done much to open up the wealth of the agricultural land of North Queensland. Trade follows the flag. Here the flag of the mercantile marine has frequently been first planted to demonstrate the certainty of trade.

Without apology, a few facts are submitted which utterly condemn the practicability of one department of island enterprise. When, after some expenditure in the purchase of plant and material, and no little labour, the couple of beehives that formed the original stock of a project for the harvesting of the nectar which had hitherto gone to waste or been disposed of by unreflecting birds, had increased to a dozen, and honey of pleasant and varying flavour flowed from the separator at frequent intervals, hopes ran high of the earning of a modest profit from one of the cleanest, nicest, most entertaining and innoxious of pursuits.

No one who takes up bees and who studies their manners and methods can allow his admiration to remain dormant. It is not the fault of the bees if he does not become ashamed of himself in some respects; nor are they to blame if the wisest men fail quite to comprehend some of the wonders they perform.

Interest in bee-culture grows; and some of the habits of the insect came to be understood and, inevitably, admired, the while all convenient vessels available, even to the never-to-be-despised kerosene-tins, were utilized to store the nectar garnered from myriads of blossoms. But as time passed the fair prospects faded. Less and less quantities of honey were stored. The separator seldom buzzed with soothing melody as the honey, whirled from the dripping frames of combs, pattered against its resonant sides. Bees seemed less and less numerous. An air of idleness, almost dissoluteness and despair, brooded over some of the hives. The strong robbed the weak; and the weak contented themselves with gathering in listless groups, murmuring plaintively. If the hives were enquiringly tapped, instead of a furious and instant alarm and angry outpouring of excited and wrathful citizens, eager to sacrifice themselves in the defence of the rights of the commonwealth, there was merely a buzzing remonstrance, indicative of decreased population, weakness and disconsolation.

The cause of so great a change in the character and demeanour of citizens who erstwhile worked as honey-carriers all day, and who during the hot, still nights did duty as animated ventilating fans to maintain a free circulation of air through the hive, had to be investigated. Soon it was revealed in the presence of two species of birds, the Australian bee-eater (*Merops ornatus*) and the white-rumped wood-swallow (*Artamus leucogaster*). The former is one of the handsomest of the smaller birds of Australia, its chief colouring being varying shades of green with bronze-brown and black head and blue back; and to add to its appearance and pride two graceful feather-shafts of black protrude from the green and yellow of the tail. It travels in small companies of, say, from four and five to a couple of dozen, and in its flight occasionally seems to pause with wings and tail outspread, revealing all its charms. Fond of perching on bare twigs commanding a wide survey, it darts thence with unerring precision to catch bees and other insects on the wing. If its prey takes unkindly to its fate, the bird batters it to death on its perch ere swallowing it with a twitter of satisfaction.

The wood-swallow wears a becoming suit of soft pearly grey and white, to contrast with its black head and throat. It has a graceful, soaring flight and a cheerful chirrup. At certain seasons scores congregate on a branch, perching in a row, so closely compact that their breasts show as a continuous band of white. When one leaves his place to catch an insect, the others close up the ranks and dress the line, and on returning, wrangle and scold as he may, he needs must take an outside place. Let a bush fire be started, and flocks of wood-swallows whirl and circle along the flanks of the circling smoke, taking flying insects on the wing, or deftly pick "thin, high-elbowed creatures", scuttling up tree-trunks out of the way of the flames.

Those were the marauders who confounded anticipations of a comfortable livelihood in the decent calling of an apiarist. They devoured bees by the hundred every day. Every hive paid dreadful toll to them, for they found food so plentiful, and with so little exertion, that they made the vicinity of the hives a permanent abiding place. For a brief season I found myself confronted by a problem. I had to apply my own favourite theories and arguments to myself and weigh against them practical advantages. Honey was plentiful, and, given that the bees were protected against voracious enemies, might have been stored in marketable quantities. But was I not bound by honour as well as sentiment to protect the birds? Was not my coming hither due to a certain extent, to a wish for the preservation of bird life? Was there not in my presence an implied warranty to that effect? Had not the island since my occupancy become a sanctuary, a city of refuge, a safe abiding place, a kingdom where all the birds of the air—save tyrants and cannibals—were welcomed with gladness and enthusiasm? Had I not warned others of the dreadful consequences that would befall any disturbance of the sacred air by so much as the unauthorized report of a gun?

How then was I to deal out justice to the defenceless bees that I had hurried hither, willynilly, without consideration of their likes and dislikes, and their multitudinous descendants? How protect my investment in apiarist plant? How maintain the stock of honey, white, golden and tawny brown, excellent, wholesome, delicious food, and still preserve the natural rights, the privileges of the birds? Had not the birds the right of prior occupancy and other legitimate claims, in addition to sentimental demands upon my conscience? Not only, too, were the birds beautiful to look upon and of engaging habits; not only had they become companionable and trustful; not only were they among the primeval features of the island that I was so eager to leave unspotted from the world; but they were eminently useful in the work of keeping within bounds the rampant host of insects to which mankind is in the habit of applying the term injurious.

It took no long time to make up my mind. Gladly came the determination to abandon the enterprise rather than do violence to the birds. Fortunately, a kindly friend took the entire plant and the hives off my hands. We are the worse off in respect of honey; but we have the birds, and the thought comes that there are now hundreds of colonies of bees from the original stock, here and on the mainland, working out their own destinies. Had the enterprise been allowed to flourish, it would have been at the cost of the lives of hundreds of graceful birds; and hundreds of others that now merrily make so free would have been scared away. The money that would have been spent in cartridges is applied to the purchase of honey from foreign parts. No one is much the worse off. Indeed, my friend who purchased the stock is the richer by my abandonment of the calling, and am not I conscious of consistency?

So, these my vocations drift into the gentle and devious stream of inconsequence. It would be vain-glorious, no doubt, to assert that there is placid indifference to vainglory, which Carlyle declares to be, with neediness and greediness, one of the besetting sins of mankind; but am I not free from the cares that obtrude on those of tougher texture of mind who find joy in the opposite to this peace and unconcern for the rewards and honours of the world? Better this isolation and moderation in all things than, racked with worries, to moan and fret because of non-success in the ceaseless struggle for riches, or the increase thereof; better than to bow down to and worship in the "soiled temple of Commercialism" that haughty and supercilious old idol Mammon; better than to offer continual sacrifices of rest, health, and the immediate good of life to appease the exacting and silly deities of fashion and society.

There may be some who, in a disparaging tone, will at this stage of my confessions enter an accusation of impracticableness. To such a charge I would plead guilty; but to those who proffer it, I neither appeal nor do I fear their judgment. These writings are for those who see something in life beyond the mere "getting on in the world", or making a din in it.

CHAPTER II

For the Beachcomber, when not a mere ruffian, is the poor relation of the artist.

IN justification of the assumption of the title of "Beachcomber", it must be said that, having made good and sufficient provision against the advent of the wet season (which begins, as a rule, during the Christmas holidays), the major portion of each week was spent in first formal and official calls, and then friendly and familiar visits to the neighbouring islands and the mainland.

Duty and inclination constrained me to find out what were the states and moods of all the bays and coves of all the isles; the location and form of rocks and reefs; the character of shrubs and trees; the nature of the jungle-covered hilltops; the features of bluffs and precipices; to understand the style and manner and the conversation of unfamiliar birds; to discover where the turtle most did congregate; the favourite haunts of fishes. I was in a hurry to partake freely of the novel pleasure of the absolute freedom of isles uninhabited, shores untrodden; eager to know how nature, not under the microscope, behaved; what were her maiden fancies, what the art with which she allures.

But there was an excuse, rather an imperious command, for all the apparent waste of time. Before the rains came thundering on the iron roof of our little hut, the washed-out and enfeebled town-dweller who gave way to bitter reflections on the first evening of his new career, could hardly have been recognized, thanks to the robustious, wholesome effects of the free and vitalizing life. Fourteen, frequently sixteen, hours of the twenty-four were spent in the open air, ashore and afloat.

What a glowing and absolutely authentic testimonial could be written as to the tonic influence of the misrepresented climate of the rainy belt of North Queensland on constitutions that have run down! According to popular opinion, malaria ought to have discovered an exceptionally easy prey. Ague, if the expected had happened, should have gripped and shaken me until my teeth rattled; and after alternations of raging fever and arctic cold, I ought to have gone to my long home with the fearful shapes of delirium yelling in my ears. But there are places other than Judee where they do not know everything. At the fraction of the fee of a fashionable doctor, and of the cost of following his fashionable and pleasing advice—a change to one of the Southern States—in three months one of the compelling causes for the desertion of town life had been disposed of by agreeable processes. None of the bitter after-taste of physic remained. I knew my island, and was on terms of friendly admiration—born of knowledge of beauty spots—with all the others. I had become a citizen of the universe.

During this period of utter abandonment of all serious claims upon time and exertion came the conviction that the career of the Beachcomber, the closest possible "return to Nature" now popularly advocated, has charms none other possesses. Then it was that the lotus-blossom was first eaten.

Unfettered by the laws of society, with the means at hand of acquiring the few necessaries of life that nature in this generous part of her domain fails to provide ready-made, a Beachcomber of virtuous instinct, and a due perception of the decency of things, may enjoy a happy life. Should, however, he be of the type that demands a wreck or so every month to maintain his supplies of rum or gin, and other articles of his true religion, and is prepared if wrecks do not come with regularity to assist tardy nature by means of false lights on the shore, he will find no scope whatever among these orderly isles.

The Beachcomber of tradition parades his coral islet barefooted, bullying guileless natives out of their copra, coconut oil and pearl-shell; his chief diet, turtle and turtle eggs and fish; his drink, rum or coconut milk—the latter only when the former is impossible. When a wreck happens he becomes a potentate in pyjamas, and with his dusky wives, dressed in bright vestiture, fares sumptuously. And though the ships from the isles do not meet to "pour the wealth of ocean in tribute at his feet", he can still "rush out of his lodgings and eat oysters in regular desperation". A whack on his hardened head from the club of a jealous native is the time-honoured fate of the typical Beachcomber.

Flotsam and jetsam make another class of Beachcomber by stimulating the gaming instincts. Is there a human being, taking part in the rough and tumble of the world, who can honestly make confession and say that he has completely suffocated those inherent instincts of savagedom—joy and patience in the chase, the longing for excitement and surprise, the crude selfishness, the delight in getting something for nothing? When the sea casts up its gifts on these radiant shores, I boldly and with glee give way to my beachcombing instincts and pick and choose. Never up to the present have I found anything of real value; but am I not buoyed up by pious hopes and sanguine expectations? Is not the game as diverting and as innocent as many others that are played to greater profit? It is a game, too, that cannot be forced, and therefore cannot become demoralizing; and having no nice feelings nor fine shades, I rejoice and am glad in it.

And then what strange and varied things one sees! Once a "harness-cask", hostile to every sense, came trundled by waves eager to expel it from the vicinity of these oxless but scented isles. It overcame us as we sailed by, twenty yards off, and the general necessity for temperate diet and restricted dishes came as a sweet and a comforting reflection. No marvel if the ship whence it was ejected was in bad odour among the sailors. Leaving, as it lurched along, a greasy, foul stain on the sea, it may have poisoned multitudes of fishes during its evil course.

Occasionally a case of fruit, washed from the decks of a labouring steamer, drifts ashore. One was the means of introducing a valuable addition to the products of the island. It gave demonstration of how man may unwittingly, and even in opposition to his wit, assist in scattering and multiplying blessings on a smiling land—blessings to last for all time, and perhaps to amend or ameliorate the environment of a budding nation.

Again, a German barque, driven out of its course, found unexpectedly a detached portion of the Great Barrier Reef two hundred miles away to the south. When the south-easters came, they pounded away so vigorously with the heavy guns of the sea that in a brief space nothing was left of the big ship save some distorted fragments of iron jammed in among the nigger-heads of coral and the crevices of the rocks. A few weeks after, portions of the wreck were deposited on Dunk Island, and the beach of the mainland for miles was strewn with timber. That wreck was the greatest favour bestowed me in my profession of Beachcomber. Long and heavy pieces of angle-iron came bolted to raft-like sections of the deck; various kinds of timber proved useful in a variety of ways. What? was I to leave it all, unclaimed and unregarded—in excess of morality and modesty—on the beach, to be honeycombed by white ants or to rot? or to honestly own up to that sentiment which is the most human of all? Without affectation or apology, I confess that I was overjoyed—that my instincts, pregnant with original sin, received a most delightful fillip. I wallowed for the time being in the luxury of beachcombing.

Upon sober reflection, I cannot say that I am of one mind with the pastor of the Shetland Isles who never omitted this petition from his long prayer—"Lord, if it be Thy holy will to send shipwrecks, do not forget our island"; nor yet with the Breton fishermen, who to this day are of opinion that wreckage is the gift of God, and who therefore take everything that comes in a reverential spirit, as a Divine favour, whether casks of wine or bales of merchandise. But, after all, who am I that I should claim a finer shade of morality than those, with their sturdy widespread hands and perpetual blessing? My inherent powers of resistance to such temptations as the winds and tides of Providence put in their way have never been subject to proof. Does virtue go by default where there is no opportunity to be otherwise than virtuous? The very first pipe of port, or aum of Rhenish, or bale of silk, which comes rolling along may wrestle with my morality and so wrench and twist it as to incapacitate it for ordinary usage for months, or may even permanently disable it. And must not I, venturing to regard myself as a truthful historian, frankly admit a sense allied to disappointment when the white blazing beaches are destitute of the most trivial of temptations?

No, the grating of the battered barque, upon which many a wet and weary steersman had stood, now fulfils placid duty as a front gate. No more to be trampled and stamped upon with shifty, sloppy feet—no more to be scrubbed and scored with sand and holystone; painted white, it creaks gratefully every time it swings —the symbol of security, the first outward and visible sign of home, the guardian of the sacred rights of private property, the embodiment of the exclusive. Better so than lying inert underfoot on the deck of the barque thrashing through the cold grey seas of the Baltic, or scudding before the unscrupulous billows of Biscay.

Moreover, what notable and precise information this derelict timber gave as to the strength and direction of ocean currents. The wreck took place on 26 October 1900, in 18 deg. 43 min. S. lat., 147 deg. 57 min. E. long., $72\frac{1}{2}$ miles in a direct line from the port of Townsville, and about two hundred miles from Dunk Island. She broke up, after all the cargo had been salvaged, early in January 1901, and on Tuesday, 5 February, at 10 a.m., the seas landed the first of the broken planks in Brammo Bay. Then for a few days the arrivals were continuous. For over fifty miles along the coast the wreckage was scattered, very little going farther north.

Nothing goes south on this part of the coast. Yes, there is one exception during my experience. A veritable cataclysm coincided with a stiff north-easterly breeze, and hundreds of bunches of bananas from plantations on the banks of the Johnstone River—twenty-five miles away—landing-stages and steps, and the beacons from the mouth of the river, drifted south. Most of the more buoyant debris, however, took the next tide back in the direction whence it came.

When there are eight or ten islands and islets within an after-noon's sail, and miles of mainland beach to police, variety lends her charms to the pursuit of the Beachcomber. Landing in one of the unfrequented coves, he knows not what the winds and the tides may have spread out for inspection and acceptance. Perhaps only an odd coconut from the Solomon Islands, its husk riddled by cobra and zoned with barnacles. The germ of life may yet be there. To plant the nut above high-water mark is an obvious duty. Perhaps there is a paddle, with rude tracery on the handle, from the New Hebrides, part of a Fijian canoe that has been bundled over the Barrier, a wooden spoon such as Kanakas use, or the dusky globe of an incandescent lamp that has glowed out its life in the state-room of some ocean liner, or a broom of Japanese make, a coal-basket, a "fender", a tiger nautilus shell, an oar or a rudder, a tiller, a bottle cast away far out from land to determine the strength and direction of ocean currents, the spinnaker boom of a yacht, the jib-boom of a staunch cutter. Once there was a goodly hammer cemented by the head fast upright on a flat rock, and again the stand of a grindstone, and a trestle, high and elabor-ately stayed. Cases, invariably and disappointingly empty, come and go, planks of strange timber, blocks from some tall ship. A huge black beacon waddled along, dragging a reluctant mass of iron at the end of its chain cable, followed by a roughly-built "flatty" and a huge log of silkwood. A jolly red buoy, weary of the formality of bowing to the swell, broke loose from a sandbank's apron-strings, bounced off in the ecstasies of liberty, romped in the surf, rolled on the beach, worked a cosy bed in the soft warm sand, and has slumbered ever since to the soothing hum of the wind, indifferent to the perplexities of mariners and the fate of ships. The gilded mast-head truck of a smart yacht, with one of her cabin racks, bespoke of recent disaster, unknown and unaccounted, and a brand new oar, finished and fitted with the nattiness of a man-o'-war's man, told of some wave-swept deck.

That which at the time was the most eloquent message from the sea came close to our door, cast up on the snowy-white coral drift of a little cove, where it immediately attracted notice. Nothing but an untrimmed bamboo staff nearly thirty feet long, carrying an oblong strip of soiled white calico between two such strips of red turkey twill. Tattered and frayed, the flags seemed to tell of the desperate appeal for help of some forlorn castaway; of a human being, marooned on a lonely sandbank on the Barrier, without shelter, food or water, but not altogether bereft of hope. Bêche-de-mer fishers have in times past been marooned on the Reef by mutinous blacks, and left to die by slow degrees, or to be drowned by the implacable yet merciful tide. A makeshift rudder well worn bespoke strenuous efforts to steer a troubled boat to shelter, but this crude signal staff, deftly arranged, told of present agony and stress. It might have been the emblem of a tragic event that the Beachcomber, single-handed, was not able to investigate. As a matter of fact, it was only a temporary datum of one of His Majesty's surveying ships engaged in attempting to set the bounds of the Barrier.

Rarely do we sail about without enjoying the zest of the chance of getting something for nothing. Not yet has the seaman's chest, brass-bound, with its secret compartments full of "fair rose-nobles and bright moidores", been lighted upon; but who can say? Perhaps it has come ashore but now, after leagues of aimless wanderings, and awaits in some cosy cove the next beachcombing expedition. That from the ill-fated *Merchant* came hither years before my time, and was, in any case, pathetically unromantic.

Peradventure there are many who deem this solitary existence dull? Why, it is brimful of interest and sensation. There are the tragedies of the bush to observe and elucidate; all cannot be foreseen and prevented, or even avenged. A bold falcon the other day swooped down upon a wood-swallow that was imitating the falcon's flight just above my head, and bore it bleeding to a tree-top, while I stood shocked at the audacity of the cannibal. A bullet dropped the murderous bird with its dead victim fast in the talons. There are comedies, too, an you have the wit to see them, and in these beachcombing expeditions expectation fairly effervesces.

One lucky individual—a mere amateur—casually picked up a black-lip mother-of-pearl shell on an island some little distance away. It contained a blue pearl, the price of which gave him such a start in life that he is now an owner of ships. May not other tides cast up on other shores other oysters whose lives have been rendered miserable by the presence of pearls?

The Beachcomber wants no extensive establishment. His possessions need never be mortgaged. The cost of living is measurable by a standard adjustable to individual taste, wants and perceptions. The expenditure of a little manual labour supplies the omissions of and compensates for the undirected impulses which prevail, and the pursuit—if not the profession—leads one to ever-varying scenes, to the contemplation of many of the moods of unaffected, unadvertised Nature. Ashore, one dallies luxuriously with time, free from all the restrictions of streets, every precious moment his very own; afloat in these calm and shallow waters there is a never-ending panorama of entertainment. Coral gardens —gardens of the sea nymphs, wherein fancy feigns cool, shy, chaste faces and pliant forms half-revealed among gently swaying robes; a company of porpoise, a herd of dugong; turtle, queer and familiar fish, occasionally the spouting of a great whale, and always the company of swift and graceful birds. Sometimes the whole expansive ocean is as calm as it can only be in the tropics and bordered by the Barrier Reef—a shield of shimmering silver from which the islands stand out as turquoise bosses. Again, it is of cobalt blue, with changing bands of purple and gleaming pink, or of grey-blue—the reflection of a sky pallid and tremulous with excess of life.

These chronicles are toned from first to last by perceptions which came to the Beachcomber—perceptions which lead, mayhap, to a subdued and sober estimate of the purpose and bearing of the pilgrimage of life. Doubts become exalted and glorified, hopes all rapture, when long serene days are spent alone in the contemplation of the splendours of sky and sea, and the enchantment of tropic shores.

Was there not an explicit contract that some of the experiences and events of a settler's life should be duly described and recorded?

Well, the life of a settler—the man who drags his sustenance, all and every part of it, from the soil—in tropical Queensland, as a mere settler very closely resembles that of others who cultivate. If an abstract of the universal experience were obtainable, it would very likely be found to go towards the establishment of a standard from which many would cheerfully desire many cheerful changes. After all, that represents a condition not altogether monopolized by settlers.

Yet, when once the life is begun, how few there are who attempt to withdraw from it? It grows on the senses and faculties. It appeals to the emotional as well as to the stolid humours. The cares of this world as expounded in town life, and the sinfulness of never-to-be-acquired riches are foreign to the free, bland air which has filtered through the myriad leaves of the mountain, and which smacks so strongly of freedom. Sometimes the settler takes up studies and relieves the sameness of his duties by pastimes. One never went to his maize field, along narrow gloomy aisles through the jungle, without a net for the capture of butterflies. His humble home was as resplendent as the show-cases of a natural history museum. But he was singularly favoured. A lovely waterfall was the jewel on his estate. That was the shape of beauty that moved away the pall from his dark spirit and gave colour to his life and actions. Another took to collecting birds' eggs; another to the study of botany; another to photography. Each wreathed, according to his predilections, a flowery band to bind him to the earth, finding that even the life of a settler may be filled with "sweet dreams, and health and quiet".

Many become great readers and are knowing and knowledge-able. Those who drift away from country life are for the most part men who hustle after the coy damsel fortune by searching for minerals, and just as many who have succeeded in that arduous passion settle quietly on the land. Each may and does desire amendments to and amelioration in his lot. There is still left to all the healthy impulse of achievement, the desire for something better, the noble and inspiriting virtue of discontent.

Rare is a deserted home. Even the first rough dwelling of a

settler possessing the slenderest resources is invested with tender sentiments. There is his home—a poor one, perhaps, but his own, and to it he clings with desperation, sees in and about it attractions and beauty where others perceive nothing but untoned dreariness, unrelieved hopelessness. His little bit of country may be remote and isolated, but nature is warm and encouraging, and profuse of her stimulants here. She responds off-hand without pausing to reflect, but with an outburst of goodwill and purpose to appeals for sustenance. She has no despondent moods. She never lapses in prolific purposes. She may be wayward in accepting the interferences of man, but all her vigorous impulses are expended in productiveness. She cannot sulk or idle. Kill, burn and destroy her primeval jungle, and she does not give way to sadness and despair, nor are any of her infinite forces abated. Spontaneously she begins the work of restoration, and as if by magic the scar is covered with as rich and riotous a profusion of vegetation as ever. Nature needs only to be restrained and schooled and her response is an abundance of various sorts of food for man.

The routine that cultivators of the soil have to obey is diverse, but the life of the dweller in the country in tropical Queensland can be asserted with perfect safety to be more comfortable than that of the average settler in any other part of Australia. There are no phases of agricultural enterprise devoid of toil, save perhaps the growing of vanilla, the very poetry of the oldest of pursuits, in which one has to aid and abet in the loves and in the marriage of flowers. But vanilla production is not one of the profitable branches of agriculture here yet. We have to deal only with things that are at present practicable.

Whether the settler grows maize, or fruit or coffee, or as a collateral exercise of industry gets log timber, or raises pigs or poultry, the life has no great variations. If he farms sugar-cane, being resident within the zone of influence of a mill, he belongs to a different order—an order with which it is not intended to deal. My purpose refers only to men who do not employ labour, who have to depend almost solely upon their own hard hands.

I am fearful of entering upon a description of the cultivation of maize, or bananas, or citrus fruits, or pineapples, or mangoes, or coffee, or even sweet potatoes, because experience teaches me that others know of all the details in a far more practical sense.

Would it not be presumptuous for a mere idler, an individual whose enterprise and industry have been sapped by the insidious nonchalance of the Beachcomber, to tell of practical details of cultural pursuits—the enthusiasm, the disappointments, the glowing anticipations, the realization of inflexible facts, the plain emphatic truths which others have reason to know ever so much more keenly?

But it may be forgiven if I generalize and say that the minor departments of rural enterprise in North Queensland are in a peculiar stage—a stage of transition and uncertainty. Coloured labour has been depended upon to a large extent. Even the poorest settler has had the aid of aboriginals. But with the passing of that race, and prohibition against the employment of any sort of coloured labour, the question is to be asked: Can tropical products be grown profitably unless consumers are willing to pay a largely increased price—a price equivalent to the difference between the earnings of those who toil in other tropical countries and the living wage of a white man in Australia?

Fruit of many acceptable varieties can be grown to perfection with little labour in immense quantities. Coffee is one of the most prolific of crops. Timber is obtainable in magnificent assortment and unrealizable quantities. Poultry and pigs multiply extraordinarily. Apart from bananas the fruit trade is shifty and treacherous. The markets are far away and inconstant, the means of transport not yet perfect. Many assert that not half the pineapples and oranges, and not one-hundredth part of the mangoes, produced in North Queensland are consumed. That the quantity grown is trivial in comparison with what would be, were the demand regular and consistent, is evident. We want population to eat our produce, and then there will be no complaint.

In coffee it is as with many other features of rural life in Australia. The men who undertake the production are for the most part those who have gained their knowledge by personal experience on the spot. Reading and the advice of experts who have graduated in countries where climatic conditions are diverse and where the labour is cheap, yet skilled by reason of generation after generation of occupation in it, do not complete necessary knowledge. Problems have to be faced that have no theoretical nor official solution, and blunders paid for, until by the process of the elimination of mistakes the right way is discovered. Losses mount up until either patience and means are exhausted, or success crowns the application of intelligent enterprise. Then, when the coffee planter, self-taught, in each and all of the departments of culture and preparation, glories in the assurance of his capabilities to offer to the world an article of indubitable character, he discovers that the vulgar world, for the most part, prefers its coffee duly adulterated; indeed has become so warped and perverted in perception that the pure and undefiled article is looked upon with suspicion and distaste. Its flavour and aroma are quite foreign to the ordinary coffee drinker. The contaminated beverage is regarded as pure, and the genuine article is soundly condemned as an imposition, and the seller of it is liable to be accused of fraud.

But there are other branches of tropical agriculture to which the settler may devote himself. Rubber offers belated fortune. Cotton, rice, tobacco and fibre-plants flourish exceedingly, and in the production of ginger and some sort of spices and medicinal gums, profit may be possible. It is amply demonstrated that butter quite up to the standard of exportation is to be manufactured in tropical Queensland.

No one need starve or pine for lack of wholesome appetising and nutritious food while the banana grows as it does in North Queensland, and common as it is, the banana is one of the curiosities of the vegetable world. One writer says: "It is not a tree, a palm, a bush, a vegetable, nor a herb; it is simply a herbaceous plant with the stature of tree, and is perennial." He adds that the fruit contains no seed, though he qualifies the latter statement by remarking that he has heard of fully developed seeds occasionally appearing in the cultivated fruit "when left to ripen on the tree", and further that wild varieties of the banana which propagate themselves by seed are reported to be found in some parts of eastern Asia.

There are three if not more species of bananas native to Queensland, and they form a conspicuous feature of the jungle. With remarkable rapidity one of the species shoots up a ruddy symmetrical, slightly tapering stem—smooth and polished where the old leaf-sheaths have been shed—to a height of twenty and thirty feet, producing leaves fifteen feet long and two feet broad, small and crude flowers, and bunches of dwarf fruit containing little but shot-like seeds. The energy of these plants seems to be concentrated in the production of an elegant and proud form, the fruit being a mere after-thought. But the effect of the broad pale green leaves, even when frayed and ragged at the edges, in and among the dark entanglement of the jungle is so fine that the absence of edible fruit may be almost forgiven.

In the most popular of the cultivated varieties, the far-famed *Musa cavendishii*, there is little of graceful form, save the broad leaves mottled with brown. All the vitality of the plant is expended in astonishing results. A comparatively lowly plant, its productions in suitable soil are prodigious. In nine or ten months after the planting of the rhizome, it bears under favourable conditions a bunch weighing as much as one hundred and twenty pounds to one hundred and sixty pounds, and comprising as many as forty-eight dozen individual bananas. So great is the weight that to prevent the downfall of the plant a stake sharpened at each end —one to stick in the ground and the other into the soft stem—is needed to buttress it. Before the fruit has fully developed, other shoots have appeared; but each plant bears but one bunch, and when that is removed the plant is decapitated and slowly decays, and the second and third and fourth shoots from the rhizome successively arrive at the bearing stage and are permitted to mature each its bunch and then fated to suffer immediate decapitation. And so the process goes on for five or seven years, by which time the vigour of the soil has been exhausted, and moreover the rhizomes, originally planted about a foot deep, have grown up to the surface, and are no longer capable of supporting a plant upright. Then a fresh planting of rhizomes elsewhere takes place. It must not be thought that the banana defertilizes the soil. Phenomenal crops of sugar-cane are produced on a "banana-sick" land.

A traveller relating his tropical experiences glorifies the banana, stating that he has eaten it "ripe and luscious from the tree". In North Queensland bananas ripening on the plant frequently split, and seldom attain perfect flavour. The ripening process takes place after the fully-developed bunch is removed and hung up in a cool, shady, well-aired locality. Then the fruit acquires its true lusciousness and aroma. Other climes, other results, perhaps; but a banana "ripe and luscious from the tree" is not generally expected in North Queensland. The fruit may mature until it falls to the ground, yellow and soft, yet lack that delicate finish, that benign essential, the craft of man bestows. It would seem that the plant has been cultivated for so long a period that it has become dependent upon man not only for its existence but for the excellence of its crowning effort. An abandoned banana grove soon disappears, for although seeds are undoubtedly produced, the occasions are so rare that the reproduction of the cultivated varieties depends solely upon the rhizome, and these very speedily deteriorate if neglected.

Each and all of the branches of cultured industry mentioned (with the exception of the growth of sugar-cane) were at disposal for trial here. Soil, climate and aspect are extremely favourable when not approaching absolute perfection, while the advantages of direct communication with the markets are unique. But my disposition, "that rash humour which my mother gave", impelled me to disregard all the encouraging prospects of fortune, and to easily tolerate circumstances and conditions under which few would remain content. True, some few acres of jungle have been cleared and various sorts of fruit-trees planted, corn and potatoes are grown, and there are evidences of work; but no one is better qualified than I to realize the insignificance of the results of my labours in comparison with what they might have been, had the accomplishment of them been undertaken with harder hands and more determined purpose.

SOME DIFFERENCES

The weather may be extremely fine; but not without such varieties as shall hinder it from being tiresome.

Do we reflect that Australia includes some of the driest tracts in the world, as well as areas in which the rainfall approaches the phenomenal—that not very much more than half of the territory of the Commonwealth lies within the temperate zone—that there are as marked differences between Tasmania and North Queensland as between the South of England and Ceylon? That the one is the land of the potato, apple, apricot, cherry, strawberry and blackberry, and the other the land of sugar-cane, coffee, the pineapple, mango, vanilla and cocoa; that though there exist no imposing geographical boundaries, such as chains of lofty mountains or great rivers to emphasize climatic distinctions, these distinctions nevertheless exist, and that they imply special policies on the parts of government and administrations?

Do we realize that the voice of the tropic half of Australia is drowned in the torrent of the temperate? It may be possible to misrepresent opinions and to obscure the fair view of things, to defeat aspirations; but are we to be denied the right of being heard and of explaining ourselves? Politicians to whose loud and profane voices electors listen, have declared that North Queensland shall become a desolate and silent wilderness rather than that their views shall be gainsaid. Do such as these reflect that North Queensland is a fruitful country, capable of producing food and immense wealth, and giving employment to millions, and that other nations will not stand idly by and see the worth of so much land wasted because of the vanity of men who do not, and who apparently will not, endeavour to comprehend the magnificence of its extent and the width of its capabilities? The world is not so vast that any part of it—still less a part so situated and so highly favoured as this—can be left unpeopled.

Young Australians were once taught that Australian trees cast no shade—that the edges of the leaves were presented to the sun to avoid the heat of the cruel luminary; that Australian flowers had no scent, and Australian birds no song; that the stones of Australian cherries grew on the outside of the fruit, that the bees had no sting, and that the dogs did not bark. In those days a gentleman with a military title improved upon the then popular list of contradictions by asserting that in Australia the compass points to the south, the valleys are cold, the mountain-tops warm, the eagles are white, and so on. Many accordingly took their natural science as "Tomlinson" did his God—from a printed book—and that compiled in England. Until they began to investigate they were puzzled by contradictions. The first prompt bee-bite—there are many varieties of Australian bees, some pugnacious and pungent—diverted attention from the school-book romances. It was discovered that thousands of square miles of Australian soil never catch glimpses of the sun in consequence of the impenetrableness of the shade of Australian trees; that the scent of the wattles, the eucalypts, the boronias, the hoyas, the gardenias, the lotus, etc., are among the sweetest and cleanest, most powerful and most varied in the world; that many of the birds of Australia have songs full of melody; and that the so-called Australian cherry is no more a cherry than an acorn.

As to climate, will general credence be given to the statement that Dunk Island is more "temperate" than Melbourne? We experience neither the extreme heat nor the extreme cold of the metropolis of Victoria—nearly two thousand miles to the south; we have four or five times the volume of rain, yet a greater number of fine days—days without rain. The general principle that where the rainy days are fewest the amount of rain is greatest, is apt to be forgotten. During 1903 the rainfall of Dunk Island amounted to 153 inches.

Some of the denizens of a dry area in Victoria find it hard to credit the simple facts recorded by my rain-gauge. The rainfall for the month of January 1903 on Dunk Island was 26.60 inches, only 0.76 inches short of the mean for the whole year in Victoria, and more than twice the quantity that blessed the thirsty soil in some parts of Queensland. The total rainfall of the wettest locality in Victoria was 42.11 inches. Here the month of March alone gave 44.90 inches.

At Thargomindah (south-western Queensland) 11.37 inches were registered for 1903, and 9.82 inches for 1904. The two driest months of Dunk Island fell short by a trifle more than 2 inches of the total fall for 1904 for that parched area. At Eulolo (mid-western Queensland) 13.68 inches represented the sum of the blessing for 1903, while during 24 hours in December that year the Dunk Island gauge registered just 11 inches, and that quantity was 3 inches more than could be spared for Eulolo for the whole of 1904.

During 1904 Cape Otway Forest (Victoria), registered 40.92 inches, Townsville (North Queensland) 26.32 inches, and Dunk Island—only one hundred and ten miles from Townsville—94.14 inches. That was a dry year with us. What is known in this neighbourhood as "the drought year" gave just 60 inches. Plants unaccustomed to such hardship, and therefore devoid of inherent powers of resistance, then gave way with pitiful lack of resource, and as speedily recovered on the return of normal conditions. Yet the 60 inches of "the drought year" represented more than twice the average rainfall of London.

Australia is big—there is bigness in our differences.

Here in the tropics we have the finer weather—no excess of either heat or cold, no sudden, constitution-shattering changes. At Wood's Point (Victoria) rain fell on one hundred and eighty-five days in 1903, and on one hundred and sixty-six days in 1904. At Dunk Island rain occurred on one hundred and seven days in 1903 and on ninety-two days in 1904. We had many more days of picnic weather, notwithstanding our overwhelming superiority in quantity of rain. Moreover, in the tropics the bulk of the rain falls after sun-down. After a really fine day in the wet season the hours of darkness may account for several inches of rain. Here over 12 inches have been collected between sundown and nine o'clock the following morning.

Dunk Island has a mean temperature of about 69 deg.; January is the hottest month, with a mean of 87 deg., and July the coolest, mean 57 deg. Taking the official readings of Cardwell (twenty miles to the south), I find the greatest extremes on record occurred in one year, when the highest temperature was 103.3 deg. and the lowest 36.2 deg. At Innisfail (twenty-five miles to the north) the extremes were 96 deg. and 43.4 deg.

Rainfall and temperature, the proportion of clear to cloudy skies, calms, the direction, strength and the duration of winds, do not wholly comprehend distinctive climatic features. There are other conditions of more or less character and note, some hard to define yet ever present. Here the air is warm and soothing, seldom is it crisp and never really bracing. Hot dry winds are unknown, but in the height of the wet season—which coincides with the dry season of the southern States—the moisture-laden air may be likened to the vapour of a steam bath. While the rain thunders on the roof at the rate of an inch per hour, inside the house it may be perspiringly hot. After a fortnight's rain the damp saturates everything. Neglected boots and shoes grow a rich crop of mould, guns demand constant attention to prevent rust, and clothes packed tight in chests of drawers smell and feel damp. But the atmosphere is so wholesome that ordinary precautions for the prevention of sickness are generally neglected without any fear of ill consequence.

Warm as the rains are, they bring to the air coolness and refreshment. Clear, calm, bright days, days of even and not high temperature, and of pure delight, dovetail with the hot and steamy ones. The prolifigacy of vegetation is a perpetual marvel; the loveliness of the land, the ineffable purity of the sky, the glorious tints of the sea—green and gold at sunrise, silvery blue at noon, purple, pink and lilac during the all too brief twilight—are a perpetual feast.

During the cool season—a generous half of the year—dews are common—not the trivial barely perceptible moisture called dew in some parts, but most ungentle dew, which saturates everything and drips from the under-sides of verandas as the sun warms the air; dew which bows the grass with its weight, soaks through your dungarees to the hips, and soddens your thick bluchers, until you feel and appear as though you had waded through a swamp; dew which releases the prisoned odour of flowers irresponsive to the heat of the sun, which keeps the night cool and sweet, which with the first gleam of the sun makes the air soft and spicy and buoyant, and inspires thankfulness for the joy of life.

Are we not all apt to fall into the error of estimating the character of a country by its extravagances rather than its average and general qualities?

North Queensland has the reputation of being the home of malaria and the special sport of any cyclone that may have mischief in view. Being tropical, we have malaria, but it is of no more serious consequence than any one of the ills to which human flesh is heir in temperate climes. It does not exact such a toll of suffering and death as influenza, nor as typhoid used to do in crowded cities; nor is it as common as rheumatism in New Zealand, where the thermometer ranges from 100 deg. in the shade to 24 deg. of frost.

Even in the matter of cyclones—often quoted as one of its detriments—North Queensland has nothing to hide. At intervals nature does indulge in a reckless and violent outburst, but not more frequently here than in other parts of the world. Year after year the seasons are passive and pleasant, and in every respect considerate of humanity and encouraging to humanity's undertakings. Then, abandoning for a few hours her orderly and kindly ways, nature runs amok, raving and shrieking. These twenty-year-interval storms comb out superfluous leaves and branches, cut out dead wood, send to the ground decayed and weakly shoots, and scrub and cleanse trunks and branches of parasitic growths. All is done boldly, yet with such skill that in a few weeks losses are hidden under masses of clean, insectless, healthy, bright foliage. The soil has received a luxurious top-dressing. Trees and shrubs respond to the stimulus with magical vigour, for slumbering forces have been roused into efforts so splendid that the realism of tropical vegetation is to be appreciated only after nature has swept and sweetened her garden.

Many have told of the thin forests of Queensland, the open

plains, and the interminable downs whereon the mirage plays with the fancies of wayfarers; and of the dust, heat and sweat of cattle-stations. Who has yet said or sung of the mystery of the half-lit jungles of our coast, in contrast to the vivid boldness of the sun-sought, shadeless western plains; of our green, moist mountains, seamed with gloomy ravines, the source of perennial streams; of the vast fertile lowlands in which the republic of vegetation is as an unruly, ungoverned mob, clamouring for topmost places in unrestrained excess of energy; of still lagoons, where the sacred pink lotus and the blue and white water-lily are rivals in grace of form, in tint and in perfume?

ISLAND FAUNA

While the bird life of our island is plentiful and varied, mammals are insignificant in number. The echidna, two species of rats, a flying fox and two bats comprise the list. Although across a narrow channel marsupials are plentiful, there is no representative of that typical Australian order here, and the Dunk Island blacks have no legends of the existence of kangaroos, wallabies, kangaroo rats or bandicoots in times past. But there are circumstantial details extant that the island of Timana was an outpost of the wallaby until quite a recent date. A gin (the last female native of Dunk Island) who died in 1900, was wont to tell of the final battue at Timana, and the feast that followed, in which she took part as a child. This island, which has an area of about twenty acres, bears a resemblance to a jockey's cap—the sand-spit towards the setting sun forming the peak, a precipice covered with scrub and jungle, the back. Here, long ago, a great gathering from the neighbouring islands and the mainland took place. Early in the morning all formed up in line on the sand-spit. Diverging, but maintaining order, men, gins, piccaninnies, shouting, yelling, and screaming, and clashing nulla-nullas (throwing-sticks), supported by barking and yelping dogs, swept the timid wallabies up through the tangle of jungle, until like the Gaderene swine they ran, or rather hopped, down a steep place into the sea, or fell on fatal rocks laid bare by the ebb-tide. Those who partook of the last of the wallabies have gone the way of all flesh, and the incident is instructive only as an illustration of the manner in which animals may suddenly disappear from confined localities, leaving no relic of previous existence.

The largest and heaviest four-footed creature now existent on Dunk Island is the so-called porcupine (spiny ant-eater or echidna). An animal which possesses some of the features of the hedgehog of old England, and resembles in others that distinctly Australian paradox, the platypus, which has a mouth which it cannot open—a mere tube through which the tongue is thrust—which in the production of its young combines the hatching of an egg with the suckling of a mammal, and which also has some of the characteristics of a reptile, cannot fail to be an interesting object to every student of the marvels of nature. When disturbed, the echidna resolves itself into a ball, tucking its long snout between its forelegs, and packing its barely perceptible tail close between the hind ones, presenting an array of menacing prickles whencesoever attacked. While in this ball-like posture, the animal, as chance affords, digs with its short strong legs and steel-like claws, tearing asunder roots, and casting aside stones, and the ease and rapidity with which it disappears in soft soil are astonishing. The array of prickles presented as it digs an undignified retreat, and the tenacity with which it holds the ground, have given rise to the fiction that no dog is capable of killing an echidna. No ordinary dog is. He must be cunning, daring, brave, insensible to pain, and resourceful. Then the feat is quite ordinary. The long tubular nose of the echidna is the vital spot. This is guarded with such shrewdness and determination as to be impregnable. But the dog which pursues the proper tactics, and is wily and patient, sooner or later—regardless of the alleged poisonous spur—seizes one of the hind-legs, and the conflict quickly comes to an end.

By the blacks the echidna, which is known as "Coom-bee-yan", is placed on the very top of the list of those dainties which the crafty old men reserve for themselves under awe-inspiring penalties.

Next in size to the echidna is the white-tipped rat, water-loving, nocturnal in its habits, fierce and destructive. A collateral circumstance revealed absolute proof of its existence, which had previously depended upon vague statements of the blacks. Cutting firewood in the forest one morning, I came across a carpet snake, twelve feet long, laid out and asleep in a series of easy curves, with the sun revealing unexpected beauty in the tints and in the patterns of the skin. Midway of its length was a tell-tale bulge, and before the axe shortened it by a head, I was convinced that here was a serpent that had waylaid and surprised or beguiled a fowl. Post-mortem examination, however, proved once more the unreliability of uncorroborated circumstantial evidence. The snake had done good and friendly service instead of ill, for it had swallowed a white-tailed rat—the only specimen that I have seen on the island.

Next comes the little frugivorous rat of russet brown, with a glint of gold on its fur tips. A delicate, graceful creature, nice in its habits, with a plaintive call like the cheep of a chicken; preferring ripe bananas and pineapple, it consents to nibble at other fruits, as well as grain. The mother carries her young crouched on her haunches, clinging to her fur apparently with teeth as well as claws, and she manages to scuttle along fairly fast, in spite of her encumbrances. The first that I saw bearing away her family to a place of refuge was deemed to be troubled with some hideous deformity aft, but inspection at close quarters showed how she had converted herself into a novel perambulator. I am told that no other rodent has been observed to carry its young in this fashion. Perhaps the habit has been acquired as a result of insular peculiarities, the animal, unconscious of the way of its kind on the mainland, having invented a style of its own, "ages ahead of the fashion".

Mr C. W. de Vis, M.A., of the Queensland Museum, who has considerably examined specimens of this rat, pronounces it to be extraordinary, in that it combines types of three genera—the teeth of the mus, the mammae of the mastacomys and the scales on the tail of the genus *Uromys*. In the bestowal of a name he has favoured the latter genus. The animal has been introduced to the scientific world under the title *Uromys banfieldi*, by Mr de Vis, who, referring to it as "eccentric", says: "The female first sent to us as an example of the species had no young with her, nor were her mammae much in evidence; consequently, the advent of a specimen caught in the act of carrying young was awaited with interest. Fortune at length favoured our correspondent with an opportunity of placing the correctness of his observation beyond question. (A mother with a pair of infants attached to the teats was chloroformed and sent to Brisbane.) On arrival, the young were found detached. The conical corrugated nipples are, compared with the size of the animal, very long; one, especially, 20 mm. in length, calls to mind a marsupial teat."

By the examination of adult specimens the age at which the young disassociate themselves from the mother has been ascertained. Long after the time of life at which other species of rats are nibbling an independent way through the world, *U. banfieldi* clings resolutely to its parent, obtaining from her its sole sustenance. Not until the "infant" is nearly half the size of the mother does it begin to earn its living and trust to its own means of locomotion.

CHAPTER III

As the sweet voice of a bird,
Heard by the lander in a lonely isle
Moves him to think what kind of bird it is,
That sings so delicately clear, and make
Conjecture of the plumage and the form.

FRANKLY it must be admitted that the idea of retiring to an island was not spontaneous. It was evolved from a sentimental regard for the welfare of bird and plant life. Having pondered upon the destructive instinct which prevails in mankind, having seen that, though the offences which man commits against the laws of nature are promptly detected and assuredly punished, they are yet repeated over and over again, and having more pity for the victims of man's heartlessness and folly than regard for the consequences which man suffers in the blows that nature inflicts as she recoils, the inevitable conclusion was that moral suasion was of little purpose—that there must be more of example than precept. In this particular case how speedy and effective has been the result will be seen later on.

It was resolved, as other phases of island life matured, that one of the first ordinances to be proclaimed would be that forbidding interference with birds. That ordinance prevails. Our sea-girt hermitage is a sanctuary for all manner of birds, save those of murderous and cannibalistic instincts. We give all a hearty welcome and make friends of them if possible. During the eight years of our occupancy many shy creatures have become quite bold and familiar; though I am fain to admit, with disappointment, that but slight increases in the species represented have been noticed. Four strange species of terns, which are wont to lay on the bare reef patches of the Barrier, now visit Purtaboi regularly every season, depositing their eggs among those of two other species, which, in spite of disturbance by the blacks, year after year refused to abandon the spot. Possibly the fact that a haven of refuge has been established has not been widely promulgated among our friends. Those who are with us or visit us have peace and security, and are for the most part friendly and trustful.

55

Before there is any visible sign of the break of day, some keener and finer perception than man possesses reveals it to the noisy pitta, or dragoon bird, which in duty bound makes prompt proclamation. Man trusts to mechanism to check off the watches of the night; birds to a self-contained grace more sensitive if not so viciously exact. The noisy pitta bustles along the edge of the jungle rousing all the sleepy heads with sharp interrogative whistles before there is the least paling of the eastern sky. His version of "Sleepers, wake" echoes in the silence in sharp, staccato notes. Seldom heard during the heat of the day, they are oft repeated at dusk and late in the evening. Of all the birds of the day his voice is the last as well as the first, and from that the natives derive his name, "Wung-go-bah".

As the dawn hastens a subdued fugue of chirps and whistles, soft, continuous and quite distinct from the cheerful individual notes and calls with which the glare is greeted, completes a circle of sounds. Wheresoever he stands the listener is in the centre of ripples of melody which blend with the silence almost as speedily as the half lights flee before the pompous rays of the imperial sun. This charming melody is but a general exclamation of pleasure on the recovery of the day from the apprehension of the night, a mutual recognition, an interchange of matutinal compliments. Those who take part in it may be jealous rivals in a few minutes, but the first impulse of each new day is a universal paean, not loud and vaunting, but mellow, sweet and unselfish.

THE MEGAPODE

The cackle and call of the scrub fowl are nocturnal as well as sounds of the day, being repeated at intervals all through the night. Rarely venturing out of the shades of the jungle, the eyesight of this bird is, no doubt, specially adjusted to darkness and subdued lights, and is thus enabled to detect and prey upon insects which during the day lurk under leaves and decayed wood, or bury themselves in the surface of the ever-moist soil. Astonishment is excited that there can by any possibility be any grubs or beetles, centipedes and worms, scorpions and spiders left to perpetuate their species, when the floor of the jungle is raked over with such assiduity by this powerful and active bird. During the day the megapode is mostly silent, but ever and anon it gives way to what may in charity be presumed to be a crow—an uncouth, discordant effort to imitate the boastful, tuneful challenge of the civilized rooster. In common with "Elia" (and others) the megapode has no ear for music. It seems to have been practising "cock-a-doodle-doo" all its life in the solitary corners and undergrowth, and to have not yet arrived within quavers of it.

The inclusion among the birds of the air of such an inveterate land lover, a bird which seldom takes flight of its own motive, is permissible on general principles, while its practical exercise of rare domestic economy entitles it to special and complimentary notice. Reference is made elsewhere to the surpassing intelligence of the megapode in taking advantage of the heat caused by the fermentation of decaying vegetation to hatch out huge eggs. Long before the astute Chinese practised the artificial incubation of hens' and ducks' eggs, these sage birds of ours had mastered it. Several birds seem to co-operate in the building of a mound, which may contain many cartloads of material, but each bird appears to have a particular area in which to deposit her eggs. The chicks apparently earn their own living immediately they emerge fully fledged from the mound, and are so far independent of maternal care that they are sometimes found long distances from the nearest possible birthplace, scratching away vigorously and flying when frightened with remarkable vigour and speed, though but a few hours old.

I come gladly to the conclusion that the megapode is a sagacious bird, not only in the avoidance of the dismal duty of incubation, but in respect of the making of those great mounds of decaying vegetable matter and earth which perform the function so effectively. In a particularly rugged part of the island is a mound almost completely walled in by immense boulders. In such a situation the birds could hardly have found it possible to accumulate by kicking and scratching so great a quantity of debris. The material was not available on the site, and as the makers do not carry their rubbish, it was puzzling to account for it all, until it was noticed that the junction of two boulders with an inclination towards each other formed a natural flume or shute down which most of the material of the mound had been sent. As the rains and use flatten the apex fresh stuff is deposited with a trifling amount of labour, to afford an illustration of "purposive conscious action".

The megapode seems to delight in flying in the face of laws to which ordinary fowls are obedient. While making a law unto herself for the incubation of eggs, she scandalously violates that which provides that the size of the egg shall be in proportion to the size of the bird. Though much less in weight than an average domestic fowl, the egg that she lays equals nearly three of the fowl's. Comparisons between the egg of the cassowary (one of the giants among birds) and of the common fowl with that of the megapode, are highly complimentary to the latter. A fair weight for a full-grown cassowary is one hundred and fifty pounds, and the egg weighs one pound six ounces. A good-conditioned megapode weighs three pounds, the egg five and a quarter ounces; ordinary domestic fowl, four pounds, egg two ounces. The egg of the cassowary represents 1 per cent of the weight of the bird, the domestic fowl's $3\frac{1}{8}$ per cent, and that of the megapode no less than $11\frac{1}{2}$ per cent of its weight.

When these facts are considered, we realize why the horny head of the great cassowary, the layer of the largest of Australian eggs, is carried so low as she bursts through the jungle, why the pair converse in such humble tones; and why, on the other hand, the megapode exults so loudly, so coarsely, and in such shocking intervals, careless of the sentiments and of the sense of melody of every other bird.

Though the powers of flight of this bird are feeble, it inhabits islands three and four miles farther out to sea than their most adjacent neighbours. The laboured way in which a startled bird flies across the narrow expanse of my plantation proves that a long journey would never be undertaken voluntarily. Not many months ago some blacks walking on the beach on the mainland had their attention attracted by a bird flying low on the water from the direction of Dunk Island, two and a half miles away. It was labouring heavily, and some little distance from land fell exhausted into the sea. When it drifted ashore—a god-send to the boys—it was found to be a megapode—and the feat was camp talk. None could credit that a "kee-rowan" could fly so far.

SWAMP PHEASANT

The swamp pheasant, or pheasant-coucal is also an early bird, and a bird of varied linguistic capabilities. Folks are apt to associate with him but one note, and that resembling the mellow gurgle of cream from a bottle, "Glooc! glooc! glooc! glooc!" An intimate knowledge of his conversational powers leads one to conclude that there are few birds more widely accomplished in that direction. He does use the fluid phrase mentioned, but his notes and those of his consort cover quite a range of exclamations and calls.

Just as I write a pair appeal for a just recognition of their accomplishments. That which I assume to be the lord and master utters a loud resonant "Toom! toom! toom! toom!" a smooth trombonic sound, "hollow to the reverberate hill", which his consort answers with a series of "Tum! tum! tum! tum!" on a higher but still harmonious key, and in accelerated tempo. This, I fancy, is the lover's serenade, and the soft assenting answer; almost invariably the loud hollow sound is the opening phrase of the duet. "Sole or responsive to each other's note", the birds make the forest resound again during the day, especially in the prime months, and even these notes find varied and pleasing expression. Free and joyous as a rule, occasionally they seem to indicate sadness and gloom. During and after a bush fire the birds give to the notes a mournful cadence like the memories of joys that are past, a lament for the destruction of the grass among which last year's dome-shaped nests were hidden. The swamp pheasant also utters a contented, self-complacent chuckle, that resembles the "Goo! goo! goo!" of a happy infant, and occasionally a succession of grating, discordant, mocking sounds, "Tcharn! tcharn! tcharn!" The chuckle may be an expression as if gloating over the detection of some favourite dainty, and the harsh notes a demonstration of rivalry, anger and hostility. The more familiar and more frequent note is the "Toom", repeated about fourteen or sixteen times, and the thinner, softer response.

The bird resembles in plumage a pheasant. He is a handsome fellow, the ruling colours being glossy black, brown and reddish chestnut. One writer describes the bird as half hawk, half pheasant; another as a non-parasitic cuckoo; and another as "really a cuckoo". Without attempting to dispute any of these descriptions, I may say that the bird is a decided character and possesses the charm of originality. He has become so confiding that he will perch on the gate-post as one enters, assuming a fierce and resentful aspect, and he will play "hawk" to the startled fowls. He eats the eggs of other birds and kills chicks; but his murderous instincts are rarely exhibited. He does not (as far as my observation goes) kill for food, but merely because nature gives him at certain times and seasons a fiery, jealous disposition, and a truculent determination to protect his family.

"GO-BIDGER-ROO!"

As the sun shines over the range, the plaintive cooing of the little blue dove, such as picked the rice grains from the bowl beside rapt Buddha's hands, comes up from among the scented wattles on the flat, the gentlest and meekest of all the converse of the birds. The nervous yet fluty tones are as emphatic a contrast to the vehement interjections and commands of the varied honey-eater—now at the first outburst—as is the swiftly foreshortening profile of the range to the glare in which all the foreground quivers.

Once aroused, the varied honey-eater is wide awake. His restlessness is equalled only by his impertinent exclamations. He shouts his own aboriginal title, "Go-bidger-roo!" "Put on your boots!" "Which—which—which way—which way—which way you go!" "Get your whip!" "Get your whip!" "You go!" "You go!" "None of your cheek!" "None of your cheek!" "Here—here!" Then he darts out with a fluster from among the hibiscus bushes on the beach away up to the top of the melaleuca tree; pauses to sample the honey from the yellow flowers of the gin-gee; and speeds on to the scarlet blooms of the flame tree, across the pandanus palms and to the shady creek for his morning bath and drink, shouting without ceasing his orders and observations. He is always with us, though not always as noisy as in the prime of the year—a cheerful, prying, frisky creature, always going somewhere or doing something in a red-hot hurry, and always making a song of it. His lovemaking is passionate and impulsive, joyous almost to rowdyism.

BULLY, SWAGGERER, SWASHBUCKLER

The drongo-shrike is another permanent resident; glossy black, with a metallic shimmer on the shoulders, long-tailed, sharp of bill and masterful. He has a scolding tongue, and if a hawk hovers over the bloodwoods he tells without hesitation of the evil presence. He is the bully of the wilderness of leaves, bouncing birds vastly his superior in fighting weight and alertness of wing, and chattering his jurisdiction to everything that flies. When the nest on the nethermost branch of the Moreton Bay ash is packed with hungry brood, his industry is exhilarating. Ordinarily he gets all the food he wants by merely a superficial inspection; but with a family to provide for, he is compelled to fly around, shrewdly examining every likely looking locality. Clinging to the bark of the bloodwood, with tail spread out fan-wise as additional support, he searches every interstice, and ever and anon flies to the Moreton Bay ash and tears off the curling fragments of crisp bark which afford concealment to the smaller beetles, grubs and spiders.

With the loose end of bark in his bill, tugging and fluttering, using his tail as a lever with the tree as a fulcrum, and objurgating in unseemly tones, as the bark resists his efforts, the drongo assists the Moreton Bay ash in discarding worn-out epidermis, and the tree reciprocates by offering safe nesting-place on its most brittle branches.

The drongo is a bird of many moods. Silent and inert for months together, during the nesting-season he is noisy and alert, not only the first to give warning of the presence of a falcon, but the boldest in chivvying from tree to tree this universal enemy.

He is then particularly partial to an aerial acrobatic performance, unsurpassed for gracefulness and skill, and significant of the joy of life and liberty and the delirious passion of the moment. With a mighty effort, a chattering scream and a preliminary downward cast, he impels himself with the ardour of flight— almost vertically—up above the level of the tree-tops. Then, after a momentary, thrilling pause, with a gush of twittering commotion and stiffened wings preternaturally extended over the back and flattened together into a single rigid fin, drops—a feathered black bolt from the blue—almost to the ground, swoops up to a resting-place, and with bowing head and jerking tail gloats over his splendid feat.

The spangled drongo has no rival in the peculiar character of the notes and calls over which he has secure copyright. The shrill stuttering shriek which accompanies his aerial acrobatic performances, the subdued tinkling tones of pleasure, the jangle as of cracked china, the high-pitched tirade of jarring abuse and scolding at the presence of an enemy, the meek cheeps, the tremulous, coaxing whistles when the young first venture from the nest —each and every sound, totally unlike that of any other bird, indicates the oddity of this sportive member of the crow family.

Perhaps the most interesting and entertaining of all the birds of the island is that commonly known as the weaver or friendly bird, otherwise the metallic starling, the shining calornis of the ornithologist, the "Tee-algon" of the blacks. Throughout the coastal tract of North Queensland this bird is fairly familiar. It could not escape notice and comment, for it is an avowed socialist establishing colonies every few miles. There are four on Dunk Island, and though not permanent residents, spending but little more than half the year with us, they are among the few birds who have permanent homes. In some lofty tree they build perhaps two hundred nests in groups of from two to six. With all these nests weighting its thinner branches the tree may look wearied and afflicted, but it obtains direct benefit from the presence of the birds. The nests, deftly built of tendrils and slender creepers and grass are domed, the entrance being at the side, and so hidden and overhung as almost to escape notice. Each August the birds appear, coming from the north, and until the middle of March, when they take their departure, they do not indulge in many leisure moments. There are the old nests to renovate and new ones to build in accordance with the demand of the increasing population, and loads of fruits and seeds and berries to be conveyed from the jungle to the colony. The shining calornis is a handsome fellow, gleaming black, with purple and green sheen. The live bird differs so greatly from the dull, stuffed specimen of the museum that one is tempted to endeavour to convey by similitude its wonderful radiance. A soap bubble, black yet retaining all its changing lights and flashing reflections, is the nearest approach to a just description, and then there are to specify the rich, red eyes, eyes gleaming like polished gems. Until after the first year of their existence the young are brown-backed, and mottled white and bluish-grey of breast, and would hardly be recognized as members of the colony but for the shrill notes and restless activity and those flaming eyes—living gems of wondrous radiance, which epitomize the life of the bird.

Twenty or thirty may be peering about in a bloodwood, and with a unanimous impulse and a call in unison they slip through the forest, and shoot into the jungle, flashing sun-glints. Eager, alert, always under high pressure, the business of the moment brooks of no delay. The flocks come and go between the home and the feeding-ground with noisy exclamations and impetuous haste. With whirr of wings and jeering notes they swoop close overhead, wheeling into the wilderness of leaves with the rapidity of thought, and with such graceful precision that the sunlight flashes from their shoulders as an arc of light. Work, hasty work, is a necessity, for their wastefulness is extreme, or, rather, do they not unconsciously perform a double duty, being chief among the distributing agents—industrious and trustworthy though unchartered carriers for many helpless trees. When the company darts again out of the jungle, each with a berry in its bill and each shrilly exulting, many a load is dropped by the way, and many another falls to mother earth in the act of feeding the clamorous young. Berries and seeds having no means of self-transportation are thus borne far from parent trees to vegetate in sweet unencumbered soil. Other birds take part in this generous disposal, but none engages in it so systematically or so openly.

Beneath the tree which is the head centre of the colony is a carpet of debris several inches thick. Old and discarded nests, fragments of unused building materials, the nutmeg with its lacing of coral-red mace, the blue quandong, the remains of various species of figs, hard berries, chillies, degenerated tomatoes, the harsh seed-vessels of the umbrella-tree, samples of every fruit and berry of attractive appearance, however hot and acrid, all go to form a mulching of vegetable matter such as no other tree of forest or jungle gets. Prodigal and profuse as she may be, nature is the rarest of economists. Out here in the forest is springing up an oasis of jungle, every plant of which owes its origin to the shining calornis.

It must not be thought that all the notes of these most engaging birds, symbolic of light in plumage and in flight, are shrill and strident. When they feed—and they seem always to be feeding or carrying food—their chatter is perpetual and varied in tone. Occasionally a male bird sets himself to beguile the time with song. Then his flame-red eyes flash with ardour, his head is thrown back, a sparkling ruffle appears on his otherwise satiny-smooth neck; and the tune resembles that of a well-taught canary—more fluty but briefer. But the song is only for the ears of those who know how to overcome timidity and shyness. Birds naturally so impetuous are restless and uneasy under observation. One must pose in silence until his presence is forgotten or ignored. Then the delicious melody, the approving comments of the songster's companions, and the efforts of ambitious younsters to imitate and excel, are all part of a quaint entertainment.

THE NESTFUL TREE

All the forest brood do not plot mutual slaughter. Some live in strict amity. Here in the Moreton Bay ash, taken advantage of by the shining calornis, a white-headed, rufous-backed sea-eagle nests, and the graceful, fierce-looking pair come and go among the glittering noisy throng without exciting any special comment. Of course it would be impossible to detect any certain note of remonstrance, for the smaller birds are generally commenting on something or other in acidulous tones.

Another occupant of this nestful tree is the sulphur-crested cockatoo, whose eggs are laid deep down in a hollow. Two or three hundred of the shining colonists, a brood of sea-eagles—white-headed, snowy-breasted and red-backed—and a couple, perhaps three, screeching white cockatoos, represent the annual output of this single tree, in addition, of course, to its own crop of sweet-savoured flowers (on which birds, bees, beetles and butterflies, and flying-foxes feast) and seeds in thousands in cunning cups.

"STATELY FACE AND MAGNANIMOUS MINDE"

How feeble and ludicrous are the voices of the fierce hawks and eagles! The white-headed sea-eagle's puking discordant twang, the feeble cheep of the grey falcon—the cry of a sick and scared chicken—the harsh protest of the osprey, are sounds distinctive but frail, conveying no notion whatever of the demeanour and characteristics of the birds.

Now, the white-headed sea-eagle, with its sharp incurved beak, terrible talons, and armour-plated legs, is a friend to all the little birds. He has the "stately face and magnanimous minde" that old writers were wont to ascribe to the Basilik, the King of Serpents. They know and respect, almost venerate him. A horde of them never seeks to scare him away with angry scolding and feeble assaults, as it does the cruel falcon and the daring goshawk. Domestic fowls learn of his way, and are wise in their fearlessness of him. But I was not well assured of the reasons for the trustful-

64

ness and admiration of the smaller birds for the fierce-looking fellow who spends most of his time fishing, until direct and conclusive evidence was forthcoming. Two days of rough weather, and the blue bay had become discoloured with mud churned up by the sea, and the eagle found fishing poor and unremunerative sport. Even his keen eyesight could not distinguish in the murky water the coming and going of the fish. Just below the house is a small area of partly cleared flat, and there we saw the brave fellow roaming and scooping about with more than usual interest in the affairs of dry land.

At this time of year green snakes are fairly plentiful. Harmless and handsome, they prey upon small birds and frogs, and the eagle had abandoned his patrol of the sad-hued water to take toll of the snakes. After a graceful swoop down to the tips of a low-growing bush, he alighted on the dead branch of a bloodwood one hundred and fifty yards away. With the help of a telescope, his occupation was revealed—he was greedily tearing to pieces a wriggling snake, gulping it in three-quarter-yard lengths. Here was the reason for the trustfulness and respect of the little birds. The eagle was destroying the chief bugbear of their existence— the sneaking greeny-yellowy murderer of their kind and eater of their eggs, whose colour and form so harmonizes with leaves and thin branches that he constantly evades the sharpest-eyed of them all, and squeezes out their lives and swallows them whole. But the big red detective could see the vile thing fifty and even one hundred yards away, and once seen—well, one enemy the less.

Briskly stropping his beak on the branch of the tree on which he rested, and setting his breast plumage in order, much as one might shake a crumb from his waistcoat, the eagle adjusted his search-lights and sat motionless. In five minutes a slight jerk of the neck indicated a successful observation, and he soared out, wheeled like a flash, and half turning on his side, hustled down in the foliage of a tall wattle and back again to his perch. Another snake was crumpled up in his talons, and he devoured it in writhing, twirling pieces.

The telescope gave unique advantage during this entertainment, one of the tragedies of nature, or rather the lawful execution of a designing and crafty criminal. Within ten minutes the performance was repeated for the third time, and then either the supply of snakes ran out or the bird was satisfied. He shrewdly glanced this way and that, craning and twisting his neck, and seeming to adjust the lenses of his eyes for near and distant observation. No movement among the leaves seemed to escape him. Two yards and a half or perhaps three yards of live snakes constituted a repast. At any rate, after twenty minutes' passive watchfulness, he sailed up over the trees and away in the direction of his home in the socialistic community of the shining calornis.

The white-headed sea-eagle is a deadly foe to the pugnacious sea-serpent also. On the beach just above the high water-mark was the headless carcass of one that must have been fully five feet long, and while it was under inspection an eagle circled about anxiously. Soon after the intruders disappeared the bird swooped down and resumed his feast, and presently his mate came sailing along to join him. The snake must have weighed several pounds, and apparently was not as dainty to the taste as the green arboreal variety, for after two days' occasional feasting there was still some of the flesh left.

Shrewd as is the observation of the white-headed sea-eagle he is not exempt from blunders. Though he pounces with authoritative certainty and precision, he does not discriminate until the capture is complete, between the acceptable and the unacceptable. Generally whatsoever is seized is carried off, apparently without inspection. Perhaps the balloon fish is the only one that is promptly discarded. The sea porcupine, which shares with that repugnant creature the habit of exemplifying the extent to which the skin of a fish is capable of distention without bursting, is frequently picked up from the shallow water it favours. Short sharp needles stand out rigidly from its skin, forming a complete armament against most foes. The sea-eagle does not always devour the sea porcupine, which at the very best is nothing more than a picking. Amongst such a complex labyrinth of keen bones a hasty meal is not to be found, and the sea-eagle is not a leisurely eater. He likes to gulp; and so when he has indiscreetly blundered on a porcupine he frequently unlocks his talons and shakes himself free, while the fish, inflated to the last gulp, floats away high and light, bearing on its tense silvery-white side the crimson stigmata of the sea-eagle.

When misguided fish have blundered into the trap in the corner of the bay, the sea-eagle demands a share of the easily-gotten spoil. Perched on the tallest stake, he faithfully indicates the presence of feed that he cannot obtain unless by goodwill; yet who would deny the bird of his right? Having fulfilled his duty as sentinel, he soars to an adjacent tree, uttering that sneering twang which is his one paltry attribute, and when a fish is thrown into the shallow water he swoops down and is away with it to his eyrie. If the sand is bare, however, he cannot, owing to his length of wing, pick up the fish in his flight. Unbecoming as it may be to tantalize by trickery so regal a bird, a series of trials was undertaken to ascertain the height from the surface whence a fish could be gripped. Twelve successive swoops for a mullet flopping on the sand failed, though it was touched at least six times with the tips of the eagle's outstretched talons. Consenting to failure, the bird was compelled to alight undignifiedly a few yards away, to jump awkwardly to the fish, and to eat it on the spot; for however imperious the sea-eagle is in the air, and dexterous in the seizure of a fish from the water, he cannot rise from an unimpressionable plane with his talons full.

On another occasion a fish was raised four inches on a slender stake. The sea-eagle dislodged it several times, but could not grasp it. Raised a further four inches the fish was seized without fumbling. Eight inches or so, therefore, seems to be about the minimum height from which a bird with six feet of red wing and a nice determination not to bruise or soil the tips, may grip with certainty.

WHITE NUTMEG PIGEON

No birds of the air which frequent these parts attract more attention than the white nutmeg or Torres Strait pigeons, which resort to the islands during the incubating season. White, with part of each flight feather black, and with down of pale buff, they are handsome birds, strong and firm of flesh, and possess remarkable powers on the wing. Half of the year is spent with us. They come from the north in their thousands during the first week of September, and depart during March. While in this quarter they seek rest and recreation, and increase and multiply on the islands, resorting to the mainland during the day for food. Their flights to and from are made in companies varying from four to five to as many as a hundred—but the average is between thirty and forty. Purpose and instinct guide them to certain islands, and to these the companies set flight.

Towards the end of the breeding season, when the multitude has almost doubled its strength by lusty young recruits, for an hour and more before sunset until a few minutes after, there is a never-ending procession from the mainland to the favoured islands—a great, almost uncountable host. Soon some of the tree-tops are swaying under the weight of the masses of white birds. The whirr and rush of flight, the clacking and slapping of wings, the domineering "coo-hoo-oo" of the male birds and the responsive notes of the hens, the tumult when in alarm all take wing simultaneously and wheel and circle and settle again with rustling and creaking branches, the sudden swoop with whistling wings of single birds close overhead—all this creates a perpetual din. Then, as darkness follows hard upon the sinking of the sun, the birds hustle among the thick foliage of the jungle, with querulous, inquiring notes and much ado. Gradually the sounds subside, and the subdued monotonous rhythm of the sea alone is heard.

An endeavour, from the outset destined to be futile, has been made each season in succession to estimate the number of nutmeg pigeons passing a given point per minute on their evening flight. With so methodical a bird, it was to be expected that the companies would have favoured points of departure from the mainland, and would fly along precise routes to a common destination. There are thousands of stragglers all along the coast, but the main bodies keep to particular routes. Most of those which rest on the islands in this neighbourhood quit the mainland between Clump Point and Tam o' Shanter, the trend of numbers being towards the latter point. Six miles separate these headlands, but the channel between Tam o' Shanter and Dunk Island is little more than two and a half miles, so that the pigeons here become concentrated to a certain extent. Early in the season they pass Dunk Island at the rate of about three hundred per minute, during the hour and a half preceding sunset. To speak more definitely, but well within the mark, those flying south, easily within range of sight from the sand-spit here, may be calculated at something like twenty-seven thousand. But in reality the procession of birds may cover a breadth of two miles, while only those flocks nearest to the observer are included in the estimate. No doubt fully one hundred thousand come and go evening and morning. When the incubating season is at its height the number lessens; when all the young are hatched the unmarshalled procession trails along with but brief intervals between the companies—some flying low over the water, others high and wide.

Great as the company of birds seems, it is small compared with the myriads that favoured the islands in years gone by. Pioneers tell of the days when blacks were wont to make regular expeditions, returning to the mainland with canoes laden with fledglings and eggs, which in accordance with tradition were devoured by the older men and women. The youngsters of the tribes were nurtured in the belief that if they partook of such luxuries all the pigeons would fly away, never to re-visit their haunts. Strange as it may seem, the vast quantities eaten by the blacks did not seem to decrease the numbers. But since the advent of the white man, with his nerve-shattering gun, a remarkable diminution has been observed in some localities. No doubt it could be successfully maintained that the gun is responsible for an insignificant toll compared with that taken by the blacks of the past. But the birds were then deprived of their nestlings and eggs quietly, if remorselessly, while the noise of the gun is more demoralizing to the species as a whole than are the numbers actually killed.

Nutmeg pigeons are frequently shot by the hundred as they reach their nesting-places and mass themselves on the trees. Some of their nurseries lie far away from the usual tracks of the sportsman. Yet a single expedition during the breeding season to one of the islands may cause immense destruction and unprofitable loss of life. Though in lessening numbers they venture much farther along the coast to the south, they keep well within the tropical zone. The most favoured resorts within many miles are the Barnard Islands, fourteen miles to the north of Dunk Island. The whole of the tribes, therefore, though scattered for feeding over an immense area of the coast congregate on four or five islands—miles apart—to rest and breed. The assemblages are indeed prodigious; but they represent the gathering of clans which have a very wide dispersal. Crowded together the host appears innumerable, but on the mainland during the day (when only the hen birds stay at home) the pigeons seem scarce. An occasional group may be met with, and they may be heard fluttering and flapping on the tree-tops (they are generally silent when feeding), but they are too thinly distributed to afford sport. Any other species of native bird which took to gregarious habits might seem as numerous as this. If all the sulphur-crested cockatoos, scrub turkeys, and scrub fowls scattered over an area of the mainland corresponding in extent with the feeding-ground of the nutmeg pigeons were massed each night in four or five communities, the numbers would seem startling; but because the poor pigeon, conspicuous and heedless, has the instinct or habit of association, it is argued that they outnumber all the other birds, that their legions are infinite, and that that fact is sufficient licence for the destruction of thousands during the breeding season. Compared with some species, nutmeg pigeons may be considered scarce, although their breeding establishments extend over hundreds of miles of the eastern coast of North Queensland. But it must be remembered that the birds breed only on the islands. To preserve them effectually certain islands should be proclaimed sanctuaries, and genuine sportsmen will never indulge their propensities when haunted by the thoughts of the consequent cruelty.

The food of the nutmeg pigeon is multifarious. All sorts of nuts and seeds and even fruits are consumed—quandongs, various palm seeds (including those of the creeping-palm or lawyer-vine, *Calamus*), nutmeg (*Myristica insipida*, not the nutmeg of commerce, though resembling it), the white hard seeds of the native cabbage, the Burdekin plum, and all sorts of unpromisingly tough and apparently indigestible, innutritious woodeny nuts and drupes. Moreover, it fattens on such diet, but still the wonder grows at the happy provision which enables nuts proportionately of such enormous size to be swallowed by the bird, and ejected with ease after the pulp or flesh has been assimilated. As the birds alight on the island after their flight from the mainland, a portion of the contents of the crop seems to be expelled. A shower of nuts and seeds comes pattering down through the leaves to the ground as each company finds resting-place. Perhaps those only who are suffering from uncomfortable distention so relieve themselves. The balance of the contents of the crops seems to go through the ordinary process of digestion. Thus, by the medium of the pigeons, there is a systematic traffic in and interchange of seeds between the mainland and the islands.

The nutmeg pigeon resorts to islands where there is no fresh water, and builds a rude platform of twigs, and occasionally of leaves, on all sorts of trees, in all sorts of localities. Palms and mangroves, low bushes, rocky ledges, saplings, are all favoured, no particular preference being shown. It rears generally two, and sometimes three young, one at a time, during the long breeding season, which continues from the end of September until the end of January, and for each successive egg a fresh carpet of twigs or leaves is spread. A rare nest was composed of fresh leaves of the Moreton Bay ash, with the petioles towards the centre, forming a complex green star. No doubt the arrangement of the leaves was accidental, but the white dumpy egg as a pearl-like focus completed a quaint device. Another egg reposed carelessly at the base of a vigorous plant of *Dendobrium undulatum*, the old-gold plumes of the orchid fantastically shading it.

Those pigeons who elect to incubate on the ground discard even the rude platform of twigs, which generally represents the nest of those who prefer bushes and trees, but gradually encircle themselves with tiny mounds of ejected seeds, until the appearance of a nest is presented. At the termination of the breeding season these birth-places of the young are indicated by circular ramparts, in the composition of which the aromatic nutmeg predominates. Personal experiments on the spot prove that these nutmegs germinate less readily than those taken direct from the tree. Planted with the red mace still adherent the nuts are quite reliable; others which have been swallowed by the pigeon and ejected, though submitted to like conditions, fail in considerable proportion. So that the oft-repeated theory that the Queensland nutmeg requires primarily to undergo some chemical process similar to that which takes place in the crop of the pigeon to ensure germination, has no foundation whatever in fact. The part the pigeon performs is to transport the nut to free, unstifled soil.

No bird is more precise and punctual in its visits. It comes to its nesting-places and departs with almost almanac-like regularity. It is a large bird as pigeons go, and becomes wonderfully tame and trustful when undisturbed. Specimens may be procured in thousands. Blacks, understanding their habits, climb particular trees known to be well patronized, and as the birds swoop down to rest, kill them easily with a swoop of a long slender stick, or hurl nulla-nullas into the home-coming flocks, just as they alight. It is not a good table bird, the flesh being dark, tough, and of an earthy flavour—far inferior to the generality of pigeons, and not to be compared with ground or aquatic game.

FRUIT-EATERS

The tyrannical fig-tree of the species referred to elsewhere, in full fruit—pink in colouring, until it attains purple ripeness—attracts birds from all parts, and for nearly a quarter of the year is as gay as a theatre. From sunset to sunrise birds feast and flirt with but brief interludes. A general dispersal of the assemblage occurs only in the tragic presence of a falcon, whose murderous deeds are transiently recorded by stray painted feathers. But the fright soon passes, and the magnificent fruit pigeon—green, golden-yellow, purplish-maroon, rich orange, bluish-grey, and greenish-yellow, are his predominant colours—resumes his love-plaint in bubbling bass. "Bub-loo, bub-loo, maroo",* he says over and over again in unbirdlike tone, without emphasis or lilt. "Bub-loo, bub-loo, maroo", a grievance, a remonstrance and a threat in one doleful phrase; but to the flattered female, it is all compliment and gallantry. That other, known as the allied—so like his cousin that his dissonant accents, "quok—quok—quoo", are more to be relied upon as ready means of identification than any striking difference in plumage; the white-headed, the pheasant-tail, the gorgeous "superb", the tranquil dove, Ewing's fruit pigeon—most timorous of the order—are regular patrons, and each of the family has the distinctive demeanour and note. All save the allied—which is too full of assurance and fruit to be disconcerted by the presence of man—may flutter into the jungle, and then, as the momentary disturbance subsides, a study, whimsical and rich, begins.

With one exception the fruit pigeons, however gay the colouring of the throat and breast and under parts generally, are green of back, that passing falcons may be deceived by resemblance to leafy environment. Yet the "superb" and Ewing's and Swainson's have the richest of crowns—pink or shimmering rosy purple. Why this fanciful decoration if not to carry the delusion farther by resemblance to a flower?

These glorious pigeons are but a few of the many birds that come to the tree with its millions of pink figs, and enliven the scene with soft notes and eager whistles. Varied and mangrove honey-eaters, Jardine caterpillar-eaters, the tiny swallow dicaeum, in a tight-fitting costume of blue-black and red (who must bruise and batter the fruit to reduce it to gobbling dimensions), the yellow white-eye (who pecks it to pieces), the white-bellied and the varied graucalus, the drongo, the shining calornis—these and others have been included time after time in the one enumeration.

---

*Settlers know this pigeon as the "wampoo", or "Bubbly Mary".—A.H.C.

Cockatoos do not visit the fig-trees as systematically as might be expected. When they come they waste almost as lavishly as the flying-foxes at night, nipping off branchlets and dropping them after eating but two or three of the figs.

When the grey falcon soars overhead the birds display varied forms of strategy. The inconspicuous pigeons crouch motionless but alert, their eyes fixedly following the circles of the enemy; the readily detected graucalus fly straight to a forest tree, whence there is a clear get-away; the companies of yellow white-eyes, with a unanimous note of alarm, dart into the jungle; the caterpillar-eaters and the honey-eaters, peering about, drop discreetly down among the lower branches; and silence prevails.

No serious heed is taken of the white-headed sea-eagle. Though the fruit-eaters do not recognize the lordly fellow on the instant of his appearance, he may perch on the topmost branches of the tree to scrutinize the shallows, and they will resume their feasting and noise. But a falcon is as a death's-head, and alas! too often a san-guinary disturber of the peace, as the tufts of painted feathers tell.

AUSTRALIA'S HUMMING-BIRD

One of the most self-assertive of birds of the island is also one of the least—the sun-bird. Garbed in rich olive green, royal blue, and bright yellow, and of a quick and lively disposition, small as he is, he is always before his public, never forgetful of his appear-ance or regardless of his rights. Feeding on honey and on insects which frequent honey-supplying flowers, the sun-bird is generally seen amid surroundings quite in keeping with the splendour of his plumage. The best part of his life is passed among blossoms, and he seems to partake of their beauty and frailness. The gold of the gin-gee, the reds of the flame-tree, the umbrella-tree, and of the single and double hibiscus are reflected from his shining feathers, as he flutters and darts among the blooms, often sipping on the wing after the habit of the humming-bird—which he resembles even to the characteristic expansion of the tail feathers.

When in September the flame-tree is a dome of red, sun-birds gather by the score—the gayest of all the revellers. Uncommon length of bill enables them to probe recesses of flowers forbidden others, and they seem proud of the superiority. The varied honey-eater visits flower after flower with something of method. The sun-bird flashes from raceme to raceme, sampling a dozen blooms, while his noisy rival sips with the air of a connoisseur at one. There is a spell in the nectar of the flame-tree as irresistibly attractive to the taste of birds as the colour is to the sight of man. Although the tree bursts into bloom with truly tropical ardour, they await the coming banquet with unaffected impatience. Then one of the prettiest frolics of the sun-bird is revealed. Time cannot lag with such gay, saucy creatures, so while they wait half a dozen or more congregate in a circle and with uplifted heads directed towards a common centre sing their song in unison. Whether the theme of the song is of protest against the tardiness of the tree, or of thanks in anticipation, or of exultation in race, or of rivalry, matters not; but one is inclined to the last theory, for none but males take part in it. The sun glints on their burnished breasts, their throats throb, their long bills quiver with enthusiastic effort, and the song still matters not, for it is but a thin twittering, so feeble and faint as to be inaudible a few yards off. With a squeak in chorus the choir disperses, to meet and sing again in a few minutes in another part of the reddening tree.

"MOOR-GOODY"

Aptly imitating its most frequent note, blacks have given the name of "Moor-goody" to a sedate little bird rarely seen away from the jungle, and then only in the shadiest of bushes. Many of the birds are distinguished and named in accordance with their notes. "Wung-go-bah" describes the noisy pitta; "Wee-loo" the stone plover; "Coo-roo" the tranquil dove; "Piln-piln" the large-billed shore plover; "Kim-bum-broo" the mangrove honey-eater; "Cal-loo-calloo" the manucode; "Go-bidger-roo" the varied honey-eater; and so on.

"Moor-goody" (shrike-thrush) has the most tuneful and mellow call of all, and in obedience to the general law which forbids beauty to sweet-voiced birds, is soberly clad in two shades of brown, cinnamon the breast, dust the back. But it is of graceful form, and soft of flight as a falling leaf; the eyes are large and singularly tender and expressive. Often terminating in a silvery chirrup, the note, varied with melodious chuckles and gurgles of lulling softness, is exceedingly pleasing, the expression of a bird of refinement, content and sweet temper. Coming at frequent intervals from the jungle or the heart of the mango trees or acalypha bushes, and wheresoever foliage is thickest, the sound is always welcome, as it tells of some of the most desirable features of the tropics—quiet, coolness, and the sweet security of shade. It tells, too, of the simple life spent in seclusion in contradistinction to the "envious court" of the roysterers in the glare of the leafless flame-tree.

THE FLAME-TREE'S VISITORS

A final note in reference to the flame-tree may be permitted. As it is the popular rendezvous during September, pleasure was taken in cataloguing the greatest variety and number of birds congregated there at one and the same time. Several lists were compiled, the most comprehensive being:

Sulphur-crested Cockatoo	White-rumped Wood-swallow
Honey-eaters (varied, mangrove, and dusky)	Australian Bee-eater
	Black-headed Diamond-bird
Friar-bird (two species)	Sun-bird
Shining Calornis	Pied Caterpillar-eater
Drongo-shrike	

Honey-eaters were represented by a dozen or more; but were not as numerous as the sun-birds, which were difficult to accurately enumerate, owing to their sprightly behaviour. Next came the shining calornis (about ten), friar-birds (about eight), wood-swallows (six, all in a row—a band of white among the red flowers); bee-eaters (about the same number), and so on down the list in ever-shifting places and varying numbers.

The birds were more numerous about 8 a.m. This hour may seem late, in consideration of familiar habits, but the flame-tree is in the shadow of the highest peak of the island, and consequently does not receive the earliest of the benedictions of the sun. Birds come and go to it in irregular pulsations. Their presence is constant, but their number variable. Comparative silence may exist for an hour or so after the first joyful feast of the day, to be broken by quite a gush of the sounds of revelry, and then the tree becomes again for a space as noisy as a merry-go-round.

RED-LETTER BIRDS

To the manucode is ascribed practical interference with the laws of nature. This handsome bird, of jet black glossy plumage, comes hither in September, adding to the pleasant sounds of the jungle a loud rich note, which closely resembles the frequent repetition of the name bestowed upon it by the blacks, "Calloo-calloo". As are its visits so are its notes—casual, coming in erratic bursts and sudden sallies of whirling spiral sound. Its advent is hailed with satisfaction, for the belief exists that it causes the bean-tree—the source of a much-esteemed food—to grow more quickly. This faith has a substantial origin, for shortly after the bird's first fluty notes are heard the bean-tree blossoms, renewing the promise of plenty. While here, the calloo-calloo is remarkably shy, very rarely venturing out of the seclusion of the thickest jungle, and warning off intruders with a curious note of alarm, half purr, half hiss.

When the clattering corcorax puts in an appearance the blacks lift up their eyes unto the hills, firm in the faith that the birds cause in them an increase in height, or to put it in the vernacular —"Look out! Mountain jump up little bit!" When the flame-tree flowers, it is to tell of the coming of the nutmeg pigeon, when eggs and dainty young are to be obtained with little trouble.

Yet another red-letter time on the calendar is the laying season of the terns. Then the fancies of the blacks lightly turn to thoughts of "Tan-goorah" (bonito) and other strong-flavoured fish. So that the young shall not lack, nor suffer hunger, the hatching is coincident with the appearance of immense shoals of young fish which the bonito perpetually harrass, driving them to the surface for the terns, with sharp screams of satisfaction, to dart upon. What with the strong, far-leaping fish, and the agile, acrobatic birds, the existence of the small fry is one of perplexity and terror.

Six species of tern take part in these gyrating, foraging campaigns. Three show almost purely white as they fly; the others, less numerous, as dark flakes in the living whirlwind. Ever changing in position and in poise—some on the swift seaward cast, some balancing for it with every fraction of brake power exerted in beating wings and expanded tail, some recovering equilibrium lost through a fluky start, some dashing deep, some hurrying away (after a spasmodic flutter of dripping feathers) with quivering slips of silver—the perpetual whirl keeps pace with the splashes of the bonito and the ripples of the worried small fry.

Could they enjoy the satisfaction of the fact the little fish might snigger when the terns are called upon to exert all their agility and tricks, vainly endeavouring to elude the slim-winged frigate-bird. This tyrant of the upper air observes, as it glides in steady, stately circles, the noisy unreflecting terns, and with arrow-like swiftness pursues those which have been successful. Dodge and twist and double as it may—and no hare upon land is half so quick or resourceful as the wily tern in the air—the frigate-bird follows with the audacity and certainty of fate, until the little fish is abandoned, to be snapped up by the air-ranger before it reaches the sea. As an exhibition of fierce and relentless purpose, combined with sprightliness and activity, the pursuit of a tern by the fearless frigate-bird, and the impetuous swoop after and seizure of the falling fish, cannot be matched in nature.

As the cries of the circling tern mark the movements of the distracted shoals, the blacks in canoes fit into the scheme of destruction, taking a general toll. So pre-occupied are the bonito, that they fall a comparatively easy prey to the skilled user of the harpoon. Sharks continue the chain of destruction by dashing forays on the bonito, and occasionally man harpoons a shark. With his frail bark canoe tugged hither and thither by the frightened but still vicious fish, the black, endowed with nerve, then enjoys real sport. Not the least in dread of the shark, his only fear being for the safety of his harpoon and line as the lithe fish leaps and snaps, the black plays with it until it submits to be towed ashore.

The birds' eggs on the coral banks also make an item in the blacks' bill of fare; while the frantic little fish hustled towards the shore are captured by the million in coffer-dams made of loosely twisted grass and beach trailers.

CASUAL AND UNPRECISE

These observations of mine are admittedly casual and unprecise. Not the life of a single bird or insect has been sacrificed to prove "facts" for personal edification or entertainment. Cases in which points were inconclusive have been allowed to remain undecided. The face of the administrator of the law here is rigidly set against the enforcement of the death penalty, simply because the subject is beautiful, or rare, or "not understood". With the aid of a good telescope and a compact pair of field-glasses, birds may be studied and known far more pleasurably than as stark cabinet specimens, and, perhaps, with all the certainty that the ordinary observer needs. Patience and a magnifying-glass put less constraint on insects than lethal bottles and pins.

An observer who was prepared to satisfy doubts with the gun

might, possibly with ease, bring up the bird census of the island to one hundred and fifty. Such a one may find pleasure in the future in demonstrating how much more than a seventh of the birds of Australia dwell upon or visit the spot. The present era of strict non-interference has resulted in an increase, however small, in the species represented. Whereas in years gone by but two species of sea-birds nested on Purtaboi, now at least six avail themselves of that refuge.

Birds that were driven to remote reefs and banks of the Barrier now make themselves at home for three months of the year within hailing distance. Tidings of goodwill towards the race generally are beginning to spread. Gladness compels me to record a recent development of the protective laws. Space for the rearing of families at the headquarters of the terns—Purtaboi—having been gradually absorbed during recent years, the overflow—comprising perhaps a thousand amorous birds—has taken possession of the sand-spit of Dunk Island. So calm are they in the presence of man, so sure of goodwill, that when temporarily disturbed, they merely wheel about close overhead, remonstrating against intrusion in thin tinny screams, and settle again on their eggs before the friendly visit is well over. Not for ten years at the least have sea-birds utilized this spot. Realizing their privileges elsewhere in the immediate neighbourhood, they have thrust themselves under official protection. They crowd me off a favourite promenade, mine by right of ten years' usage. They scold every boat, affront passing steamers, and comport themselves generally as on the assurance of counsel's opinion on the legality of their trespass.

And so it has come to pass that the example of the uninfluential beachcomber, in the establishment of an informal and unofficial refuge for birds, has been warranted and confirmed by the laws of the country. A proclamation in those terms, those good set terms, which time and custom approve, forbids shooting on this and two neighbouring groups of islands. Is there not excuse in this flattery for just a little vainglory?

CHAPTER IV

GARDEN OF CORAL

BRAMMO BAY has its garden of coral—a border of pretty, quaint and varied growth springing up along the verge of deep water. It is not as it used to be—no less lovely than a flower-garden of the land. Terrestrial storms work as much havoc in the shallow places of the sea as on the land. Pearl-shell divers assert that ordinary "rough weather" is imperceptible at a depth of two fathoms; while ten fathoms are generally accepted as the extreme limit of wave action, however violent the surface commotion. Yet in the shallow sea within the Barrier Reef, in times of storm and stress, not only are groves of marine plants torn and wrenched up, but huge lumps of coral rock are shattered or thrown bodily out of place and piled up on the beaches.

A storm in a particular March which did scarcely any damage to vegetation ashore, destroyed most of the fantastic forms which made the coral garden enchanting. In its commotion, too, the sea lost its purity. The sediment and ooze of decades were churned up, and, as the agitation ceased, were precipitated—a brown, furry, slimy mud, all over the garden—smothering the industrious polyps to which all its prettiness was due. Order is being restored, fresh and vigorous shoots sprouting up from the fulvid basis; but it may be many years before the damage is wholly repaired and the original beauty of the garden restored, for the "growth" of coral—the skeletons of the polyps—is methodical and very slow. We speak of coral as if it were a plant, yet the reproduction is by means of eggs, and the polyp is as much an animal as a horse or an elephant.

In times past the marine garden comprised several acres in which were plants of almost every conceivable shape and form, and more or less bright and delicate in colour. Fancy may feign shrubs, standard and clipped; elaborate bouquets, bunches of grapes, compact cauliflowers, frail red fans. Rounded, skull-like protuberances with the convolutions of the brain exposed, stag-horns, whip-thongs yards long, masses of pink and white resembling fanciful confectionery, intricate lace-work in the deepest

79

indigo blue, have their appointed places. Some of the spreading plant-like growths are snow-white, tipped with mauve, lemon-coloured tipped with white, white tipped with lemon and pale blue.

On the rocks rest stalkless mushrooms, gills uppermost, which blossom as pom-pom chrysanthemums; rough nodules, boat- and canoe-shaped dishes of coral. Adhering to the rocks are thin, flaky, brittle growths resembling vine-leaves, brown and golden-yellow; goblets and cups, tiered epergnes, distorted saucers, eccentric vases, crazily-shaped dishes. Clams and cowries and other molluscs people the cracks and crevices of coral blocks, and congregate beneath detached masses and loose stones. In these fervid and fecund waters life is real, life is earnest. Here, are elaborately armoured crayfish upon which the most gaudy colours are lavished; grotesque crabs; fish brilliant in hue as humming-birds. Life, darting and dashing, active and alert, crawling and slithering, slow and stationary, swarms in these marine groves.

A coral reef is gorged with a population of varied elements viciously disposed towards each other. It is one of nature's most cruel battlefields, for it is the brood of the sea that "plots mutual slaughter, hungering to live". Molluscs are murderers and the most shameless of cannibals. No creature at all conspicuous is safe, unless it is agile and alert, or of horrific aspect, or endowed with giant's strength, or encased in armour. A perfectly inoffensive crab, incapable of inflicting injury to anything save creatures of almost microscopic dimensions, assumes the style and demeanour of a ferocious monster, ready at a moment's notice to cry havoc and let loose the dogs of war. Another hides itself as a rugged nodule of moss-covered stone, its limbs so artfully stowed away that detection would be impossible did it not occasionally betray itself by a stealthy movement. The pretty cowrie, lemon-coloured and grey and brown, throws over its shining shoulders a shawl of the hue of the rock on which it crawls about, grey or brown or tawny, with white specks and dots which make for invisibility—a thin filmy shawl of exquisite sensitiveness. Touch it ever so lightly, and the helpless creature, discerning that its disguise has been penetrated, withdraws it, folding it into its shell, and closes its door against expected attack. It may feebly fall off the rock, and, simulating a dead and empty shell, lie motionless until danger is past. Then again it will drape itself in its garment of invisibility, and slide cautiously along in search of its prey. Under the loose rocks and detached lumps of coral for one live shell there will be scores of dead ones. The whole field is strewn with the relics of perpetual conflict, resolving and being resolved into original elements.

We talk of the strenuous life of men in cities. Go to a coral reef and see what the struggle for existence really means. The very bulwarks of limestone are honeycombed by tunnelling shells. A glossy black, torpedo-shaped creature cuts a tomb for itself in the hard lime. Though it may burrow inches deep with no readily visible inlet, cutting and grinding its cavity as it develops in size and strength, yet it is not safe. Fate follows in insignificant guise, drills a tiny hole through its shell, and the toilsomely excavated refuge becomes a sepulchre. All is strife—war to the death. If eternal vigilance is the price of liberty among men, what quality shall avert destruction where insatiable cannibalism is the rule? There is but one creature that seems to make use of the debris of the battlefield—the hermit crab, which, but half armoured, must to avert extermination fit itself into an empty shell, discarding as it grows each narrow habitation for a size larger.

Disconsolate is the condition of the hermit crab who has outgrown his quarters, or has been enticed from them or "drawn" by a cousin stronger than he, or who has had the fortune to be ejected without dismemberment. The full face of the red bluespotted variety is an effective menace to any ordinary foe, and that honourable part is presented at the front door when the tenant is at home. For safety's sake the flabby gelatinous, inert rear end must be tucked and hooked into the convolutions of the shell, deprived of which he is at the mercy of foes very much his inferior in fighting weight and truculent appearance. The disinterested spectator may smile at the vain, yet frantically serious, efforts of the hermit to coax his flabby rear into a shell obviously a flattering misfit. But it is not a smiling matter to him. Not until he has exhausted a programme of ingenious attitudes and comic contortions is the attempt to stow away a No. 8 tail into a No. 5 shell abandoned. When a shell of respectable dimensions is presented, and the grateful hermit backs in, settles comfortably, arrays all his weapons against intruders, and peers out with an expression of ferocious content, smiles may come, and will be out of place only when the aches of still increasing bulk force him to hustle again for still more commodious lodgings.

A frilled clam in its infancy seals or anchors itself in a tiny crack or crevice, and apparently by a continuous but imperceptible movement analogous to elbow-rooming, deepens and enlarges its cavity as it develops. Should it survive in defiance of all its foes, just taking from the sea the sustenance for which it craves with gaping valves, it may increase in bulk, but its apartment in the limestone never seems too large—just a neat fit. In its abiding-place it presents an irregular strip of silk, green as polished malachite, or dark green and grey, or blue and slaty green, mottled and marbled, with crimped edges and graceful folds—an attractive ornament in the drab rock. Touch any part—there is a slow, suspensory withdrawal, and then a snap and spurt of water as the last remnant of the living mantle disappears between the interlocking valves of porcelain white.

Apart from the bulk and the fantastic shapes of coral structures, there is the beauty of the living polyps. That which when dry may have the superficial appearance of stone plentifully pitted—a heavy dull mass—blossoms with wondrous gaiety as the revivifying water covers it. The time to admire these frail marine flowers is on an absolutely calm day. All the sediment of the sea has been precipitated. The water is as transparent as rock crystal, but like that mineral slightly distorts the object unless the view is absolutely vertical. It is a lens perfect in its limpidity. Here is a buff-coloured block roughly in the shape of a mushroom with a flat top, irregular edges, and a bulbous stalk. Rich brown algae hangs from its edges in frills and flounces. Little cones stud its surface, each of which is the home of a living, star-like flower, a flower which has the power of displaying and withdrawing itself, and of waving its fringed rays. Each flower is self-coloured, and may represent a group of animals. There are blues of various depths and shades from cobalt to lavender, reds, orange and pinks, greens, browns and greys, each springing from a separate receptacle. All are alike in shape—viewed vertically, many-rayed stars; horizontally, fir-trees faultlessly symmetrical in form and proportion. These flowers, all blossom, or trees, or stars, are shy and timorous. A splash and they shrink away. The hope of such wilderness—as barren-looking as desert sandstone—ever blossoming again seems forbidden. Quietude for a few moments, and one after another the flowers emerge, at first furtively but gathering courage in full vanity, until the buff rock becomes as radiant as a garden-bed.

The congested state of a coral reef, and the inevitable result thereof—perpetual war of species and shocking cannibalism—have been referred to. Another result of the overcrowding has yet to be mentioned. Possibly there may be those who are disinclined to credit the statement that some of the denizens take in lodgers. But the fact remains. Having ample room and to spare within their own walls, they offer hospitality to homeless and unprotected strangers, whom graceless nature has not equipped to take part in the rough-and-tumble struggle for existence outside. A tender-hearted mollusc accepts the company of a beautiful form of mantis-shrimp—tender, delicate, and affectionate—which dies quickly when removed from its asylum, as well as a singular creature which has no charm of character, and must be the dullest sort of lodger possible to imagine. It is a miniature eel, which looks as if it had been drawn out of rock crystal or perfectly clear glass. There is no apparent difference between the head and the tail, save that one end tapers more gradually than the other. Very limited power of motion has been bestowed upon it. It cannot wriggle. It merely squirms in the extremity of laziness or lassitude. These two keep the mollusc company—the lively shrimp, pinkish brown and green with pin-point black eyes, and the little eel as bright and as transparent yet as dull and insipid as glass. One of the oysters attracts the patronage of a rotund crab, which in some respects resembles a tick, and a great anemone a brilliant fish—scarlet and silver defined with purple hair-lines—which on alarm retires within the ample folds of its host.

The flowers of a coral reef live. A bouquet of lavender-coloured, tender, orderly spikes has a gentle rhythmical, swaying movement. A touch, and by magic the colour is gone—naught remains but a dingy brown lump on the rock, whence water oozes. Another form of plant-like life takes the colour of rich green—the green of parsley, and faints at the touch, as does the sensitive plant of the land. Another strange creature, roughly saucer-shaped, but deep grey mottled with white and brown, continuously waves its serrated edges and pulsates at the centre. It starts and stops, contracts and withdraws steadily into the sand upon interference.

One of the shrimps (*Gonodactylus chiragra*) in my experience found only far out on the reef at dead low-water winter spring-tides, might be taken as a display collection in miniature of those gems of purest ray serene which the dark unfathomed caves of ocean bear. The emerald-green tail is fringed with transparent golden lace; the malachite body has the sheen of gold; the chief legs are of emerald with ruby joints, and silvery claws; the minor as of amber, while over all is a general sheen of ornamentation of points and blotches of sapphire blue. Long white antennae, delicate and opaque, spring from the head. The decorative hues are not laid on flat, but are coarsely powdered and springled as in the case of one of the rarest of Brazilian butterflies—and they live. Picture a moss-rose with the "moss" all the colours of the rainbow, on which the light plays and sparkles, and you have an idea of the effect of the jewellery of this lustrous crustacean. Yet it is not for human admiration. Its glints speedily dim in the air. To be gobbled up by some hungry fish is the ordinary fate of the species. Possibly splendour is bestowed upon the shrimp as a means by which certain fish distinguish a particularly choice dainty, and the fish show the very acme of admiration by "wolfing" it. Thus are the examples of high art in nature remorselessly lavished.

Quite distinct is the unconscious genius which now demands brief reference to its perfections. Though a brilliant example of the employment of unattractive deceptive features, it has no individual comeliness—not an atom of grace, no style of its own. Every feature, attitude and movement is subordinate to the part it plays. Death being the penalty, it may not blunder. Behold, among acres of similar growth, a trivial collection of rough, short weeds of the sea—grey, green and mud-coloured. This microcosm glides and stops. The movement is barely perceptible; the intervals of rest are long and frequent. An untimely slide as the chance gaze of the observer is directed to the spot, betrays that here is the centre of independent life and motive. The dwarf, unkempt weeds cloak a meek, weak, shrinking crab, whose frail claws and tufted legs are breeched with muddy moss, and whose oddly-shaped body is obscured by parasitic vegetation and realistic counterfeits thereof. Inspection, however critical, makes no satisfactory definition between the real and the artificial algae, so perfectly do the details of the moving marine garden blend with the fringes and fur of the animal's rugged and misshapen figure and deformed limbs. As an artistic finish to a marvellous piece of mummery, in one of the crude green claws is carried a fragment of coral, green with the mould of the sea. It and the claw are indistinguishable until, in the faintest spasm of fright, the crab abandons the coral, and, shrinking within itself, becomes inanimate—as steadfast a patch of weeds as any other of the reef. Recovering slowly from its fright, and conscious of the necessity for each detail of its equipment and insignia, the lowly crustacean timidly re-grips the coral, and, holding it aloft, glides discreetly on its way, invisible when stationary, most difficult to detect when it moves.

To see the coral garden to advantage you must pass over it— not through it. Drifting idly in a boat in a calm clear day, when the tips of the tallest shrubs are submerged only a foot or so, and all the delicate filaments, which are invisible or lie flat and flaccid when the tide is out, are waving, twisting, and twining, then the spectacle is at its best. Tiny fish, glowing like jewels, flash and dart among the intricate interlacing branches, or quiveringly poise about some slender point—humming-birds of the sea, sipping their nectar. A pink translucent fish no greater than a lead-pencil wriggles in and out of the lemon-coloured coral. Another of the John Dory shape, but scarcely an inch long, blue as a sapphire with gold fins and gold-tipped tail, hovers over a miniature blue-black cave. A shoal darts out, some all old-gold, some green with yellow damascene tracery and long yellow filaments floating from the lower lip. A slender form, half coral pink, half grey, that might swim in a walnut shell, displays its transparent charms. Conspicuous, daring colours here are as common as on the lawn of a race-course. Occasionally on the edge of a reef there comes the fish of frosted silver, with hair like purple streamers floating from the dorsal fin a foot and more behind. Some call it the "lady" fish, because of its beauty and grace, and others the diamond trevally (*Alectis ciliaris*). More frequently is seen the "sleepy fish", salmon-shaped, of resplendent copper, with bright blue blotches and markings, which remains motionless in the water, and so often awakens not until the spear of the hungry black is fast in its shoulders.

Another handsome creature of olive green with blue wavy stripes and spots (*Fistularis serratus*) has the shape of a garfish, and to counterbalance a long tubular snout, a slender filament resembling the bare feather-shaft of some bird of paradise extending from the tail.

With all its fantastic beauty a coral reef is cruel. Nearer the shore the stony blocks are overspread by masses of that singular skeletonless coral, known as alcyonaria—partaking of the nature of rubber and of leather—an ugly, repulsive, tyrannous growth, over-running and killing other and more delicate corals, as undesirable pests crowd out useful and becoming vegetation. It occurs in varying colours and forms—sickly green and grey, bronze and yellow, brown and pink. Loathsome, resembling offal in some aspects as the receding tide lays it bare, it becomes pretty and interesting when covered with calm, limpid water, and its dull life flourishes with star-like, living flowers.

Before our coral garden was as familiar as it is, it was said that on one of the reefs of Dunk Island there reposed a colossal clam —one of the giants of the variety known to science as *Tridacna gigas*. So prodigious was the alleged specimen, that no one had been able to remove it, and it was dimly suggested that the occupant of the island would easily become possessed of a very marvel among molluscs. So far, its resting-place has not been discovered, though all the reefs have been explored many times; nor do any of the natives know of its existence. Very few reefs, if all reports are to be credited, are without monstrous clams, but they seem to acquire the habit of suddenly disappearing—quite foreign to their bulk and stay-at-home character—when the time of anticipated capture aproaches. One, up a little north, was stated to be over ten feet long, and to weigh at least a ton, and fourteen feet was alleged to be the size of another. But all disappear like will-o'-the-wisps when the search-party arrives on the scene, and none but ordinary specimens, which have no reputation to maintain, are there to flout the ardour of the collector.

Circumscribed as it is, the garden of coral in Brammo Bay, now slowly recovering its lost loveliness, supplies an excellent field for the observation of some of the most wonderful of the processes of nature. In many respects it is a miniature, as most fringing reefs seem to be, of the Great Barrier.

It would be hopeless to attempt to describe the many varieties of coral and fish and crabs and strange grotesque creatures low in the scale of life which are unceasingly at work within "coo-ee". The complexity of the subject from a scientific aspect is sufficient justification for reluctance to set down anything beyond casual experiences and personal observation, and the record of ever-recurring pleasure obtained from the delights of the marine garden. Special attainments and varied lore must be at the command of the student who would attempt to classify the marvels of a coral reef of even limited scope. When it is remembered that the Great Barrier Reef of Queensland—"one of the most valuable possessions of the state"—has a length of one thousand two hundred and fifty miles; that some of its outlying reefs extend as far from the coast as one hundred and fifty miles; that some approach as close as ten or twelve miles; that the average distance of the outer edge from the coast-line is thirty miles; that it embraces an area of eighty thousand geographical square miles; and that its corals, continuous and detached and isolated, teem with life, it is impossible to repress feelings of astonishment, wonder, and admiration.

QUEER FISH

A strange fish! Were I in England now (as once I was), and had but this fish painted, not a holiday fool but would give a piece of silver.

Of curious and pretty shells there are so many varieties in these warm waters, that one must be well versed in conchology before daring to attempt an enumeration even of the commonest. I frankly admit "a little learning is a dangerous thing" in this interesting branch of natural science, and therefore cannot pledge myself to give details, while eager to set forth a few of the objects of interest, which present themselves to the open-minded though uninformed observer of sea-beaten rocks, mud flats, coral reefs, and the open sea.

Well may the dabbler despair when nine titles are necessary to catalogue the oysters alone—oysters which vary from the size, independence, and toughness of the clam, to delicate morsels, so crowded and cemented in communities together that they form bridges between severed rocks and shelves and cornices broad and massive; oysters flatter than plates, oysters tubular as service gas-pipes; the gold-lipped mother of pearl, the black-lipped mother of pearl, the cockscomb, the coral rock oyster, the small but sweet rock oyster, two varieties of the common rock oyster, besides the trap-door, the hammer, and another of somewhat similar shape whose official and courtesy title are both alike unknown, but which furnished knives and sharp-edged tools of various shapes to the original inhabitants of the island. The gold-lipped mother of pearl is rarely found, favourable conditions for it—deep water and strong currents—not being general. An occasional stray shell is picked up, and so far none has betrayed the presence of a valuable pearl. The black-lip occurs on the reefs, but not in any great quantity, and the most plentiful variety of the edible oyster is bulky in size and somewhat coarse in flavour.

Apart from the rarity and beauty of some of the denizens of the reefs, there are others that are singular and interesting, and some whose intimate acquaintance is quite undesirable, save from a scientific and safe standpoint. A miniature marine porcupine decorates its slender spines of white with lilac tips, sharp as needles, brittle as spun glass, and charged with an irritant which sets all the nerves tingling. On the reefs uncouth fish pass solitary, isolated lives in hollows and crevices of the coral, sealed up as are the malodorous hermits in rocky cells at Lhassa, and dependent for doles upon the profuse and kindly sea. Their bodies seem to mould themselves roughly to the shape of the hollows to which each has grown accustomed as crude but almost inanimate castings. To obtain perfect specimens the mould must be shattered. If the body does not yet fill the hollow, the inhabitant clings desperately to it, wedging itself with wonderful plasticity into odd corners and against niches, resisting to the last efforts at eviction. Torn from its home the fish is a feeble, helpless creature, incapable of taking care of itself, quite unfit to be at large, though apparently belonging to the self-reliant shark family.

More than one species of fish, it is said, inhabit these coral grottoes. A compact creature with prominent rodent teeth ejects a spurt of water when its retreat is approached at low tide, while about its front and only door are strewn the shells of the crustaceans and molluscs it has devoured.

Stones hide creatures of forbidding but varying shape and colour —diminutive bodies ovate and round—brown, grey, glossy black with brown edgings, pink with grey quarterings and grey fringe, whence radiate five sprawling slender "legs", a foot or so long. Though doubtful in appearance, more in consonance with the creepy imagery of a nightmare than a reality of the better day, these are merely the shy and innocent brittle stars. They are endowed with such exquisite sensitiveness that to evade capture they sacrifice, apparently without a pang, their wriggling legs piece by piece, and each piece, large or small, squirms and wriggles. The poet says that when the legs of one of the heroes of "Chevy Chase" were smitten off, "he fought upon their stumps". The voluntary dismemberment of the brittle star may be even more pitiful—in fact almost complete, yet it still strives to pack away its forlorn body in some crevice or hollow of the coral rock. It has been asserted that no one has ever captured by hand a brittle star perfect in all its members. "One baffled collector," said a highly entertaining London journal, "who thought that he had succeeded in coaxing a specimen into a pail, had the mortification of seeing it dismember itself at the last moment, and asserts that the eye which is placed at the end of a limb gave a perceptible wink as he picked up the fragment."

Here too, most of the "brittle stars" are self-conscious to the point of self-obliteration. But some, though still quite worthy of the specific title *fragilissima*, which science has bestowed upon the tribe, may, if taken up tenderly, be handled without the loss of a single limb; and a limb more or less can hardly be of consequence to a creature which, no greater than half a walnut shell, possesses five, each twelve or fourteen inches long, and supplied with innumerable feet. Further, so far none of the vestiges of those that have committed the form of *hara-kiri* fashionable among the species has been observed to behave in any way unbecoming the shyest, most retiring and most sensitive of creatures. The brittle star discards its limbs, or the best part of them, in the meekest manner possible.

To enumerate the smaller and lowlier of the many creatures that live on the coral reef would be a task utterly beyond ordinary capability. The reader must be content with reference to a few of the more conspicuous of the denizens.

THE WARTY GHOUL

Beware of the stone fish (*Synanceia horrida*), the death adder of the sea, called also the sea-devil, because of its malice; the warty ghoul because, perhaps, of its repulsiveness; the lion fish, because of its habit of lurking in secret places; the sea scorpion for its venom; and by the blacks "Mee-hee". Loathsome, secretive, inert, rough and jagged in outline, wearing tufts and sprays of sea-weed on its back, scarcely to be distinguished from the rocks among which it lurks, it is armed with spines steeped in the cruellest venom. Many fish are capable of inflicting painful and even dangerous wounds, but none is to be more dreaded than the ugly and repulsive "stone fish". Fortunately, it is comparatively rare. Conceal itself as it may among the swaying seaweed as it lies in ambush ready to seize its prey, or partially bury itself in the mud, it seldom eludes the shrewd observation of the blacks. With a grunt of satisfaction it is impaled with a fish-spear and placed squirming on a rock to be battered to pulp with its prototype—a stone. Utter destruction is the invariable fate of any stone fish detected in these waters, the belief of the blacks being that in default fatal effects follow a wound. But a black who suffers the rare chance of contact fortifies his theoretical cure of pulverizing the offending fish by immersing the injured foot or hand in running water for a whole day, the popular treatment for all venomous wounds. As to the effect of the wound they say, "Suppose that fella nail go along your foot, you sing out all a same bullocky all night. Leg belonga you swell up and jump about? Bingie (belly) belonga you, sore fella. Might you die". One boy described the detested creature—"That fella like stone. Head belonga him no good—all hole". A graphic way of detailing a rugged depression in the head, which conveys the idea that the bones have been staved in by a blow with a hammer.

The stone fish resembles in character and habits the death adder. Its disposition is pacific, it has no forwardness of temper; is never willing to obtrude itself on notice, trusting to immobility and to its similitude to the grey rocks and mud and brown algae to escape detection. Unless it is actually handled or inadvertently trodden upon, it is as innocent and as harmless as a canary. Why then should it be furnished with such dreadful weapons of offence? A full dozen of the keenest of spines, all in a row, extend from the depression at the back of the head towards the tail, each spine hidden in a jagged and uneven fringe, which, when the fish is in its natural element, can scarcely be distinguished from seaweed. Not until the warty ghoul acquires the sagacity which accompanies ripe age and experience, does it encourage deceptive plumes of innocent algae to anchor themselves to its back. Then it is that detection is beyond ordinary skill, and its presence fraught with danger. In a specimen eight inches long, the first spine, counting from the head, can be exposed half an inch, the second and chief fully three-quarters, and the remainder graduate from half to a quarter of an inch. Each spine—clear opal blue—is surrounded by a sac of colourless liquid (presumed to contain the poisonous element), which squirts out as the spine is unsheathed. On the sides, and in lesser numbers on the belly, are irregular rows of miniature craters which on being depressed eject, to a distance of a foot or more, a liquid resembling in colour milk with a tinge of lavender. Fast on the points of a spear the fish gives an occasional and violent spasmodic jerk, when the prettily tinted liquid is ejected from all the little cones. After a pause, during which it seems to concentrate its energies, there is another and another twitch, each the means of sprinkling broadcast what is said to be a corrosive liquid, almost as virulent as vitriol. From almost any part of the body this liquid exudes or can be expelled.

With its upturned cavernous mouth (interiorly a forbidding sickly green), its spines, its cones, its eruptions, its ejecta, its great fan-shaped pectoral fins, and its deformities generally, the stone fish well deserves the specific title of *horrida*. Moreover, has it not a gift which would have brought it to the stake a few score years ago, as a sinful, presumptuous and sacrilegious witch—that of living for an hour or two out of its natural element? It deserves the bad eminence to which it has been raised by the blacks on account of looks alone, and if the poisonous qualities are in line with its hideousness, one can but ponder why and wherefore such a creature has existence in "this best of all possible worlds". But it is known that to the Chinese it is dainty. They pay for it with good grace as much as 2s. 6d. per lb., and the flavour is said to resemble crab.

"BURRA-REE"

Another inhabitant of the coral garden to be avoided is the balloon fish (*Tetraodon ocellatus*), which distends itself to the utmost capacity of its oval body when lifted from the water. The flesh is generally believed to be poisonous, though of tempting appearance. Authorities assert that the pernicious principle is confined to the liver and ovaries, and that if these are removed as soon as the fish is captured the flesh may be eaten with impunity. Let others, careless of pain and tired of life, experiment. Middle-aged blacks tell that when a monstrous "Burra-ree" was speared here, notwithstanding its evil repute, some of the hungry ones cooked and ate of it. All who did so died or were sick unto death. Some years ago two Malays in the vicinity of Cairns partook of the flesh and died in consequence. No black will handle the fish, and a dog which may hunt one in shallow water, and mouth it, partakes of a prompt and violent emetic. Blacks are very careful to avoid touching it with anything shorter than a fish-spear, being of opinion that the poison resides in or on the skin, and that the flesh becomes impregnated when the skin is broken.

The balloon fish is toothless, the jaws resembling the beak of a turtle, and in some species both the upper and the lower jaws have medial sutures like those of a snake. Was there not a Roman statesman or warrior whose jaws were fitted with a consolidated and continuous structure of ivory instead of the ordinary separate teeth?

The balloon fish depends upon its inconspicuousness and harmony with its environment in the struggle for existence, for, no doubt, there are in the sea fish so strong of stomach as to accept it without a spasm. It will allow a boat to be paddled over it as it floats—a brown balloon—almost motionless in the water without evincing alarm, but it makes a commotion enough for a dozen when a spear is fast in its back.

FOUR THOUSAND LIKE ONE

Among the more remarkable fish that frequent these waters is a species that does not come within the limits of my limited reading on the curious things of nature. No doubt it is well known to the initiated, but I take the opportunity of saying that these notes are not penned with the presumptuous notion of enlightening the learned and the wise, but for the edification, mayhap, of those who do not know, who have no means of acquiring information first hand, to whom text-books are unavailable, and who are not above sharing the pleasures of one whose observations are superficial, and to whom hosts of common things in nature are rare and entertaining.

In the clear water of Brammo Bay, a greenish black object, a yard across by about a yard and a half long, moved slowly along, swaying this way and that, but maintaining a fairly accurate course consistent with the shore. As the boat drifted, it seemed as if an unsophisticated sting-ray had lapsed into the blissfulness of ease, careless alike of mankind, and of its enemies in the water. When within reach the boat-hook was used as a spear more to startle the indolent fish than in the vain hope of effecting its capture. The boat-hook passed through what appeared to be the middle of the creature with a splash, and four or five fish, about eight inches long, and of narrow girth, floated away, stunned, killed by the shock. Then it was realized that the apparently solid fish was really a compact mass of little fish, moving along with common impulse and volition, each fish having a sinuous, wriggling motion. So closely were they packed that it was impossible without careful scrutiny to discern individual members of the group, and so intimate their association and so remarkable their mutual sympathy, that they seemed to possess minds with but a single thought, hearts that beat as one. Here were not forty, not four hundred, but more likely four thousand living, moving, and having their being as a single individual. Dispersed for an instant as the boathook or paddle was driven through it, the mass coalesced automatically and instantly as if controlled by mechanical force, or composed of some resilient substance, and swayed again on its course, while the dead and stunned drifted away.

Examining the specimens procured, it was found that they resembled lampreys in shape, olive green in colour, with pale lemon-coloured streaks and marks. Each of the gill cases terminated in a two-edged spur, transparent as glass, and keen as only nature knows how to make her weapons of defence.

Presently in obedience to some instinct the shoal left the shallow water inshore, and we watched it glide among the brown waving seaweed to the line of dull red, which indicated the outer edge of the coral reef and saw it no more. This, my piscatorial pastor and master says, was no doubt a community of striped cat-fish (*Plotosus anguillaris*).

THE BAILER SHELL

Adhering to a rock by a short stumpy stalk, sometimes sealed firmly to a loose stone, you may find an object in form and structure resembling an elongated, coreless pineapple, composed of a leathery semi-gelatinous, semi-transparent substance, dirty yellow in colour. It is the spawn-case or the receptacle of the ova (if that term be allowable), and the cradle of what is commonly known as the bailer shell (*Cymbium oethiopicum*) the "Ping-ah" of the blacks, one of the most singular and interesting features that these reefs have for the sightseer. In its composition there may be fifty more or less cohering, conic sections, each containing an unborn shell in a distinct and separate stage of development. At the base, the shells are, perhaps, just emerging each from its special compartment, as a young bee emerges from its cell—each a thin frail shell, about half an inch long, white with pale yellow and light brown markings. In time, should it survive all the accidents and assaults by which on entering the world it is beset, the tiny shell will develop into an expansively mouthed vessel. The next succeeding row will be in a less matured state, and so the development diminishes towards the apex. Some of the compartments are occupied by shells transparent, colourless and fragile in the extreme, some by shells having merely the rudiment of form, until at the apex the cells contain but a drop or so of sparkling, quivering jelly.

The bailer shell alive is like an egg, in the fact that it is full of meat. Many marine shells have surprisingly diminutive fleshy occupants, however great their tenacity and strength. The animal inhabiting a large-sized bailer weighs several pounds, the flesh being tough, leathery and of unwholesome appearance. When it has decayed, the shell being thin, the cavity is phenomenally capacious. Large specimens contain a couple of gallons of water, and as the shape is most convenient, and there is neither rust nor moth to corrupt, their aptitude as effective and durable bailers for boats is apparent. Some name them the boxer shell, tracing resemblance to a boxing-glove, others the "boat", and others again the melon shell. Blacks use them for a variety of purposes—bailers, buckets, saucepans, drinking-vessels, baskets, and even wardrobes. They represent, perhaps, the only utensil in which a black can boil food, and it is an astonishing though not edifying spectacle when the fat-layered intestine of a turtle, sodden in salt water just brought to a boil in a bailer shell, is eagerly devoured by hungry blacks.

A RIVAL TO THE OYSTER

Down the caverns of the submerged rocks and blocks of coral are two or three species of *Echinus* (sea-urchins), with long and slender spines radiating from their spheroid bodies. One (*Diadema setosa*) is distinguished by what appears to be precious jewels of sparkling blue—believed to be visual organs—which lose their brilliancy immediately on removal from the water. Another has a centre of coral pink. The black spines, ten inches or so long, are exquisitely sharp and brittle in the extreme. Some believe that the animals are endowed with the power of thrusting these weapons forward to meet the intrusive hands, for unless approached with caution they prick the fingers while yet seemingly out of reach. Admitting that I have never yet attempted rudely to grasp this creature (which certainly is capable of presenting its array of spines whither it wills) while submerged, for the mere purpose of testing its ability to defend itself—my enthusiasm being tempered by the caution of the mere amateur—it may be said that some of the spines appear to be blunt. All could hardly be "sharper than needles", for being used as a means of locomotion among and over and in the crevices of the coral and rocks, some are necessarily worn at the points. With care they may be handled without injury, though at first glance it would seem impossible to avoid the numerous weapons. Imagine a brittle tennis ball stuck full of long slender needles, many tapering to microscopic keenness at the points, climbing stiffly along the edges of rocks by a few of the stilt-like needles, and a very fair figure of *Echinus* is presented. As a curious and beautiful creature he is full of interest, and as an adjunct to one's diet he is, in due season, full of excellent meat. We take the ugly and forbidding oyster with words of gratitude and flattery on our lips, and why pass with disrespect the creature that is beautiful and wonderful as well as savoury? To enjoy it to perfection, extricate the creature from his lurking place far down in the blue crevice of the coral, with a fish-spear. Don't experiment with your fingers. On the gunwale of your boat divest it of its slender black spines, and with a knife fairly divide the spheroid body, and a somewhat nauseous-looking meat is disclosed; but no more objectionable in appearance than the substance of a fully ripe passion fruit. The flavour! Ah, the flavour! It surpasseth the delectable oyster. It hath more of the savour and piquancy of the ocean. It clingeth to the palate and purgeth it of grosser tastes. It recalleth the clean and marvellous creature whose life has been spent in cool coral grottoes, among limestone and the salty essences of the pure and sparkling sea, and if you be wise and devout and grateful, you forthwith give praise for the enjoyment of a new and rare sensation.

Echinus is said to be essentially herbivorous, but my cursory observation leads me to the opinion (very humbly proffered) that it fulfils a definite purpose in the order of nature, too, and depends for sustenance, or for the building up of its structure, upon certain constituents of the coral. Does it not break and grind down to powder the ramparts of coral? Clumsy and ill-shaped as it appears to be in other respects, it has jaws of wonderful design, and known to the ancients as "Aristotle's lantern". They are composed of five strips of bony substance, with enamel-like tips overlying each other in the centre of the disk-shaped mouth. With this splendid instrument the creature grips and breaks off or gnaws off, or bores out crumbs of coral which you find, apparently in process of digestion, as you render him an acceptable morsel. Scientific observers affirm that by means of an acid which the *Echinus secretes*, it disintegrates the rock, and that the jaws are used merely to clear away the softened rubbish. How is it then that the globular cavity is often well-ballasted with tiny crisp chunks of coral rock? Possibly to the assimilation of the lime is due, in some measure, the singularly sweet and expressive savour. So we see the coral-reef-building polyps toiling with but little rest, almost incessantly labouring to raise architectural devices of infinite design, and other creatures as industriously tearing them down to form the solid foundation of continents.

Another species of *Echinus* eludes its enemies by the adoption of a cumbersome and forbidding mask. Ineffectively armed, the spines though numerous being short and frail, it holds empty bivalve shells on its uppermost part. The unstudied accumulation of debris—a fair sample of the surrounding ocean floor—would fail to fix notice, but that it moves bodily and without apparent cause. Inspection penetrates the disguise. Wheresoever *Echinus* goes—its progress is infinitely slow—it carries a self-imposed burden, the refuse of dead and inanimate things, that it may, by imposition upon its foes, continue in the way of life.

Local blacks have no fear of sharks. They take every care to avoid crocodiles, exercising great caution and circumspection when crossing inlets and tidal creeks. So shrewd are their observations that they will describe distinctive marks of particular crocodiles and indicate their favourite resorts. Their indifference to sharks is founded on the belief that those which inhabit shallow water among the islands never attack a living man. Blacks remain for hours together in the water on the reefs when bêche-de-mer fishing, and the record of an attack is rare indeed. They are far more fearful of the monstrous groper, which, lying inert among the coral blocks and boulders of the Barrier Reef, bolts anything and everything which comes its way, and which will follow a man in the water with dogged determination, foreign to the nervous, suspicious shark. Recently a vigorous young black boy was attacked by a groper while diving for bêche-de-mer. The fish took the boy's head into its capacious mouth, mauling him severely about the head and shoulders, and but for his valiant and determined struggles would doubtless have succeeded in killing him.

Even such an incident as the following does not convince blacks that the sharks of the Barrier Reef are dangerous. The captain of a bêche-de-mer cutter was paddling in a dinghy along the edge of a detached reef not many miles from Dunk Island, while several of his boys were swimming and diving. Suddenly one of them was seized and so terribly mutilated that he died in a few minutes. Although the captain was within eight or ten feet of the boy, and three of his mates not more than a few yards off; though all were wearing swimming goggles which enable them when diving to distinguish objects at a considerable range; though the sea was calm and clear and the water barely ten feet deep, no one saw a shark or any other fish capable of inflicting such injuries as had caused the death of "Jimmy", nor was there any disturbance of the surface of the water.

Years before a countryman of the unfortunate Jimmy was mauled by a small shark, but got away, though crippled for life. By some quaint process of reasoning the companions of the boy who was killed connected his death with the attack upon the other, the scene of which was two hundred miles distant, and became convinced that he had been the victim of "nother kind altogether"—a sort of mysterious marine "debil-debil", not known to entire satisfaction by the best-informed black boy, and quite beyond the comprehension of the dull-witted white man. Having thus conclusively to their minds set at naught the theory that a shark was responsible, it was absolutely unreasonable to fear sharks generally. Why should they blame a shark when it was established beyond doubt that nothing but a "debil-debil" could have killed Jimmy? Their opinion was founded on this invincible array of logic: if a shark had killed Jimmy, it must have been seen. Nothing was seen; therefore it must have been a "debil-debil". And the incident was accepted as a further and most emphatic proof of the contention that sharks do not "fight" live black boys. The single instance at Princess Charlotte Bay was an exception.

Our tame sharks seem to have no fear of animals larger even than man. A shallow stretch of water half a mile broad separates the islets of Mung-un-gnackum and Kumboola from Dunk Island. At low-water spring-tides two connecting bands are exposed—a sand-bank and a broad, flat coral reef, between which is a lagoon, in which the water may be six or seven feet deep. The horses of the estate are in the habit of making excursions to Kumboola, the desire for change being manifested so strongly that occasionally they will swim across when the tide is full. One of the horses was returning from an outing when there was a depth of about three feet on the sand-bank. As it approached the beach a shark, apparently making out from the lagoon, was seen suddenly to change its course, and follow the horse at a discreet distance. When only fifty yards from the beach the shark made an impetuous rush, and snapped at one of the horse's forefeet. The horse swerved, plunged and lashed out vigorously, and with such excellent precision that the shark was kicked like a football out of the water. It appeared to be five or six feet long, and to be quite satisfied that the horse, like a black, was not to be molested until it was past resistance. The horse bore the marks of the affray on the pastern for weeks.

Again, when a favourite dog jumped overboard from the boat in an eager but ridiculous venture after a "skipper", a shark detected the dog and shadowed it. As we went about to pick up the dog the dorsal fin of the shark indicated the wily, leisurely way in which it was keeping pace, reconnoitring and waiting until its prey was exhausted, while the dog did not appear to realize that a "frightful fiend" did close behind him swim. As the boat approached, the shark swerved off flippantly, but hovered in the vicinity, unsatisfied as to the identity of the new and strange animal that had so unaccountably appeared in its natural element and as suddenly disappeared. A rifle bullet, a little to the rear of the base of the dorsal fin, however, made it wobble and bustle away on a most eccentric route.

The term "skipper", purely local, is intended to distinguish that singular fish, of the "long Tom" (*Zylosurus*, s.p.) or alligator-pike, which shoots from the water and skips along by striking and flipping the surface with its tail, while keeping the rest of its pike-like body rigid and almost perpendicular. Each stroke is accomplished by a ludicrous wriggling movement. It would seem that by the impact of the tail upon the water the fish maintains its abnormal position and also sustains for a time its initial velocity. For a hundred yards or so its speed is considerable, equal to the flight of a bird, but the length of each successive skip rapidly diminishes, as the original impulse is exhausted, and then the fish disappears as suddenly as it shot into view. The "skipper" is an exceptionally supple fish. It is excellent eating, probably the sweetest fish of these waters, and it is much appreciated by blacks, who call it by the pretty name of "Curram-ill", and spear it whensoever chance affords.

The most gorgeous denizen of these waters is also one of the most curious—a fish resembling the surf parrot fish, but seeming to surpass even that brilliant creature in colouring. It subsists on limpets and may be seen, a lustrous blue, at half tide feeding in favourite localities. The shape of the head and shoulders reveals something of the character of the fish, though the purpose of its resplendent appearance may not be obvious. Both head and jaws typify strength and leverage power. The mouth resembles the beak of a turtle or rather that of a balloon fish (*Tetraodon*). The under jaw protrudes slightly, and is fitted (in the case of the male) with two prominent canine teeth; the upper jaw has also a pair of projecting teeth of similar character. Each of the jaws consists of two loosely sutured segments, the articulation of the lower being much the freer. The gullet is horny and rasp-like, and in its exterior opening is an auxiliary set of teeth of most remarkable formation. The upper part of this interior set in some respect resembles the under jaws of a land animal, but there are marked distinctions. It consists of two bony structures, slightly curved outwards, lying parallel to each other and bound together by tough ligaments which not only permit a certain amount of independent lateral movement, but also independent action forwards and backwards. Each of the structures is fitted with a dozen to sixteen closely packed teeth, and at the rear of each is a magazine charged with five or six more, ready to move up and forward into position for active service as those ahead are worn away. The principle of modern magazine-rifles is surprisingly exemplified by these reserve teeth. The lower jaw, or rather dental plate, resembles a flattened palate, the whole surface being studded with teeth, the edges of which overlap. It may be described as a piece of mosaic work in white and ivory. There are between sixty and seventy teeth resembling incisors on the dental plate. The whole seem to be in a state of perennial renewal to compensate for wear and tear. As those of the front row are broken or worn down, the next succeeding row occupies the frontal position. The teeth are deeply set in the bony base of the inverted palate, or rather obtrude but slightly above the surface, their office being to break down and grind to powder flinty food.

The outward and visible teeth of the male are apparently given as weapons of defence, since they do not occur in the female, which has four back teeth. From their prominent position the teeth of the male must also be used for grasping and levering or pulling steadfast limpets from rocks. They needs must be hard and have strength as well as science at the back of them, for a limpet can resist a pulling force of nearly two thousand times its own weight. The sutures of the jaws of the fish enable it to accommodate its grip to the various sizes of limpets, and to take a fair and square hold, while the lower jaw seems to act as a fulcrum when the leverage is applied. But the exterior jaws and teeth are devoid of interest, compared with the interior set, which form an ideal pulverizing apparatus. To those who are versed in ichthyology, these are known as pharyngeal teeth, because they are connected with the pharynx. Such teeth are present in some form or other in all true fish, but usually in a degraded form. In the rainbow and parrot fish they are highly specialized, otherwise the pulverization of the hard shell of molluscs would be impossible. The interior of the mouth of certain species of the shark family, given specially to a diet of oysters, is thickly set with a series of uniformly diffused minute teeth, and another fish of these seas has a gizzard composed of an intensely tough material, lined with membrane resembling shark's fin. This fish swallows cockles and such like molluscs whole, and grinds them in its gizzard.

And the colouring of this wonderful creature! The semi-transparent dorsal fin, which extends without a break from the back of the head to the tail, is broad and slightly scalloped. It displays an upper edging of radiant blue, a broad band of irridescent pink with greenish opal-like lights, and a narrow streak of the richest emerald green, close along the back. The body is covered with large scales, the colouring of which conveys a general appearance of an elaborate system of slightly elongated hexagons, generally blue outlined with pink, sometimes golden-yellow combined with green; and the colours flash and change with indescribable radiance. The head is decorated with bands of pink, orange and green; the pectoral fins are pale green with a bold medial stripe of puce, and the tail is a study of blue-green and puce. When the fish is drawn from the water the colours live, the play of lights being marvellously lovely. The colours differ, and they also vary in intensity in individuals. Though the prevailing tint may be radiant blue, it will be shot with gold in one and with pink in another.

The flesh is edible, though (as is common with parrot fish) not particularly admirable with regard to flavour. It is wonderful and beautiful. Are not these qualities all-sufficient? Must everything be good to eat? To the natives of the island this jewel of the sea is known as "Oo-ril-ee", and to scientists as belonging to the *scaroid* family.

TURTLE GENERALLY

Three species of turtle frequent these waters—the loggerhead (*Thalassochelys caretta*), the hawksbill (*Chelone imbricata*), and the green (*Chelone mydas*). Both of the latter are herbiverous and edible; but the flesh of the first-named, a fish and mollusc eater, is rank and strong, and it is therefore not hunted, the shell being of little if any value. Loggerhead, however, is not disregarded by the blacks, though to the unaccustomed nose the flesh has a most repulsive smell. It is powerful and fierce when molested. One, which was harpooned, on being hauled up to the boat seized the gunwale and left the marks of its beak deep in the wood. The creature seems also to be endowed with greater vitality than the other species, and this fact may excite the wonder of those who have seen the heart of a green turtle pulsate long after removal from the body, and the limbs an hour after separation shrink from the knife and quiver.

The hawksbill furnishes the tortoiseshell of commerce, and is much sought after. The flesh is highly tainted with the specific flavour of turtle, and therefore objectionable, though blacks relish it. Farther north, in some localities, it is generally believed that the flesh of the hawksbill may be imbued with a deadly poison. Great care is exercised in the killing and butchering, lest a certain gland, said to be located in the neck or shoulder, be opened, as flesh cut with a knife which has touched the critical part becomes impregnated. Here, though the blacks take precautions in the butchering of a hawksbill (being aware of its bad repute elsewhere), they have had no actual experience of the unwholesomeness of the flesh. One old seafarer acknowledges that he nearly "pegged out" as the result of a hearty meal of the liver of a hawksbill. As is well known, fish which are edible in one region may be poisonous in another; the same principle may apply to the turtle.

The flesh of the luth or leathery turtle (*Dermochelys coriacea*) which diets on fish, crustacea, molluscs, radiates, and other animals, causes symptoms of poisoning; but the luth does not appear to be common in this part of the Pacific, though it occurs in Torres Strait.

In a standard work on natural history it is asserted that the natives remove the overlapping plates of tortoiseshell from the hawksbill by lighting a fire on the back of the creature, causing them to peel off easily. "After the plates have been removed, the turtle is permitted to go free, and after a time it is furnished with a second set of plates." Surely this might be classed among the fabulous stories of Munchausen. As the lungs of the turtle lie close to the anterior surface of the carapace, the degree of heat sufficient to cause the plates to come off would assuredly be fatal. Possibly there is explanation at hand. The turtle being killed, the carapace is removed and placed over a gentle fire, and then the plates are eased off with a knife. But that method is not generally approved. Professional tortoiseshell-getters either trust to the heat of the sun or bury the shell in clean sand, and when decomposition sets in, the valuable plates are detached freely. Exposure to fire deteriorates the quality of the product unless great care is exercised.

The green turtle, with thin dovetailing plates, is the most plentiful and valued principally for food. But all green turtle are not acceptable. An old bull is so rank, that "there is no living near it —it would infect the North Star". There are many Europeans who cannot relish even good green turtle, however tender, delicate and sweet it may be. The worthy chaplain of Anson's fleet who "wrote up" the famous voyages, has some shrewd observations on the subject of green turtle, which he refers to as the most delicious of all flesh, "so very palatable and salubrious", though proscribed by the Spaniards as unwholesome and little less than poisonous. He suggests that the strange appearance of the animal may have been the foundation of "this ridiculous and superstitious aversion".

Perhaps the poor Spaniards of those days happened in the first instance upon an ancient bull, or a hawksbill, and tapped the poison gland, or a loggerhead or a luth, and came ever after to entertain, with right good cause, a holy terror of turtle, irrespective of species.

An interesting phase in the life-history of the green turtle is the deception the female employs when about to lay eggs. Her "nests" are shallow pits in the sand. She may make several during a hasty visit to a favourite beach, while postponing the laying until the following day. Whether this is a conscious stratagem by which the turtle hopes to mislead and bewilder other animals partial to the eggs, or merely a caprice—one of those idle fancies which the feminine part of animated nature frequently indulge in at a time when their faculties are at unusual tension—does not appear to be quite understood. When serious business is intended, the turtle scoops new pits, leaving some of them partially and others quite unfilled. These also appear to be intended to delude. That in which the eggs are deposited is filled in and the surface smoothed and flattened, and in cases where the nest is any distance beyond the limits of high-water, it is frequently carelessly covered with grass and dead leaves. The heat of the sun hatches the eggs. But the guile of the turtle is limited. However artfully the real nest may be concealed, the tracks to and fro as well as the tracks to and from the many counterfeits are as unmistakable, until the wind obliterates them, as the tracks of a treble-furrow plough. The chances against an unintellectual lover of turtle eggs discovering a fresh nest off-hand are in exact ratio to the number of deceptive appearances. In a few days all the tracks are blotted out, and then none but those skilled or possessed of keen perception may detect the nest. Blacks probe all the likely spots with spears, and soon fix on the right one.

In a certain locality where the hawksbill turtle congregate in untold numbers, a remarkable deviation from the general habit has been observed. Several of the islands are composed of a kind of conglomerate of coral debris, shells and sand. With strange perversity some turtle excavate in the rock cylindrical shafts about eighteen inches deep by six inches diameter with smooth perpendicular sides. There is no adjunct to the flippers which appear to be of service in the digging, yet the holes are such that a man would find it impossible to make without the use of a chisel.

Whether they are dug with the flippers, or bored, or bitten out with the bill, does not appear to be known. Eggs varying in numbers from one hundred and twenty to one hundred and fifty are deposited in each shaft, and covered loosely with the spoil from the excavation.

When the young are hatched only those on top are able to clamber out. They represent but a very small percentage of the family. The majority die miserably, being unable to get out of what is their tomb as well as their birthplace. In the vicinity are sandy beaches on which other hawksbill turtle deposit their eggs in accordance with time-honoured plans, and successfully rear large families. Why some individuals should be at such pains to defeat the universal instinct for the propagation and preservation of their species is a puzzle. Moreover, hundreds of these anomalous nests are excavated some distance beyond high-water, in country where the growth of grass is so strong and dense as to form an almost impenetrable barrier to those infantile turtle which have the fortune to get out of the death-traps, and in obedience to instinct, endeavour to reach the sea. Is it that nature, "so careful of the type" imposes Malthusian practices to avoid the danger of over-crowding the "never-surfeited sea"? Notwithstanding the positive check upon increase, the young are produced in myriads. "Sambo", a black boy, who had visited this isle, on his return to shores where turtle are less numerous, sought to impress his master with the substantial charms of the far-away north. "When," he said, "you come close up, you look out. Hello! You think about stone. No stone; altogether turtle!"

There, to within a recent date, might be seen the bones of fourteen great green turtle side by side in a row. At first glance the scene seems a sanctified death-place for the species, until you are informed that a visitor to the isle, astonished at the number of turtle on the beach, and eager to secure an abundance of fresh meat, turned over fourteen, intending to call again for them. Circumstances prevented him from re-visiting the place, and the turtle, being unable to right themselves, perished.

Personal observation and inquiries from many men whose lives may be said to be spent among turtle on the Barrier Reef convince me that blacks never venture to get astride a turtle in the water. One more daring and agile may seize a turtle, and by throwing his weight aft cause the head to tilt out of the water. The turtle then strikes out frantically with its flippers, but the boy so counter-balances it that the head is kept above the surface continuously, until the turtle, becoming exhausted, is guided into shallow water or alongside a boat, where it is secured with the help of others. Boys who accomplish this feat are few and far between, though it is by no means uncommon for a turtle to be seized while in the water and overturned, in which position it is helpless. A turtle detected in shallow water falls a comparatively easy prey, for on being hustled it soon loses heart and endeavours to hide its head, ostrich-like, when it is easily captured. None unacquainted with the skill with which the creature can spar with its flippers, and the effectiveness of these flippers, when used as weapons of defence, should venture to grip a turtle in its natural element.

Another species, stated to have a circumscribed habitat, has a steep dome-shaped back, resembling at a casual glance a seamless metal casting, with the edges abruptly turned up. The head is large, the eyes deeply embedded in their sockets, and the animal has the power of protruding and withdrawing the head much more extensively developed than usual. The "death's-head" staring from beneath the dome-shaped back gives to the animal a most gruesome aspect. These details are supplied by the master of a bêche-de-mer schooner, to whom all the nooks and corners of the Great Barrier Reef and of the Coral Sea beyond, from New Guinea to New Caledonia, are familiar. He says that the species, as far as his observation goes, is confined to the neighbour-hood of one group of islands. To others this is known as the "bas-tard tortoiseshell". The back is not actually seamless, but age causes the plates to cohere so closely as to present that appearance.

THE MERMAID OF TO-DAY

Dugong (*Halicore australis*) still frequent these waters. The rapa-city of the blacks is a rapidly diminishing factor in their exter-mination, and the rushing to and fro of steamers, which it was thought would scare away those which remain, is becoming too familiar to be fearsome. Even in the narrow limits of Hinchinbrook Channel, through which the passing of steamers is of everyday occurrence, they still exist, though not in such numbers as in the early days. It would seem that the waters within the Great Barrier Reef may long continue one of the last resorts of this strange, uncouth, paradoxical mammal.

Half hippopotamus, half seal, yet in no way related to either, something between a pachyderm and cetacean, the dugong is a herbivorous marine mammal, commonly known as "the sea cow", because of its resemblance in some particulars to that useful domesticated animal. It grazes on marine grass, parts of the flesh very closely resemble beef, and post-mortem examination reveals internal structure similar in most details to those of its namesake. But, unlike the cow, the dugong has two pectoral mammae instead of an abdominal udder, and like the whale is unable to turn its head, the vertebrae of the neck being, if not fused into one mass, at least compressed into a small space.

In form it resembles a seal, the body tapering from the middle to the fish-like, bi-lobed tail. As with the whale, the flippers o. arms do not contribute any considerable means of locomotion, but are used, in the case of the female at least, for grasping the young. When the mother is nursing her child, holding it to her breasts, she is careful, as she rises to breathe, that it, too may obtain a gulp of fresh air, and the two heads emerging together present a strangely human aspect. Traces of elementary hind-legs are to be found in some small bones lying loosely in the flesh. The skull is singularly formed, the upper jaw being bent over the lower. The huge pendulous, rubber-like under-lip, so studded with coarse, sharp bristles as to be known as the brush, seems a development of the under-lip of the horse, and is a perfect implement for the gathering of slimy grass.

To detail further the paradoxes of the dugong, it may be said that some of the teeth resemble those of an elephant; that the males have ivory tusks and of ivory their bones are made; that parts of the flesh may hardly be distinguished from veal and other parts from fine young pork. The freshly flayed hide is fully half an inch thick, and when cured and dried resembles horn in consistency.

Reddish grey, sometimes almost olive green in colour, with white blotches and sparse, coarse bristles, the animal has no comeliness, and yet when a herd frolics in the water, rising in unison with graceful undulatory movements for air, and the sunlight flashes in helioscopic rays from wet backs, the spectacle is rare and fine. Rolling and lurching along, gambolling like good-humoured, contented children, the herd moves leisurely to and from favourite feeding-grounds, occasionally splashing mightily with powerful tails to make fountains of illuminated spray—great, unreflecting, sportful water-babes. Admiration is enhanced as one learns of the affection of the dugong for its young and its love for the companionship of its fellows. When one of a pair is killed, the other haunts the locality for days. Its suspirations seem sighs, and its presence melancholy proof of the reality of its bereavement.

For some time after birth the young is carried under one or other of the flippers, the dam hugging it affectionately to her side.

As the calf grows, it leaves its mother's embrace, but swims close beside, following with automatic precision every twist and lurch of her body, its own helplessness and its implicit faith in the wisdom and protective influence of its parent being exemplified in every movement.

Blacks harpoon dugong as they do turtle, but the sport demands greater patience and dexterity, for the dugong is a wary animal and shy, to be aproached only with the exercise of artful caution. An inadvertent splash of the paddle or a miss with the harpoon, and the game is away with a torpedo-like swirl. To be successful in the sport the black must be familiar with the life-history of the creature to a certain extent—understanding its peregrinations and the reason for them—the strength and trend of currents and the locality of favourite feeding-grounds. Fragments of floating grass sometimes tell where the animal is feeding. An oily appearance on the surface of the sea shows its course, and if the wind sits in the right quarter the keen-scented black detects its presence when the animal has risen to breathe at a point invisible to him. He must know also of the affection of the female for her calf, and be prepared to play upon it implacably. In some localities the blacks were wont to manufacture nets for the capture of dugong, and nets are still employed by them under the direction of white men; for the flesh of the dugong is worthily esteemed, and oil from the blubber—sweet, and limpid as distilled water—is said to possess qualities far superior to that obtained from the decaying livers of cod-fish in the restoration of health and vigour to constitutions enfeebled and wasted by disease.

Using a barbless point attached to a long and strong line, and fitted into a socket in the heavy end of the harpoon shaft, the black waits and watches. With the utmost caution, and in absolute silence he follows in his canoe the dugong as it feeds, and strikes as it rises to breathe. A mad splash, a wild rush! The canoe bounces over the water as the line tightens. Its occupant sits back and steers with flippers of bark, until as the game weakens he is able to approach and plunge another harpoon into it. Sometimes the end of the line is made fast to a buoy of light wood, which the creature tows until exhausted.

So contractible and tough is the skin, that once the point of the harpoon is embedded in it nothing but a strong and direct tug will release it. Some blacks substitute for the barbless point four pieces of thin fencing wire—each about four inches long, bound tightly together at one end, the loose ends being sharpened and slightly diverged. This is fastened to the line and inserted in the socket of the haft, and when it hits it holds to the death, though the animal may weigh three-quarters of a ton.

It is stated that the blacks towards Cape York, having secured the animal with a line attached to a dart insufficient in length to penetrate the hide and the true skin, seize it by the nose, and plug the nostrils with their fingers until it drowns. Here, too, the natives have discovered that the nose is the vulnerable part of the dugong, and having first harpooned it in any part of the body, await an opportunity of spearing it there, with almost invariably speedy fatal effects. The flesh of a young dugong is sweet and tender, and the blubber, dry-cured after the manner of bacon with equal quantities of salt and sugar and finally smoked, quite a delicacy.

Not long since an opportunity was given of examining the effects of a bullet on a dugong. We had harpooned a calf perhaps a year and a half old, and as it rose to the surface in the first struggle for freedom, I shot it, using a Winchester repeating carbine, 25-35, carrying a metal-patched bullet. There was no apparent wound, and on the second time of rising another bullet was lodged in the head, causing instantaneous death. When the animal came to be skinned, it was found that the first bullet had completely penetrated the body, the tough, rubber-like hide so contracting over the wounds of entry and exit as to entirely prevent external bleeding. The fatal bullet had almost completely pulverized the skull, the bones of which were ivory-like in texture. The appearance of the skull might have led to the conclusion that an explosive instead of a nickel-plated bullet had been used, while if the first bullet had not penetrated several folds of the intestines, it probably would have caused the animal very little inconvenience.

The dugong rises to the surface at frequent intervals for air, and the ancients, in the rounded heads of the mother and her offspring, fancied a resemblance to human beings, who sought to lure the unwary to their mansions beneath the waves. Hence the scientific title "Sirenia" for the family to which the dugong belongs. Unpoetical people as the coastal blacks of Queensland are, yet they were among the few who had for neighbours the shy creatures upon whose existence was founded the quaint and engaging legends of the mermaid.

But now we make prosaic bacon from the mermaid's blubbery sides! And those long tresses which she was wont to comb as she gloated over her comeliness in her oval mirror and sang those alluring strains, so soothing, so sweet, yet so deceiving—those wet and tangled locks, where are they? Is the whole realm of nature becoming bald? The hair of the mermaid of to-day is coarse, short, and spikey, with inches between each sprout. For a comb she uses a jagged rock, or cruel coral; for her vanity there is no semblance of pardon; and for her seductive plaint, has it not degenerated into a gulping unmelodious sigh, as she fills her capacious lungs with air?

BÊCHE-DE-MER

Anticipating the possibility of readers away from the Coral Sea, and to whom no reference to the subject is available, wondering as to the form and character of bêche-de-mer, let it be said that the commonest kind in these waters is an enormous slug, varying from six inches long by an inch and a half in diameter, to three feet six inches by four inches. Rough and repulsive in appearance, and sluggish in habit, it has great power of contractibility. It may asume a dumpy oval shape, and again drag out its slow length until it resembles an attenuated German sausage, black in colour. Its "face" may be obtruded and withdrawn at pleasure, or rather will, for what creature could have pleasure in a face like a ravelled mop?

Termed also trepang, sea cucumber, sea slug, and cotton-spinner, and known scientifically as Holothuroidea, no fewer than twenty varieties have been described and are identified by popular and technical titles.

The "fish" are collected by black boys on the coral reefs—dived for, picked up with spears from punts, or taken by hand in shallow water. Some prefer to fish at high-water, for then the bêche-de-mer are less shy, and emerge from nooks in the rocks and coral, and in the limpid water on the Barrier are readily seen at considerable depths. Then the boys dive or dexterously secure the fish with their slender but tough spears, four fathoms long.

At the curing-station (frequently on board the owner's schooner or lugger) they are boiled, the fish supplying nearly all the water for their own cooking. Then each is cut open lengthwise, with a sharp knife, and by a thin skewer of wood its interior surface is exposed. Placed on wire-netting trays in series the fish are smoked or desiccated in a furnace heated, preferably, with black or red mangrove wood, and finally exposed to the sun to eliminate dampness which may have been absorbed on removal from the smoke-house. When the fish leave the smoke-house they have shrunk to small dimensions, and resemble pieces of smoked buffalo hide, more or less curled and crumpled. In this condition they are sent away to China and elsewhere to be used in soup. Australian gourmands are beginning to appreciate this delicacy, which is said to be marvellously strengthening, though without elaborate cooking it is almost tasteless, and therefore unlike dugong soup, which surpasses turtle in flavour and delicacy, and would fatten up a skeleton. Bêche-de-mer is merely a substantial foundation or stock for a more or less artistic culinary effort.

Bêche-de-mer realizes as much as £160 per ton. In former days "red prickly fish" was the most highly prized on the Chinese markets, but several years ago a fisherman in the neighbourhood of Cooktown used a copper boiler. Several Chinese epicures died after partaking of soup made from a particular parcel, and red prickly was forthwith credited with poisonous qualities. The consignment was traced to its origin, and popular opinion at the time was that the boiler had, unknown to the proprietor of the station, induced verdigris. Investigation, however, gave ground for the belief that the fish in the boiling exuded juices of such corrosive qualities that the copper was chemically acted upon. Bêche-de-mer is now invariably cooked in iron vessels, the bottom half of a malt tank being a common boiler, and the red prickly, after being absolutely worthless for many years—so quaint are Oriental prejudices—is now regaining favour in that market.

Bêche-de-mer, though called fish by tradesmen, neither swims nor floats; neither does it crawl, nor wriggle, nor hop, skip nor jump. It simply "moves" on the ocean floor, when not reposing in apparently absolute and unconscious idleness like its distant relative, the star-fish. Nor does the creature possess any means of protection. Some species are rough and prickly, and are said to irritate the hand that grasps them. Others either in nervousness, or a result of shock to the system, or to amaze and affright the beholder, shoot out interminable lengths of filmy, cottony threads, white and glutinous, until one is astonished that a small body should contain such a quantity of yarn ready spun, to eject at a moment's notice like the mazes of ribbon drawn from a conjurer's hat.

While it would be idle to particularize the different varieties of bêche-de-mer that lead such lowly lives in the coral reef here, there is one more conspicuous than the others, which may be referred to without presuming to trespass on the preserves of scientific inquirers. Indeed, it is entitled to notice, for it seems to be most prominent among the few which afford examples of unconscious mimicry and sympathetic colouration to insure themselves from molestation. Bêche-de-mer does not generally give the idea of capability of even the simplest form of deception. True, the "black fish", shrinking from observation, puts on a cloak of sand, and a cousin assumes a resemblance to an irregular piece of coral —rugged, sea-stained and rotten. But the variety under notice takes a higher place in the deceptive art, for it seems to pose as an understudy to one of the most nimble and vicious habitants of the sea—the banded snake. It lies coiled and folded among the stones and coral of the reef, or partially hidden by brown seaweed, which heightens its momentary effect upon the nerves of the barefooted beachcomber. Its length is from four to five feet, girth about three inches, colour reddish brown, with darker bands and blotches. The deception is in appearance only. A touch reveals an innocent but shocking fraud—a poor despicable dummy, lacking the meanest characteristic of its alert original.

Limp and impotent, it is little more than a skin full of water, a yard and a half of intestine with no superficial indication of difference between head and tail. Watch closely, and the "face" —a much frayed mop—is shyly obtruded from one end, and there is justification for the opinion that the other end is the tail. Possibly, after all, this may not be a true variety of bêche-de-mer. In that case an apology to the rest of the tribe is necessary, though the mop-like face betrays a strong family likeness.

If this dolefully helpless creature be lifted by the middle on a stick, its liquid contents are instantly separated, forming distended, high-pressure blobs at each end of the empty, flabby, shrunken skin. Though it suffers this experiment placidly, being incapable of the feeblest resistance, it has the primordial gift of care of itself. Twists purposely made to test its degree of intelligence are artfully straightened out, and the eagerness and hurry with which water is forced throughout empty parts show that life is both sweet and precious. And what is the value of life to an animal of such homely organism and so few wants? And under what charter of rights does it slink among the coral and weed affrighting God-fearing man under the cloak of his first subtle enemy?

CHAPTER V

THE TYRANNY OF CLOTHES

*Give the tinkers and cobblers their presents again and learn to live of
yourself.*

FEW enjoy a less sensational and more tranquil life than ours.
Weeks pass, and but for the visits of the kindly steamer, and the
passing of others at intervals, there is naught of the great world
seen or experienced. A strange sail brings out the whole population,
staring and curious. Rare is the luxury of living when life is uncon-
strained, unfettered by conventionalities and the comic parade
of the fashions.

The real significance of freedom here is realized. What matters
it that London decrees a crease down the trouser legs if those garments are but of well-bleached blue dungaree? The spotless shirt,
how paltry a detail when a light singlet is the only wear? Of what
trifling worth dapper boots to feet made leathery by contact with
the clean, crisp, oatmeal-coloured sand. Here is no fetish about
clothes; little concern for what we shall eat or what we shall drink.
The man who has to observe the least of the ordinances of style
knows not liberty. He is a slave; his dress betrayeth him and pro-
claims him base. There may be degrees of baseness. I am abject
myself; but whensoever I revisit the haunts of men clad in the
few light incommoding clothes that rationalism ordains, I
rejoice and gloat over the slavery of those who have failed to catch
even glimpses of the loveliness of liberty, who are yet afeared of
opinion—"that sour-breathed hag". How can a man with hoop-
like collar, starched to board-like texture, cutting his jowl and
sawing each side of his neck, be free? He may rejoice because
he is a very lord among creation, and has trousers shortened by
turning up the ninth part of a hair after London vogue, and may
be proud of his laws and legislature, and even of his legislators,
but to the tyrannous edge of his collar he is a slave. He can
neither look this way nor that, nor up nor down, without being
reminded that he has imposed upon himself an extra to the
universal penalties of Adam.

One who lives in London tells me of the load of clothes he is compelled to wear in winter to preserve animal heat. He fights for life thus arrayed—thick woollens next to the skin, the decent shirt (badge of respectability), the waistcoat of heavy cloth, the cardigan jacket (which hides the respectable shirt), the coat of cloth, strong and heavy; the overcoat long and incommoding, the woollen comforter, the wool-lined gloves, the double-woollen socks, the half-inch soled boots, the leggings, the hat. To carry this burden of clothes all day, pursuing ordinary vocations, were surely the grossest of bondage. While my three-garment costume —is it not convenient and fashionable enough?

A smart cutter appeared in Brammo Bay. A man, apparently in a pale red shirt, let down the sails and anchor, and by and by one in a black coat buttoned to the throat paddled himself ashore in a dinghy. Like a great many worn on state occasions in country parts here, the coat had seen better days. It was black with greenish lights; the stitches round the buttonholes and along the seams brown and grey; it smelt fusty; the buttons were—well, various and assorted. An inch or two of tarry spun yarn, clove-hitched to a miniature toggle, neatly carved, was the hopeful beginning, a hasty splinter inserted pin-wise, the heedless ending of the row. Between these ranged a bleached cowrie shell, loosely looped with string; a fantastic ornament (green with verdigris) from some bygone millinery, and a cherished relic of a pair of trousers of the past in all the boldness of polished brass. But it was easy to detect that there was no shirt beneath the dingy coat; and that the coat itself was merely a concession to the evidence of civilization which had been apparent from the boat. On board the man wore neither coat nor shirt. The cheerful note of colour, so conspicuous as he sailed to the anchorage, was his sun-burnt skin. Some men burn brown, some red. He was of the red variety, and his bare skin looked a deal more respectable than his cockroach-nibbled coat. To him, clothing save for decency's sake, had become superfluous. He felt that "to be naked is to be so much nearer the being man than to go in livery". He wore no hat, no boots. Pyjama trousers of cotton composed his entire workaday costume; dungaree trousers and a musty coat his Court dress. Yet he was clean and glowing with health and cheerfulness; self-reliant, splendidly independent. Had he allowed his mind to dwell on clothing his independence would have been less. He might have required the aid of a black boy to navigate his boat, and the continual presence of a black boy in a small boat does not make for sweetness and light.

SINGLE-HANDEDNESS

Another grandly free man sailed his cutter into the bay one fine morning. He knew the water and ran her on the sand, brought his anchor ashore and shoved her off, to swing lazily the while. When I paid him a ceremonious visit, I found that he had but one arm. The empty right sleeve was the more pathetic when I saw him mixing his flour for a damper, and in the cunning twists and wriggling by which the fingers freed each other of the sticky dough and other dexterous manipulations, I soon came to recognize that with his left hand he was as deft as many men with their right and left. He had sailed the boat ladened with wire netting and heavy goods from Bowen, two hundred miles south, and was on his way to his selection, one hundred miles farther north. A wiry, slight man though a real "shell-back", one who had been steeped in and saturated with every sea, was "giving the sea best", nerve-shaken, so he said—and yet sailing a cutter with but three or four inches of free-board "single-handed". And he told the why and wherefor of his fear of the sea.

With a mate he had been, for many months, bêche-de-mer fishing, their station or headquarters a lonely islet in Whitsunday Passage, which winds about that picturesque group of islands through which Captain Cook passed in the year 1770. The twain had been out on one of the spurs of the Great Barrier Reef, and had been caught in the toils of adverse weather. After beating about for days they managed to make their station—hungry, thirsty, their souls fainting within them. Shelter and comfort were theirs, and it was no surprise to my visitor when his mate slept the next morning beyond the accustomed time. "Let him rest," he said, "he is dog-tired"; and went about the work of the day. He had himself known what it was to sleep eighteen and twenty hours at a stretch, for he had many times been worn by toil and watching and nerve-tension to the limit of endurance. And so the day passed, and the man in the bunk slept on. Peace and rest were his, and the busy man envied the calm indifference to the day's doings that he could not find in his heart to disturb.

"Won't he feel fresh when he does wake," he reflected. "He'll be a bit narked at having wasted a whole bloomin' day. I shouldn't be surprised if he was savage because I didn't call him."

When the evening meal was prepared and everything in the tiny hut made orderly, it would be a pleasure for him to wake up and discover that he had been allowed to have his sleep out.

Ah! but his sleep was very sound and very silent—almost too stillful to be natural.

A touch on his shoulders, saying, "Andrew, wake up, old fellow!"

No movement, or response. His feet cold! cold! and his chest, too, cold!

The mate had found his port after stormy seas. His heart—worn out with stress and strain—had failed within him, and all day long his companion thought tenderly of him, making but little noise, thinking that his sleep was the sleep of a day, not the sleep of eternity that no earthly din may disturb.

The weather was still boisterious, but it was essential to take the body to Bowen, to render unto the authorities there conclusive evidence that death had been the result of natural causes. My visitor's nerves were then virile. But the time of stress and strain was at hand. He found himself alone on a remote island. A grim responsibility forced upon him. Awful as the duty was, it had to be courageously faced, and performed as tenderly as might be. Instead of the enjoyment of comfort and rest, and days of busy companionship and revivifying hopes, there was the shock that sudden death inflicts, dramatic loneliness, dry-eyed grief, forced exertion, and the abandonment of brightening prospects.

With pain and infinite labour he succeeded in dragging and rolling the corpse to the beach. Thence he pushed it up a plank on to the deck of the cutter, and leaving his possessions to chance and fate, he, the wearied and bereaved one-armed man, set sail in violent weather across the open sea to the nearest port. At midnight the "great cry" of a hurricane arose. Lightning flashed over the stricken yeasty sea. A lonesome and grim quest this—full of peril. Did not nature in the trumpet tones of a furious and vengeful spirit decree the destruction of the little boat as she bounced and floundered among the crests of those awful waves? Here was booty belonging to the ocean—prey escaping from the talons of the fiercest and most remorseless of harpies. So they shrieked and swarmed about the boat, howling for what was theirs. The strife was great, but not too great for the lonely man's seamanship.

All the fiends of the sea might do their worst, but until the actual finale came, he would sail the boat—lifting her on the swell, eluding the white hissing bulk of the following sea.

When at last the boat ran into port, the sea had gained a moral victory, but the man gave to the authorities the mortal remains of his mate, to be buried decently on land.

He told me that he felt cowed—he could never face the sea again. Once before he had given up "sailorizing", not then on account of his nerves, but because ambition to possess a sweet-potato patch, pumpkins, and a few bananas, melons, mangoes, had got hold of him. He had taken up a piece of land, but having no money his flimsy fencing was no barrier to the wallabies, and he abandoned the enterprise to them. Now he had abandoned his bêche-de-mer project, had bought wire netting to keep out the wallabies, and would make a second effort to settle down. A little net-fishing would help to keep him going. "As for the sea," said he, "I have had enough—too much. It is all right while your pluck lasts, but once get a shake, and you had better give it up. And the little boat—I broke that rail as I was getting poor Andrew's body on board. She is all right, but for that—and she's for sale."

In an hour, having concocted some stew and baked his damper, the single-handed, nerve-shaken old sailor set sail, and I knew him no more.

Another of poor old "Yorky's" adventures is worth telling. While out on the Barrier Reef, the black crew of his bêche-de-mer boat mutinied, and knocking him and his mate on the head, threw them overboard. The sudden souse into the water restored Yorky to consciousness, and he swam back to the cutter whence the blacks had hastily fled in the dinghy. It was a desperate struggle for a one-armed man to cling to and clamber up the side of the boat, but Yorky has never yet failed when his life was at stake. He won the deck at last, but at the expense of a broken rib and the flesh on the best part of his side torn bare to the bones. Still dazed, he chanced to look over the side, where he saw his mate's head bobbing up and down in the water. Hard as it had been for him to save himself, it was more difficult still to rescue the body from the sharks. Frantically using rough-and-ready methods, he hauled it on board, and disposed it as decently as circumstances permitted. Yorky, great of heart, is quite unused to the melting mood. He admits that he felt pretty bad mentally. But whatever his feelings towards his sodden mate lying there with watery blood oozing from wounds on his head, exhibiting the marks of the necessarily rough-and-ready means that had been taken for his rescue, they had to be suppressed. Wet, dizzy, and sadly battered, with little more apparent reason for the possession of the breath of life than his companion, he set sail, slipped the anchor, and steered for the nearest port. Some distance on the way, to use Yorky's own and sufficient words, "The dead man came to life!" Both had to submit to the restraint of hospital treatment for many weeks ere physical repairs were complete.

How is it that a one-armed man, slight in physique, whose brains have been addled by blows with billets of firewood, whose side is raw and bleeding, and who has a broken rib hampering his movements, is able to achieve feats that would be surprising if performed by a whole and stalwart individual? Yorky has always been a wonder, and his life a series of adventures and arduous tasks, which seem to prove that the loss of a limb has been compensated for by hardihood and resourcefulness worth a great deal more.

A BUTTERFLY REVERIE

> And laugh
> At gilded butterflies, and hear poor rogues
> Talk of Court news.

There were but three men and a dog in the boat, but the boat was overburdened. Not that the dog was big, or the men either. It was all on account of the day.

It was a day in which you wanted the whole realm of nature for yourself—so full of sunshine and flitting butterflies was it—so beaming with the advent of summer, and her fervent greetings, so wondrously calm and clear. You felt selfish at the pleasure of it all. It filled you wellnigh to surfeit, yet you would have more of it. It was too delicious to squander upon others, yet how could one mind comprehend the grandeur of it all?

The white boat drifted on a blue and lustrous sea. The reef points tapped a monotonous scale as the white sails swung to the swaying of the gaff. Listlessly the boat drifted to the barely perceptible swell, regular as the breathings of a sleeping child. Sound and motion invited to slumber. The shining sea, the islands, green and purple, the soft sweet atmosphere, the full glory of a rare day, kept all the senses in tune.

There, four miles away, lay the island, and close at hand the turtle were ever and anon rising, balloon-like, from coral gardens to gulp greedy draughts of air, which not even the salty essences of the ocean could rob of its perfume.

Sometimes the boat did seem conscious of inconstancy, and anon with feminine frivolity she would coyly swing round to flirt with the islets close at hand. She would have her own way until the free breezes came, and somehow the wind still blows whereso'er it listeth, and will not be untimely wooed, though the sailor whistles with all the "lascivious pleasing of the lute".

Some atmospheric phenomenon, altogether beyond idle concern, lifted the islands afar off out of the water, suspending them in the sky. The languorous breadths of the sea gradually changed to silver, and under the purple islands the silver band extended, bright and gleaming, until it seemed to merge again into the blue of the sky. That was so, for was it not all visible—the purple islands, with the silver bands separating them from the sea? Yet u_der ordinary conditions those very islands are blue studs set in the rim of the ocean. What magic is it that uplifts them to-day ?etween the ocean and the sky?

This was a day of gushing sunshine and myriads of butterflies. They flew from the mainland, not as spies but in battalions—a never-ending procession miles broad. You could fancy you heard in the throbbing stillness the movement of the fairy-like wings— a faint, unending hum. From the odorous jungle they came, flitting in gay inconsequence, steering a course of "slanting indeterminates", yet full of the power and the passion of the moment. They flitted between the idle boom and the deck, and up the gleaming sky, in all the sizes that distance grades between nearness and infinity.

There were islands near at hand and some afar off. What instinct guided them—for butterflies are short-sighted creatures —I know not. If wind had come, as we who lolled lazily in the boat longed, the myriad host of resplendent creatures would have been scattered and millions beaten down into the sea, above which they flew with such airy levity.

What instinct guided the frail, unreflective creatures across miles of ocean to the Islands of the Blest among butterflies?

In their variety, too, they were entertaining. In great number was the pretty frailty, whose wings are compact of transparencies and purple blotches. In this full, fierce light the purple is black and the transparencies all steel-like glitter. They came across in shoals. There was neither beginning nor end. All the sky glittered with winged mosaics. Then came the great green and gold and black creature, accompanied sometimes by his less gaily decorated mate, ponderous of flight; and, anon, that insect of regal blue, that can flit as idly as any of the order, and yet dart in and out of the jungle and over the tree-tops, with swallow-like swiftness. Rarely in the throng came that scarlet and black, which makes the gaudy, flaunting hibiscus envious of its colour; but the little yellow "wanderers", ever busy and active, came low over the water, weary with the long journey, and sometimes ready to rest —shifty flecks of gold—on the white sail.

There was no end to the flight. The air was too full. One wearied of the ceaseless panorama of the gay bejewelled insects. They were the possessors of the prime of that glorious morning. Beautiful and frail, and inconsequent as they were, you envied them. They flitted on without guide or leader, venturing the dangers of water and air, flying up in the full blaze of the sun—eager, joyous, unconcerned. In the boat we were compelled to loll about between heaven and the cool coral groves, and compare enforced inactivity with the blithesome freedom of the weakest butterfly.

Occasionally a turtle would bob up from its pastures below, and catching sight of the sail, with a bubbling gulp, disappear, the white splash creating concentric rings of ripples. But the breeze came not, and the disorderly procession of butterflies, miles broad, passed on.

> Some flew light as a laugh of glee;
> Some flew soft as a low, long sigh,
> All to the haven where each would be.

I listened to the wooings of the black boys to the breeze. They liked not the prospect of sweeping the boat home. They implored for wind with cooings, with petulant whistlings, and with gentle but novel objurgations. But it came not, and so the afternoon passed and evening fell, and the butterflies, a faint, thin stratum, drifted on.

Then as a final challenge to the breeze that we longed for, and which had resisted all appeals, "Come on, big wind, and kill little boat!" exclaimed an irresponsible boy, whose ears had long ached with the day's dull silence, and who saw no prospect of hot turtle steak for supper.

As if to take up the gauntlet, a faint zephyr flicked the listless cheek of the ocean, and slapped the sails. The boom swayed and swung over, the boat, without guidance, idly headed off, and we flopped home to the placid bay before the unenergetic breeze, which was all that nature in her idle hour could spare.

THE SERPENT BEGUILED

Eve Avenged

You do yet taste
Some subtleties o' the isle that will let not you
Believe things certain.

Once upon a time—not so very long ago either—an unpretentious poultry farm was started. The idea of making, if not a rapid and bulky fortune, at least "a comfortable living" (and that phrase embodies much) out of poultry farming has been conceived, possibly, many times and oft. There was nothing novel, therefore, in the hatching out of this particular scheme. But for a paltry detail it would never have attained notoriety. We never blazon our failures—why should we? The one spark of original thought that enlightened the prosaic plans of the undertaking was this: the promoters wanted quality in the eggs of their hens as well as quantity. In order that there might be no excuse for and no degeneracy on the part of the hens, shops were ransacked for nest-eggs of proper proportions. These were placed in spots conspicuous to the hens, who, of course, understood that they were expected to lay up to them. In other words, these were patterns for the hens to lay by. No self-respecting fowl likes to be beaten by a nest-egg. She goes one, or, it may be, a dozen or two, better; but the stony-hearted egg is never to be bluffed. It is there as a standard of size, and in accordance with its dimensions so will the credit of the fowl-yard be.

In this particular yard all went well for many months. Why, the hens beat the nest-eggs with scarcely an effort, and then started making records. It was a fierce competition, and the enterprise flourished. A good beginning had been made, and the high-minded hens chuckled with pride and satisfaction. In the course of two or three months, however, a gradual deterioration in the size of the eggs took place. There was just the same amount of fuss and feathers, showing the artfulness of the hens, but the eggs soon dwindled down below plans and specifications, and then an investigation took place. Not a single nest-egg was to be found. Vainly was search made. The hens sniggered. They had fulfilled their duty, and finding it tiresome and wearing to produce abnormal eggs, had secreted those set apart for them to measure by, and had thereupon levelled their enterprise and skill down. Such sinfulness and such burglarious conduct on the part of respectable hens that had the most discreet upbringing, that had never been allowed to play in anybody else's yard, and that had never been permitted to wander from the paths of virtue, was a sore affliction.

But one day a nest-egg was found far away in the bush, and then another a quarter of a mile from the yard in the creek. Yet another was discovered underneath a hollow log. Being restored to accustomed places with due ceremony, and in sight of all the hens in convention assembled, a gratifying change in the size of eggs produced resulted in a few days. But again a slump set in. The nest-eggs had disappeared, and the hens were fulfilling their contract anyhow.

Other nest-eggs of prescribed dimensions were taken out of stock; and a yet more wonderful thing happened!

One morning about fowl-feeding time, a great cry arose:

"Sen-ake!" "Sen-ake!"

Yes, there was a snake. About half—the latter half—its length was visible outside the back of a nesting place (a box open at the front), and a blow from a shovel disabled it. Further examination showed that the snake had squeezed through a knot-hole in the box. A lusty man hauled on the snake violently. The box was heavy, and from the front the snake could be seen. It looked troubled and uncomfortable, but not inclined to back out, although the inducement in that direction was considerable. Eventually the snake parted; and in the latter half there was a bulge. Dissection revealed—What—marvellous! a nest-egg. But why did the snake show such reluctance to leave the box? The first or forward half was hooked out from among the straw, and there was another oval distention—another nest-egg! The snake had discovered elsewhere a china egg, had swallowed it, and then crawled in at the knot-hole, and got outside another. Escape was impossible, until the problem was solved by halving.

There are no more accusations of dishonourable motives on the part of the hens in doing away with the porcelain patterns to escape the arduous duty of laying. It was all the fault of the serpent. Now, the serpent is *not* wise, for any nest-egg beguiles him. It takes a long while to digest such hardware. Traps are now laid for him. An egg of china is put in a box, the open part of which is covered with small mesh-wire netting. The snake submits to the temptation of the egg coyly resting on a bunch of grass, and having made it its own, cannot let go. Then comes abhorred fate in the shape of a gleeful man with a long-handled shovel.

ADVENTURE WITH A CROCODILE

Cooling of the air with sighs,
In an odd angle of the Isle.

Now to proceed with the deliberate intention of dragging by the ears into these pages a crocodile yarn. We have not a single "alligator" in Australia, our crocodiles being wrongly so called, but this perversity of nomenclature does not affect the anecdote.

To tell of the coast of Queensland, and to omit reference to an adventure with one of those wary beasts would be to court criticism likely to cast a shadow upon the veracity of more than one of the incidents and occurrences herein to be chronicled.

I approach the duty to the readers as well as to myself with diffidence, for has it not been stated that these pages were fated to be unsensational and unromantic, and can anyone imagine an unsensational adventure with a crocodile? Therein lie the virtue of and the apology for this story.

If the reader will take the trouble to scan the revised chart of the island, he will notice on the eastern coast an indentation entitled "Panjoo", which, in the language of the blacks, seems to indicate "nice place". A steep grassy slope comes down to the sea, separated therefrom by a line of pandanus palms. To the north is a jungle-covered spur, along the foot of which is a palm-tree gully; to the south a ridge with low-growing, wind-bent acacias. The gully enters the boulder-strewn inlet under the shade of much leafage. The great Pacific gurgles at the base of giant rocks, among which a ragged palm (*Caryota*) bears immense bunches of yellow insipid fruit, each containing two coffee-like berries. Panjoo is a favourite objective, for it may be approached from various directions, each pleasant, but as a resort for a crocodile it is about as unpromising a locality as could be imagined.

Thither one bright November morning we ("Paddy", the most silent and alert of black boys, and myself) went. The tide was out, and we found a comparatively easy track close to the margin of the sea, having occasionally to wade through shallow pools and to clamber over rocks thickly studded with limpets.

Years gone by a huge log of pencil-cedar had been cast among the boulders at Panjoo, and as I looked at the log Paddy, with a start, indicated the presence of a novelty—a crocodile apparently in repose with its head in the shadow of a boulder. I was carrying a pea-rifle more for company than for anything else; for Paddy, though of a most cheerful disposition, never made remarks. His conversation for the most part was compounded of eloquent looks and expressive gestures. A monosyllable to him was a laborious sentence; four or five words a speech. But the presence of a ten-foot crocodile of unknowledgeable ferocity was a vital occasion. We hastily discussed in staccato whispers our plan of campaign. It was arranged that we should assail the enemy at close quarters. The calibre of the rifle was 22; its velocity most humble, the bullet of soft lead. Unless it entered the eye of the crocodile, and thence by luck its small brain, there was no hope of fatal effects. Yet to take home such a rare trophy as a crocodile's skull, never before known or heard of on the island, was a hope sufficient to evoke and steady the instincts to be called upon as a necessary preliminary.

Paddy armed himself with weighty stones, and so manoeuvring to cut off the creature's retreat to the sea, we silently and with the utmost caution advanced.

The crocodile moved not as we, thirsting for its blood, stealthily approached. Then, as I raised the rifle, Paddy tilted up his much-flattened nose, sniffed, and in tragic whisper said: "Dead!"

At all times a crocodile has a characteristic odour, a combination of fish and very sour and stale musk, but Paddy smelt more than the familiar scent—the scent of carrion.

Most unworthy of mortals, we had found the rarest of unprecious things—a crocodile that had died a natural death. Apparently a day, or at the most a day and a half, had elapsed since the creature had laid its head under the shadow of the boulder and died, far from accustomed haunts and kin. There was no sign of wound, bruise or putrefying sore. All the teeth were perfect. It seemed like a crocodile taking its rest, with its awful stench around it.

With poles we levered the body out of the way of the tide. Months after, when nature had done her part in the removal of all fleshy taint, we returned for the bones. The teeth are now scattered far and wide as trophies of the one and only crocodile ever acknowledged to have been discovered dead.

CHAPTER VI

IN PRAISE OF THE PAPAW

PROPERTIES varied and approaching the magical have been ascribed to one of the commonest plants of North Queensland; and yet how trivial and prosaic are the honours bestowed upon it! That which makes women beautiful for ever; which renews the strength of man; which is a sweet and excellent food, and which provides medicine for various ills, cannot be said to lack many of the attributes of the elixir of life, and is surely entitled to a special paean in a land languishing for population.

Distinctive and significant as the virtues possessed by the papaw are, yet because of its universality and because it yields its fruits with little labour, it gets but scant courtesy. It is tolerated merely; but if we had it not, if it were as far as that vast shore washed by the farthest sea, men would adventure for such merchandise and adventure at the bidding of women. How few there are who recognize in the everyday papaw one of the most estimable gifts of kindly nature?

Some who dwell in temperate climes claim for the apple and the onion superlative qualities. In the papaw the excellences of both are combined. The onion may induce to slumber, but the sleep it produces, is it not a trifle too balmy? The moral life and high standard of statesmanship of an American senator are cited as examples of the refining influences of apples. For every day for thirty years he has, to the exclusion of all other food, lunched on that fruit. Possibly the papaw may be decadent in respect to morals and politics. The grape, lemon, orange, pomelo, and the straw-berry, each in the estimation of special enthusiasts, is proclaimed the panacea for many of the ills of life. One writer cites cases in which maniacs have been restored to reason by the exclusive use of cherries. The apple, they say, too, gives to the face of the fair ruddiness, but the tint, is it not too bold, compared with maiden blush which bepaints the cheek of the beauty who rightly under-stands the use of the vital principle of the papaw? Those who have complexions to retain or restore, let them understand and be fair.

In North Queensland the plant grows everywhere. In the dry,

buoyant climate west of the coast range, and in the steamy coastal tract, on cliff-like hill-sides, on sandy beaches a few feet above high-water mark, among rocks with but a few inches of soil, and where the decayed vegetation of generations has made fat mould many feet deep, the papaw flourishes. It asks foothold, heat, light and moisture, and given these conditions a plant within a few months of its first start in life will begin to provide food—entertaining, refreshing, salubrious—and will continue so to do for years. Its precociousness is so great and its productiveness so lavish, that by the time other trees flaunt their first blossoms, the papaw has worn itself out, and is dying of senile decay, leaving, however, numerous posterity. The fruit is delicate, too, and soon resolves itself into its original elements.

The true eater of fruit is of a school apart, not to be classed with the individual who, because of the rites and observances of the table, accepts, in no exalted spirit, a portion of fruit at the nether end of a feast. He is one who has attained, or to whom has been vouchsafed, a poignant sense of all that does the least violence to the sense of taste and smell; but, moreover, who is capable of discovering edification in things as diverse as the loud Jack fruit and the subtle mangosteen.

As with many other fruits, so with the papaw. Only those who grow it themselves, who learn of the relative merits of the produce of different trees, and who can time their acceptance of it from the tree, so that it shall possess all its fleeting elements in the happy blending of full maturity, can know how good and great the papaw really is. The fruit of some particular tree is, of course, not to be tolerated save as a vegetable, and then what a desirable vegetable it is. It has a precise and particular flavour, and texture most agreeable. And as a mere fruit there are many more rich and luscious, and highly-flavoured; many that provoke louder and more sincere acclamations of approval. But the papaw, delicate and grateful, is more than a mere fruit. If we give credence to all that scientific research has made known of it, we shall have to concede that the papaw possesses social influences more potent than many of the political devices of this socialistic age.

But there may be some who do not know that the humble papaw (*Carica papaya*) belongs to the passionfruit family (*Passiflora*) a technical title bestowed on account of a fancied resemblance in the parts of the flower to the instruments of Christ's sufferings and death. And it is said to have received its generic name on account of its foliage somewhat resembling that of the common fig. An authority on the botany of India suggested that it was originally introduced from the district of Papaya, in Peru, and that "papaw" is merely a corruption of that name. The tree is, as a rule, unbranched, and somewhat palm-like in form. Its great leaves, often a foot and a half long, borne on smooth, cylindrical stalks, are curiously cut into seven lobes, and the stem is hollow and transversely partitioned with thin membranes.

One of the most remarkable characteristics of the papaw is that it is polygamous—that is to say, there may be male and female and even hermaphrodite flowers on the same plant. Commonly the plants are classed as male and female. The males largely predominate. Many horticulturists have sought by the selection of seeds and by artificial fertilization to control the sex of the plant so that the fruit-bearing females shall be the more numerous, but in vain. Some, on the theory that the female generally obtains a more vigorous initial start in life, and in very infancy presents a more robust appearance, heroically weed out weak and spindly seedlings with occasionally happy results. The mild Hindu, however, who has cultivated the papaw (or papai to adopt the Anglo-Indian title) for centuries, and likewise wishes to avoid the cultivation of unprofitable male plants, seeks by ceremonies to counteract the bias of the plant in favour of masculine attributes. Without the instigation or knowledge of man or boy, a maiden, pure and undefiled, takes a ripe fruit from a tree at a certain phase of the moon, and plants the seed in accordance with more or less elaborate ritual. The belief prevails that these observances procure an overwhelming majority of the female element. The problem of sex, which bewilders the faithless European, is solved satisfactorily to the Hindu by a virgin prayerful and pure.

On plants which have hitherto displayed only masculine characteristics, small, pale yellow, sweetly-scented flowers on long, loosely-branched axillary panicles, may appear partially or fully developed female organs which result in fructification, and such fruit is ostentatiously displayed. The male produces its fruit not as does the female, clinging closely and compact to the stem, but dangling dangerously from the end of the panicles—an example of witless paternal pride. This fruit of monstrous birth does not, as a rule, develop to average dimensions, and it is generally woodeny of texture and bitter as to flavour, but fully developed as to seeds.

The true fruit is round, or oval, or elongated, sometimes pear-shaped, and with flattened sides, due to mutual lateral pressure. As many as two hundred and fifty individual fruits have been counted on a single tree at one and the same time. The heaviest fruit within the ken of the writer weighed eight pounds eleven ounces. They hug the stem closely in compact single rows in progressive stages, the lower tier ripe, the next uppermost nearly so, the development decreasing consistently to the rudiments of flower-buds in the crown of the tree. The leaves fall as the fruit grows, but there is always a crown or umbrella to ward off the rays of the sun. When ripe, the most approved variety is yellow. In the case of the female plant growing out of the way of a male, the fruit is smaller in size, and seedless or nearly so.

Another curious, if not unique point about this estimable plant is that sometimes within the cavity of a perfect specimen will be found one or two infant naked fruits, likewise apparently perfect. Occasionally these abnormal productions are crude, unfashioned and deformed.

Ripened in ample light, with abundance of water, and in high temperature, the fruit must not be torn from the tree "with forced fingers rude", lest the abbreviated stalk pulls out a jagged plug, leaving a hole for the untimely air to enter. The stalk must be carefully cut, and the spice-exhaling fruit borne reverently and immediately to the table. The rite is to be performed in the cool of the morning, for the papaw is essentially a breakfast fruit, and then when the knife slides into the buff-coloured flesh of a cheesy consistency, minute colourless globules exude from the facets of the slices. These glistening beads are emblems of perfection. Plentiful dark seeds adhere to the anterior surface. Some take their papaw with the merest sensation of salt, some with sugar and a drop or two of lime or lemon juice; some with a few of the seeds, which have the flavour of nasturtium. The wise eat it with silent praise. In certain obvious respects it has no equal. It is so clean; it conveys a delicate perception of musk—sweet, not florid; soft, soothing and singularly persuasive. It does not cloy the palate, but rather seductively stimulates the appetite. Its effect is immediately comforting, for to the stomach it is pleasant, wholesome, and helpful. When you have eaten of a papaw in its prime, one that has grown without check or hindrance, and has been removed from the tree without bruise or blemish, you have within you pure, good and chaste food, and you should be thankful and of a gladsome mind. Moreover, no untoward effects arise from excess of appetite. If you be of the fair sex your eyes may brighten on such diet, and your complexion become more radiant. If a mere man, you will be the manlier.

So much on account of the fruit. Sometimes the seeds are eaten as a relish, or macerated in vinegar as a condiment, when they resemble capers. The pale yellow male flowers, immersed in a solution of common salt, are also used to give zest to the soiled appetite, the combination of flavour being olive-like, piquant and grateful. The seeds used as a thirst-quencher form component parts of a drink welcome to fever patients. The papaw and the banana, in conjunction form an absolutely perfect diet. What the one lacks in nutritive or assimilative qualities the other supplies. No other food, it is asserted, is essential to maintain a man in perfect health and vigour. Our fictitious appetites may pine for wheaten bread, oat-meal, flesh, fish, eggs, and all manner of vegetables, but given the papaw and the banana, the rest are superfluous. Where the banana grows the papaw flourishes. Each is singular from the fact that it represents wholesome food long before arrival at maturity.

Then as a medicine plant the papaw is of great renown. The peculiar properties of the milky juice which exudes from every part of the plant were noticed two hundred years ago. The active principle of the juice known as papain, said to be capable of digesting two hundred times its weight of fibrine, is used for many disorders and ailments.

By common repute the papaw tree has the power of rendering tough meat tender. Some say that it is but necessary to hang an old hen among the broad leaves to restore to it the youth and freshness of a chicken. In some parts of South America papaw juice is rubbed over meat, and is said to change "apparent leather to tender and juicy steak". Other folks envelop the meat in the leaves and obtain a similar effect. Science, to ascertain the verity or otherwise of the popular belief applied certain tests, the results of which demonstrated that all the favourable allegations were founded on truth and fact. A commonplace experiment was tried. A small piece of beef wrapped up in a papaw leaf during twenty-four hours, after a short boiling became perfectly tender; a similar piece wrapped in paper submitted to exactly similar conditions and processes remained hard. Few facts are more firmly established than that the milky juice softens—in other words hastens the decomposition of—flesh. Further, the fruit in some countries is cooked as a vegetable with meat, and in soups; it forms an ingredient in a popular sauce, and is preserved in a variety of ways as a sweetmeat. Syrups and wines and cordials made from the ripe fruit are expectorant, sedative and tonic. Ropes are made from the bark of the tree. By its power of dissolving stains the papaw has acquired the name of the melon bleach; the leaves, and a portion of the fruit are steeped in water, and the treated water is used in washing coloured clothing, especially black, the colours being cleaned and held fast.

And as to its beauty-bestowing attributes, an admirer's word might be quoted as a final note of praise—

"The strange and beautiful races of the Antilles astonish the eyes of the traveller who sees them for the first time. It has been said that they have taken their black, brown, and olive and yellow skin-tints from the satiny and bright-hued rinds of the fruit which surround them. If they are to be believed, the mystery of their clean, clear complexion and exquisite pulp-like flesh arises from the use of the papaw fruit as a cosmetic. A slice of ripe fruit is rubbed over the skin, and is said to dissolve spare flesh and remove every blemish. It is a toilet requisite in use by the young and old, producing the most beautiful specimens of the human race."

THE CONQUERING TREE

Inconsequent as nature appears to be at times and given to whims, fancies and contradictions, only those who study with attention her moods may estimate how truthful and how sober she really is. She is honest in all her purposes, and though changeful and gay in apparel never cheap nor meretricious.

Let a mangrove swamp be taken as an illustration of an untoward aspect of nature, and see whether among the apparent confusion, and the mud and slime and the unpleasant odours, there are not many proofs of good-humour, kindly disposition, real prettiness, and orderly and systematic purpose.

On the deltas and banks of all the rivers and creeks of North Queensland and on many of the more sheltered beaches, the mangrove flourishes, that ambitious tree which performs an important function in the scheme of nature. Its botanical title reveals its special character—*Rhizophora*. Very diverse indeed are the means by which plants are distributed. While some are borne, some fly and others float. The mangrove is maritime. While still pendant from the pear-shaped fruit of the parent tree, the seed, a spindle-shaped radicle, varying in length from a foot to four feet, germinates—ready to form a plant immediately upon arrival at a suitable locality. A sharp spike at the apex represents the embryo leaves ready to unfold, while the roots spring from the opposite and slightly heavier end. The weight is so nicely adjusted that the spindle floats perpendicularly or nearly so, when owning a separate existence from the parent tree, it drops into the water, and begins its remarkable career.

Whole battalions of living mangrove radicles fall into the rivers during February and March. Out at sea miles from the land you may cross the sinuous ranks of the marine invaders—a disorderly, planless venture at the mercy of the wind and waves. Myriads perish, hopeless, water-logged derelicts, never finding foothold nor resting-place. But thousands of these scouts of vegetation live to fulfil the glorious purpose of winning new lands, of increasing the area of continents. This arrogant plant not only says to the ocean, "Hitherto shalt thou come, but no farther: and here shall thy proud waves be stayed", but unostentatiously wrests from it unwilling territory.

Plants, like animals, require "food convenient for them", certain constituents of the soil, certain characteristics of environment, that they may flourish and fulfil their purpose. This delights in conditions that few tolerate—saline mud, ooze and frequent flooding by the salt sea. Drifting into shallow water the sharp end of the spindly radicle bores into the mud. At once slender but tough roots emerge in radiating grapples, leaves unfold at the other extremity, and the plan of conquest has begun. During the early period of its life there is nothing singular in the growth of the plant. In a few months, however, it sends out arching adventitious roots, which on reaching the mud grasp it with strong finger-like rootlets. These arching roots, too, send out from their arches other roots that arch, and the arches of these similarly repeat themselves, and so on, until the tree is underpinned and supported and stayed by an elaborate and complicated system, which, while offering no resistance of the sweep of the seas, upholds the tree as no solid trunk or stem could. Then from the plan of arches spring offshoots, in time to become trees as great as the parent. Aerial roots start a downward career from the overhanging branches, anchoring themselves in the mud. Some young seedling drops and the pointed end sticks deep in the mud, and grows forthwith, to possess arching and aerial roots of its own, and to make confusion worse confounded. The identity of the original founder of the grove is lost in the bewildering labyrinth of its own arches, offshoots, and aerial roots, and of independent trees to which it has given the mystery of life. One floating radicle with its pent-up energy, having after weeks of drifting and swaying this way and that to the slightest current and ripple, grapples Mother Earth and makes a law to the ocean. Among the interlacing roots seaweed, sodden driftwood and leaves lodge, sand collects, and as the level of the floor of the ocean is raised the sea retires, contributing by the flotsam and jetsam of each spring-tide to its own inevitable conquest.

Not to one plant alone is the victory to be ascribed. As in the army there are various and distinct branches of service, so in this ancient and incessant strife between land and water, the vegetable invaders are classified and have their appointed place and duties. Neither are all the constituents of a mangrove swamp mangroves. In the first rank will be found the hardiest and most highly specialized—*Rhizophora murcronata*, next, *Bruguiera gymnorrhiza* (a plant of slightly more lowly growth but prolific of arching and aerial roots); *Bruguiera rheedi* (red or orange mangrove). Some of the roots of the latter spread over the surface and have vertical kinks. The roots and the accessories act as natural groynes, causing the waves to swirl and to precipitate mud and sand. *Bruguiera parviflora* and *Ceriops candolleana* assist in the general scheme, the former depending upon abutments for security instead of adventitious roots. Its radicles resemble pipe-stems, or as they lie stranded on the beach, slightly curved and with the brown tapering calyx tube attached, green snakes with pointed heads.

Surprising features are possessed by the tree known as *Sonneratia alba*. The roots send up a multitude of offshoots, resembling woodeny radishes, some being forked, growing wrong end up. All the base of each tree is set about with a confusion of points—a wonderful and perfect design for the arrest and retention of debris and mud. Some of these obtrusive roots are much developed, measuring six feet in height and about four inches in diameter.

No less remarkable is the help that the white mangrove (*Avicenna officinalis*) affords in the conquest with its system of strainers. Though different in many respects from the *Sonneratia*, it too has erect, obtrusive, respiratory shoots from the roots, slender in comparison, resembling asparagus shoots or rake tines (called by some cobbler's pegs) and which strain the sea, retaining light rubbish and assisting to hold and consolidate it all. Each of the plants mentioned is equipped in a more or less efficient manner for the special purpose of taking part in the reclamation of land. In some the roots descend from the branches to the mud where roots ought to grow; in others, roots ascend from the mud to the upper air, where, ordinarily, roots have no sort of business. Each possesses varying and distinct features well designed to aid and abet the general purpose.

Other species of marine plants have their duty too. That which is known as the river mangrove (*Aegiceras majus*)—which does not confine itself to rivers—comes to sweeten the noisome exhalation of the mud, and with its profuse white, orange-scented flowers, to invite the cheerful presence of bees and butterflies. The looking-glass tree (*Heritiera littoralis*), with its large, oval, glossy, silver-backed leaves and boat-shaped fruit, stands with the river mangrove along the margin farthest from the sea, not as a rearguard, but to perform the function of making the locality the more acceptable to the presence of plants which luxuriate in sweetness and solid earth.

Another denizen of the partially reclaimed area of the mangrove swamp is the "milky mangrove", or river poison tree, *alias* "blind-your-eyes" (*Excaecaria agallocha*). In India the sap of this tree is called tiger's milk. It issues from the slightest incision of the bark, and is so volatile that no one, however careful, can obtain even a small quantity without being affected by it. There is an acrid, burning sensation in the throat, inflamed eyes and headache, while a single drop falling into the eyes will, it is believed, cause loss of sight. Yet a good caoutchouc may be prepared from it, and it is applied with good effect to ulcerate sores, and by the blacks of Queensland and New South Wales for the relief of certain ulcerous and chronic diseases; while in Fiji the patient is fumigated with the smoke of the burning wood.

Several of the plants produce more or less valuable woods. *Bruguiera rheedi* frequently grows slender shafts, favoured by blacks for harpoon handles on account of their weight and toughness. White mangrove provides a light, white tough wood eminently adapted for the knees of boats. The seeds resemble broad beans, and after long immersion in the sea will germinate lying naked and uncovered on the scorching sand, stretching out rootlets in every direction in search of suitable food, and expanding their leathery primary leaves—even growing to the extent of several inches—while yet owing no attachment to the soil. If it were not capable of surviving and flourishing under conditions fatal to most plants it could not contribute its quota to the formation of humus favourable to the progress of the advancing hosts of tropical vegetation.

Nor must it be imagined that mangrove swamps are unproductive. Fish traverse the intricacies of the arching roots, edible crabs burrow holes in the mud, and in them await your coming, and more often than not baffle your ingenuity to extricate them. Among other stalked-eyed crustaceans is that with one red, shielding claw, absurdly large, and which scuttles among the roots, making a defiant clicking noise—the fiddle or soldier crab (*Gelasimus vocans*). Oysters seal themselves to the roots, and various sorts of shellfish gather together—two or three varieties appear to browse upon the leaves and bark of the mangroves; some excavate galleries in the living trunks. The insidious cobra does not wear any calcareous covering beyond the frail tiny bivalves which guard the head—a scandalously small proportion of its naked length—but lines its tunnels with the materials whence shell is made, smooth and white as porcelain. How this delicate creature, with less of substance than an oyster—a mere worm of semi-transparent, stiff slime—bores in hard wood along and across the grain, housing itself as it proceeds, and never by any chance breaking in upon its neighbours, though the whole of the trunk of the tree be honeycombed, savours of another wonder. Authorities consider the bivalve shell too delicate and frail to be employed in the capacity of a drill, and one investigator has come to the conclusion that the rough fleshy parts of the animal, probably the foot or mantle, acting as a rasp, forms the true boring instrument. Thus, the skill of a worm in excavating tunnels in wood puzzles scientists; and the cobra is certainly among the least conspicuous of the denizens of a mangrove swamp, and perhaps far from the most wonderful.

The most remarkable if not the strangest denizens of the spot are two species of the big-eyed walking and climbing fish (*Periophthalmus koelreuteri* and *P. australis*) which ascend the roots of the mangrove by the use of ventral and pectoral fins, jump and skip on the mud and over the surface of the water and into their burrows with rabbit-like alertness. They delight, too, in watery recesses under stones and hollows in sodden wood. Inquisitive and most observant, they might be likened to Lilliputian seals, as they cling, a row of them, to a partially submerged root, and peer at you, ready to whisk away at the least sign of interference. They climb along the arching roots, the better to reconnoitre your movements and to outwit attempts at capture. Their eyes—in life, reflecting gems—are so placed that they command a complete radius, and if you think to sneak upon them they dive from their vantage points and skip with hasty flips and flops to another arching root, which they ascend, and resume their observation. It must not be assumed that the climbing fish—which seems to be more at home on the surface of the water than below—climbs up among the branches. A foot or so is about the limit of its upper wanderings.

Then, too, in what is generally regarded as a noisome, dismal, mangrove swamp, birds of cheerful and pleasing character congregate. Several honey-eaters, the barred-shouldered dove, the tranquil dove, the nutmeg pigeon, the little bittern, the grey sandpiper, the sordid kingfisher, the spotless egret, the blue heron, the ibis—all these and others frequent such places, and in their season butterflies come and go. In most of its aspects a mangrove swamp is not only the scene of one of nature's most vigorous and determined processes, but to those who look aright, a theatre of many wonders, a museum teeming with objects of interest, a natural aviary of gladsome birds.

THE UMBRELLA-TREE

Having paid, in passing, respects to the most gorgeous tree of the island, it would be sheer gracelessness to withhold a tribute to one of the commonest, though ever novel and remarkable—the umbrella-tree. Less conspicuous in its blooming than the flame-tree, it flourishes everywhere—on the beaches with its roots awash at high tide; on the rearguard of the mangroves, leaning on the white-flowered *calophyllums*; on the steep hill-sides; on the borders of the jungle, and gripping scorched rocks with naked roots. While the flame-tree—few and confined to the beaches—flashes into bloom—an improvident blaze of colour, without a single atoning green leaf—the umbrella-tree charms for several months with a combination of graceful foliage and a unique corollary of singular flowers.

From the centre of whorls of shapely glossy leaves radiate simple racemes, two feet long, as thickly set with studs of dense heads of red flowers as Aaron's rod with its magical buds. Crowned with several crowns of varying numbers of rays, rarely as few as four, frequently seven and nine and occasionally as many as twelve, each tree is a distillery of nectar of crystal purity and inviting flavour. On every ray there may be eighty red studs, each composed of twelve compact flowers, and every flower drips limpid sweetness. For months this unexcised distillation never ceases. For all the birds and dainty butterflies and sober bees there is free abundance, and every puff of wind scatters the surplusage with spendthrift profusion. Sparkling in the sunbeams, dazzling white, red, orange, green, violet, the swelling drops tremble from the red studs and fall in fragrant splashes as the wanton wind brushes past or eager birds hastily alight on the swaying rays. A rare baptism to stand beneath the tree for the cool sweet spray to fall upon the upturned face, a baptism as pure as it is unceremonious.

Red-collared lorikeets revel in the nectar, hustling the noisy honey-eaters and the querulous sun-birds. The radiant blue butterfly sips and is gone, or if it be his intent to pause, tightly folds his wings on the instant of settling, and is transformed from a piece of living jewellery to a brown mottled leaf caught edgeways among the red flowers. The green and gold butterflies are for ever fluttering and quivering. The complaining lorikeets peevishly nudge them off with red, nectar-dripping bills, the honey-eaters disperse them with inconsiderate wing sweeps; but the butterflies are not to be denied their share. After a moment's airy flight they return to the feast, quivering with eagerness. And so the weeks pass, the patient tree generating food far beyond the daily needs of all who choose to take.

By a very moderate computation—such an orderly plan of bloom lends itself to simple statistics—the average production of a fairly crowned tree is over a gallon of nectar per day. Hundreds of trees so crowned brighten all parts of the island with their red rays. And where the nectar is, there will the sun-birds be gathered together. Was ever liqueur so purely compounded? Drawn from untainted soil; filtered and purified; passed from one delicate process to another, warmed during the day, cooled by night airs, chastened by breezes which have all the virtue of whole Pacific breadths; sublimated by the sun—all to be proffered to birds and butterflies in ruddy goblets full to the brim.

THE GENUINE UPAS-TREE

Powerful as nutmeg pigeons are on the wing, some suffer lingering deaths in consequence of a singular characteristic of one of the trees of the jungle. Tall and graceful, with luxuriant glossy leaves, there is nothing uncanny about the tree. In style and appearance it is the very antithesis of "the upas-tree", upon which legendary lore cast unmerited responsibility. Yet in certain respects it would be vain to enter upon its defence. It is no myth. There is no exaggeration in the statement that the character of the Queensland tree is actually murderous, and that it counts its victims by the thousand every season. Of the great host it destroys, all save a few may be very small and very feeble, and from the human standpoint some of its death-dealing is perfectly justifiable if not laudable. Not often, locally, is a bird destroyed, but the fact that occasionally one has the ill-luck to fall foul of it and to perish miserably in consequence, places the tree in the catalogue of the remarkable. Neither spike nor poison is used, nor any sensational means of destruction, but nevertheless the tree is sure and implacable in its methods.

The seed-vessels of the Queensland upas-tree, "Ahm-moo" of the blacks (*Pisonia brunoniana*), which are produced on spreading leafless panicles, exude a remarkably viscid substance, approaching bird-lime in consistency and evil effect. Sad is the fate of any bird which, blundering in its flight, happens to strike against any of the many traps which the tree in unconscious malignity hangs out on every side. In such event the seed clings to the feathers, the wings become fixed to the sides, the hapless bird falls to the ground, and as it struggles heedlessly gathers more of the seeds, to which leaves and twigs adhere, until by aggregation it is enclosed in a mass of vegetable debris as firmly as a mummy in its cloths. Small birds as well as lusty pigeons, spiders and all manner of insects; flies, bees, beetles, moths and mosquitoes, as well as the seeds of other trees are ensnared. Spiders are frequently seen sharing the fate of the flies, fast to seeds in the humiliating posture in which Brer Fox found Brer Rabbit on the occasion of the interview with the Tar Baby.

Insectivorous plants are common enough in Australia; but the "Ahm-moo" tree does not appear to make use of the carcasses of its victims, though it kills on an exceptionally extensive scale.

On some of the islands where the tree is plentiful numbers of pigeons meet a dreary fate every season. The maturity of the seeds coincides with the hatching out of the young, and inexperienced birds pay dearly for their inexperience. The natural glutin is produced while the slim, fluted, inch-long seeds are green, but its virtue remains even after the whole panicle has withered and has fallen. So tenacious is it and prompt, that should a panicle as it whirls downward touch the leaves of lower branches of the parent, or of any neighbouring tree, it sticks and becomes a pendant swaying trap in a new position. At first glance it is not easy to identify the tree to which the obnoxious feature belongs.

The seeds occasion even dogs considerable distress, and might easily be the cause of death to them. As the dog endeavours to remove them from his feet and sides with his teeth, his muzzle is fouled, and he very soon exhibits confusion and alarm, and rolling about in frenzied attempts to free himself, gathers more and more of the seeds and accumulated rubbish.

One is led to ponder upon the purpose of this provision—to endeavour, if possible, to find its justification. Insects lured by the sweetness of the exudation are callously entrapped, and why so? Do the seeds require the presence of animal matter to ensure germination? In that case the tree is indirectly carnivorous, and therefore decidedly entitled to recognition among the curiosities of the island. Is the glutin secreted to secure the wide dispersal of the seeds? If so, the object is largely self-defeated, for seeds by the hundred cling as they fall to the branches of the parent tree, and to those of its lowly neighbours. Certainly some proportion of the seeds which reach the ground must be borne hither and thither by the agency of that eternal scratcher, the scrub fowl. But even a bird of such immensely proportionate strength may be seriously troubled by them. A case in point may be cited. A dog, retrieving a scrub fowl which had fallen in the vicinity of an "Ahm-moo" tree, emerged with it entirely enveloped with the seeds and adhering rubbish, and itself almost helpless from a similar cause. In this happy chance the seeds were eventually widely distributed. If the glutin is provided to prevent birds consuming the kernels, then the object is perfectly served; otherwise no very satisfactory reason is apparent why the tree should be invested with the means of destroying even humble forms of life. Is this one of the "lost chords" in the harmony of nature?

THE CREEPING PALM

Perhaps the most impressive feature of the jungle—that which takes fast hold, clings most tenaciously, and leaves the most irritating remembrances—is what is known as the lawyer-cane or vine (*Calamus*). It is a vegetable of tortuous ambitions, that defies you, that embarrasses with attention, arrests your progress, occasionally envelops you in a net-work of bewildering, slender, and cruelly-armed tentacles, that everywhere bristles with points, that curves back on itself, and makes loops and wriggles; that springs from a thin, sprawling and helpless beginning, and develops into almost miraculous lengths, and ramifies and twists and turns in "verdurous glooms", ascends and descends, grovels in the moist earth and among mouldy leaves, clasps with aerial rootlets every possible support, and eventually clambers and climbs above the tallest tree, twirling its armed tentacles round airy nothings. It blossoms inconspicuously, and its fruit is as hard, tough and dry as an argument on torts. Ordinary mortals call it a vine. Botanists describe it as a prickly climbing palm, and no jungle is complete without it. There are several varieties of this interesting plant, all more or less of a grasping, clinging character, and each of vital importance in the republic of vegetation.

Sometimes when it is severed with a sharp knife there flows from the cane a fluid bright and limpid as a judge's summing up; occasionally it is all as dry as dust and as sneezy, and its prickly leaf sheathes the abode of that vexing insect which causes the scrub itch.

This plant produces lengths of cane similar in every respect to the schoolmaster's weapon—familiar but immortal—varying in diameter from a quarter of an inch to an inch and a half, and in length, as some assert, to no less than five hundred and six hundred feet. Certainly three hundred feet is not uncommon, and one can readily concede an additional one hundred feet, knowing the extravagance of the remarkable palm under ordinary circumstances. And the cane weaves and entangles the jungle, binds and links mighty trees together, and with the co-operation of other clinging, and creeping, and trailing plants—some massive as ship's cables, and some thin and fine as fishing-lines—forms compact masses of vegetation to penetrate which tracks must be cut yard by yard. When this disorderly conglomeration of trees and saplings, vines, creepers, trailers and crawlers, complicated and confused, has to be cleared, as civilization demands the use of the soil, sometimes a considerable area will remain upright, although every connection with Mother Earth is severed, so interlaced and interwoven and anchored are the vines with those clinging to trees yet uncut. Then, in a moment, as some leading strand gives way, the whole mass falls—smothered, bruised, and crushed—to be left for a month and more before the fires destroy the faded relics of the erstwhile gloriously rampant jungle.

One cannot cut jungle and escape bloodshed, for the long tentacles of the lawyer catch you unawares sooner or later, and then, for all are set with double rows of re-curved points, do not endeavour to escape by strife and resistance—it is no use pulling against those pricks—but by subtlety and diplomacy. The more you pull, the worse for your skin and clothes; but with tact you may become free, with naught but neat scratches and regular rows of splinters. The points of the hooks to which you have been attached anchor themselves deep in the skin, and tear their way out and rip and rend your clothes, and your condition of mind, body and estate, is all for the worse.

But the uses of the lawyer-cane are many and various. Blacks employ it as ropes, as stays for canoes, and, split into narrow threads and woven, for baskets and fish-traps; and white men find it handy for all sorts of purposes, from boat-painters and fenders to stock-whip and maul-handles. Suppose a tree that a black wishes to climb presents difficulties low down, he will procure a length of lawyer-cane, partly biting and partly breaking it off, if he lacks a cutting implement. Then he will make a loop, so bruising and chewing the end that it becomes flexible and ties almost as readily and quite as securely as rope. Ascending a neighbouring tree, he will manoeuvre one end over a limb of that which he wishes to climb, and slip it through the loop, and run it up until it is fast. A cane fifty feet long, no thicker than one's little finger, fastened to the upper branch of a tree, has on trial borne the weight of three fairly-sized men. Thus tested, the black has no hesitation or difficulty in rapidly ascending, and in lowering down young birds, or eggs (wrapped in leaves), or whatsoever his quest.

Another cane-producing plant (*Flagellaria*), though innocent of the means of grappling, succeeds in over-topping tall trees and smothering them with a mass of interwoven leafage. Each of its narrow leaves ends in a spiral tendril, sensitive but tough, which entwines itself about other leaves and twigs. Feeling their respective ways, the tender tips of leaves of the one family touch and twist, and the grasp is for life. Though not of such extravagant character as the lawyer-vine, the *Flagellaria* seems to be endowed with perceptive faculty almost amounting to instinct in selecting the shortest way toward the support necessary for its plan of existence, which is to climb not to grovel. It spurns the ground. New shoots spring from old rhizomes in the clearings, and turn towards the nearest tree as though aware of its presence, as the tendrils of a grape vine instinctively grope for the artificial support provided for it. Progress along the ground is slow, but once within reach, the shoot rears its head, stretches out a delicate finger-tip, and clings with the grasp of desperation. A vigorous impulse thrills the whole plant. It has found its purpose in life. With the concentration of its energies, its development is rapid and merciless. Its host is rapidly enveloped in entangling embraces, smothered with innumerable clinging kisses.

STEALTHY MURDERERS

The fig-tree (*Ficus cunninghamii*) begins life as a parasite. A thin slender shoot, tremulously weak, leans lightly on the base of some tall tree, and finding agreeable conditions, clings and grows. A harmless, tender, thong-like shoot it is—a helpless plant, that could not stand alone or exist but for the hospitality of another of strength and substance. Soon a second shoot, slight and frail, emerges near the root, but at a different angle from its aspiring brother, and others as delicate as the first follow, until the trunk of the host is sprawled over by naked running shoots, grey-green in colour, crafty and insidious. As they increase in age the shoots flatten on the under surface and cross and recross. Wheresoever they touch they coalesce. The trunk becomes enveloped in living lace—in a network, rather, living, ever growing and irregular—the meshes of which gradually decrease in dimension. All the while squeezing and causing decay, the meshes close up. The trunk of the host is completely enclosed; it is the dying core of a living cylinder, for the first shoots have long since crept up among the branches, have expanded their leaves, and are busy sapping the life-blood of the tree at all points. A greedy intractable, implacable foe, it gives no quarter, but flourishes upon its dead or dying friend, upon which in its youth it leaned delicately for support. Finally it weaves its slender shoots among the topmost leaves of its victim, and having outgrown its growth, flourishes on its decay.

This vegetable usurper produces immense crops of small purple figs, the favourite food of many birds. So bountiful are its crops, and so much are they appreciated, that one perceives, almost without reflection, its due and proper place in the harmony of nature. To complete the cycle, birds frequently, after eating the fruit, "strop" their beaks on the bark of a neighbouring tree. Now and again a seed thus finds favourable conditions for its germination, and then the parasite sends exploring roots to the ground, forming as they descend intricate lace-work, while shoots repeat a similar process as they climb farther up the trunk and among the branches. Then the fate of the host seems less cruel, for the end is speedier.

Delicious fruit is produced by a somewhat similar fig (*validinervis*) growing in the locality and displaying, though not in such a cruel maner, parasitical tendencies. Passing from green to orange with deep red spots to rich purple, the fruit—about the size of an average grape—indicates arrival at maturity by the exudation of a drop of nectar. Clear as crystal, the nectar partially solidifies. Fragrant and luscious, pendant from the polished fruit, this exuberant insignia of perfection, this glittering drop of vital essence, attracts birds of all degree. It is a liqueur that none can resist, and which seems, so noisy and demonstrative do they all become, to have a highly exhilarating effect on their nerves. Birds ordinarily mute are vociferous, and the rowdy ones—the varied honey-eater as an example—losing all control of their tongues, call and whistle in ecstasy. The best of the fig-tree's life is given for the intoxication of unreflecting birds.

Few of the forest trees are more picturesque than the paper-bark or tea-tree (*Melaleuca leucadendron*), the "Tee-doo" of the blacks. It is of free and stately growth, the bark white, compacted of numerous sheets as thin as tissue paper. When a great wind stripped the superficial layers, exposing the reddish-brown epidermis, the whole foreground was transfigured. All during the night alone in the house, I heard the great trees complaining against the molestation of the wind, groaning in strife and fright; but little had I thought that the violation they had endured had been so coarse and lawless. The chaste trees had been incontinently stripped of their decent white vestiture, leaving their limbs naked and bare. In the daylight they still moaned, throwing their almost leafless branches about despairingly, their flesh-tints—dingy red —giving to the scene a strangely unfamiliar glow. This outrage was one of the most uncivil of the wrong-doings of the storm wind "Leonta". But within a week or so the trees assumed whiter than ever robes; pure and stainless, the breeze had merely removed soiled linen. The picture had been restored by the most ideal of all artists.

The blossoms of the melaleuca come in super-abundance, pale yellow spikes, odorous to excess. When the trees thus adorn themselves—and they do so twice in the year in changeless fashion, in the fulness of the wet season—the air is saturated with the odour as of treacle slightly burnt. The island reeks of a vast sugar factory or distillery. Sips of the balsamic syrup are free to all, and birds and insects rejoice and are glad. A perpetual murmur and hum of satisfaction and industry haunt the neighbourhood of the trees as accompaniment to the varied notes of excitable birds. Chemists say that insects imprisoned in an atmosphere of melaleuca oil become intoxicated. Insects and birds certainly are boldly familiar and hilarious during the time that the trees offer their feast of spiced honey.

Every tree is a fair, and all behave accordingly, chirping and whistling, humming and buzzing, flitting and fluttering, in the unrestrained gaiety of holiday and feast-day humour. Always an impertinent, interfering rascal, the spangled drongo, under the exhilarating influence of melaleuca nectar, degenerates into a blusterer. He could not under any circumstances be a larrikin;

but the grateful stimulant affects his naturally high spirits, and he is more frolicsome and boisterous than ever. The path between the coconuts to the beach passes close to two of the biggest trees, and from each as I strolled along, one sublime morning when the whole world was drenched with whiffs, strong, sweet and spirity, a drongo, flushed with excitement, flew down, bidding me begone in language that I am fully persuaded was meant to provoke a breach of the peace. The saucy bullies, the half-tipsy roysterers, tired of domineering over every participator of the feast, dared to publicly flout me, defiantly sweeping with their tails the air, as an Irishman, "blue mouldy for want of a bateing", sweeps the floor with his coat, and chattered and scolded in every tone of elated bravado. The bibacious drongo can be as demure as any. When he comes to dart among the eddying insects, glorying in the first cool gleams of the sunshine, he will take his ease on a mango branch, make jerky bows and flick the fine feathers of his tail, and "cheep" in timorous accents. He is sober then, quite parsonified in demeanour; his speech "all in the set phrase of peace", and would be scandalized by the mere mention of melaleuca nectar.

A professor of physiology asserts that rabbits are very curious when under the influence of liquor, and that a drunken kangaroo is brutally aggressive. The drongo is merely pugnacious and noisy. Having heard of the melancholy effects of over-indulgence in melaleuca nectar, I was not at all disposed to judge of the misbehaviour harshly or to take personal offence; for the drongo is a respectable bird, and the opportunities for excess come but twice a year. Are not the tenses of intoxication infinite? This is not a prohibition district, and if the happy, unreflective bird chooses to partake even to excess of the free offering of nature, the quintessence of the flowers of the tree distilled by sunshine, why should not he? Am I the only one to be "recompensed by the sweetness and satisfaction of this retreat"?

CHAPTER VII

"THE LORD AND MASTER OF THE FLIES"

AMONG the curious creatures native to the island is a fierce canni-balistic fly. Fully an inch in length and bulky in proportion, it somewhat resembles a house-fly on a gigantic scale, but is lustrous grey in colour, with blond eyes, fawn legs, and transparent irides-cent wings, with a brassy glint in them. The broad, comparatively short wings carry a body possessing a muscular system of the highest development, for the note flight produces indicates the extraordinary rapidity of the wing vibrations.

Some swift-flying insects are said to make about eight hundred down strokes of the wing per second. This big fair fellow's machinery may not be equipped for such marvellous momentum, but the high key that he sounds under certain circumstances indicates rare force and speed. No library of reference is available. The specific scientific title of the insect cannot, therefore, be sup-plied. Possibly it does not yet possess one, but it is a true fly of the family Asilidae, and being a veritable monster to merely sportful and persistent if annoying flies of lesser growth, no doubt it will continue to perform its part even though without a formal dis-tinction. Its presence is announced by an ominous, booming hum. It passes on one side with a flight so rapid as to render it almost invisible. You hear a boom which has something of a whistle, and see a yellowish glint; the rest is space and silence. In half a minute the creature returns; and thus he scoops about, booming and making innocent lightnings in the clear air. The tone is demonstrative, aggressive, triumphant; but the monster is only reconnoitring—seeing whether you have any flies about you. You may have boasted to yourself—there being no friends about to tolerate your egotistical confidences—that there are no flies about you; but the big, booming creature has his suspicions. Apparently in his opinion you are just the sort of country to attract and encourage flies, and he does not immediately satisfy himself to the contrary. But should you witlessly happen to have attracted the companionship of ever so innocent a fly, the awful presence seizes it on the wing and is away with the twang of a bullet. It will pick a fly from your sunburnt arm—no occasion for coats here—with neatness and dispatch and leave wondering comprehension far behind. And having seized its prey, it may, haply, seek as it booms along the nearest support on which to enjoy its meal.

Then you see what a terrific creature it is. One favoured me with a minute's close observation. By a hook on one of the anterior legs (it possesses the regulation half-dozen) it had attached itself to a tiny splinter on the underside of the veranda rail, and so hung, the body being at right angles to its support. Thus stretched, the leg appeared fully two inches long, and with the rest of its legs it clasped to its bosom the unfortunate little fly, shrunken with distress, the very embodiment of hopeless dismay. No sight which comes to memory's call equals for utter despair that of the little insect, which, no doubt in its day had provoked a big lump of irritation and strong but ineffective language. Hugged by its great enemy, it seemed aware of its fate, yet unreconciled to it. Pendant by the one long, slender leg, as if hung by a thread, the blond monster seemed quite at ease over its repast. That was its customary pose and attitude at meal-times. As far as observation permitted, it was pumping out the blood of its prey, but before the operation was finished it forbade closer scrutiny by humming away with a note of savage resentment—a rumble, a grumble and a growl, ending in a swelling shriek.

It would be interesting to know how many flies of the common vexing kind such a ferocious creature disposes of during the day. He preys upon the lustrous bluish-green fly, which draws blood almost on the moment of alighting, and also on the sluggish March fly, which goes about the business of blood-sucking in a lazy, dreamy, lackadaisical style; and I am inclined to acknowledge him as a friend and as a blessing to humanity generally.

A TRAGEDY IN YELLOW

Quite a distinct tragedy occurred the other day. The little yellow diurnal moth, commonly known as "the wanderer" has a partiality for the nectar of the "bachelor's button", as yellow as itself. The morning was gay with butterflies. A "wanderer" poised over a yellow cushion fluttered spasmodically, and remained fixed and steadfast with tightly-closed wings. It allowed itself to be touched without showing uneasiness, and when a brisk movement was made to frighten it to flight it was still steady as a statue. Closer inspection revealed the cause. The body was tightly gripped in the mandibles of a spider, a yellow rotund spider with long, slender greeny-yellowy legs. Under cover of the yellow flower the yellow spider had seized the yellow moth. A general inspection showed that the tragedy was almost as universal as the flowers. There were few flowers which did not conceal a spider, and few spiders which had not murdered a moth. The conspiracy between the flower and the spider for the undoing of the moth (a conspiracy from which both profited) was repeated thousands of times this bright morning, and it illustrated the profundity of nature's lesser tragedies, the sternness with which she adjusts her equilibriums.

MUSICAL FROGS

A marked feature of the wet season is the varied chant of happy frogs. During the day silence is the rule. A low gurgle of content at the sounding rain is occasionally heard on the part of a flabby, moist creature unable to restrain its sentiments until the approach of evening. But as the sun sets, each of the countless host utters a song of thankfulness and pleasure. To the unappreciative it may appear merely an inharmonious vocal go-as-you-please, in which each frog is the embodiment of the idea that upon its jubilant efforts the honour and reputation of the race as vocalists depend. But to one class of listener the opera is decently if not scientifically constituted. There is the loud and cheerful, if not shrill, bleating of the soprano, the strenuous booming of the bass, the velvety softness and depth of the contralto and the thin high tenor. Hordes of the alert, sharp-featured, far-leaping grass frog represent the chorus, and they have a perfectly rehearsed theme. Down on the flat along the edge of the pandanus grove the preliminary chords are uttered—a merry, unreflective, chirrupy strain, gay as "the Fishermen's Chorus". The motif is taken up nearer among the coconuts, and is in full swing in the pools below the terrace. Thence the sound passes on through the wattles and bloodwoods to the narrow tea-tree swamp lined with dwarf bamboos and dies in echoes in the distance. A brief interlude, and the pandanus choir gives voice again, stronger and resonant; the companions of the coconuts join lustily, the strain reverberates from the wet lands below, resounds through the forest, and is lost in the mellow distance of the tea-trees. And so the sound rises and falls, swells and dwindles away in chords and harmonies, until presently every amphibian is alert and tremulous with emotion and emulation. If an attempt be made to analyse the music, you may discover sounds sharp as those of the fife, deep and hollow as drum-beats, sonorous and acrid, tinny and mellow.

I have heard that those who are not disciples of Wagner find it necessary to undergo a process of education ere they acquire an unaffected taste for the composer's masterpieces. Possibly those who have not listened, wet season after wet season, to the light-hearted chant, may be inclined to suggest that there can be no such thing as music in the panting bellows of a North Queensland frog. But music "is of a relative nature, and what is harmony to one ear may be dissonance to another". The Chinese opera proves that "nations do not always express the same passions by the same sound". If one obtains music from the clang and clamour of full-throated frogs, may it not be because his ears are more attuned to natural than to artificial harmonies, not because of any defect in, or aberration of, hearing, or any lack of melody on the part of the frogs?

GREEN-ANT CORDIAL

White ants, black ants, red ants, brown ants, grey ants, green ants; ants large, ants small; ants slothful, ants brisk; meat-eating ants, grain-eating ants, fruit-eating ants, nectar-imbibing ants; ants that fight, ants that run away; ants that live under coldest stone, ants that dwell among the tree-tops; silent ants, ants that literally "kick up" a row; good ants, bad ants, ants that are merely so so— we have them all and would not part with any—not even the stinging green ants, which are among the most singular of the tribe, nor even the "white ant" (which is not an ant), that would literally eat us out of house and home if not rigorously excluded and warred against with poison, for they are the great scavengers of woodeny debris.

Green ants do disfigure orange- and mango-trees with their "nests", and they have the temper of furies; but they wage war on many of the insects which bother plants, and clear away insect carrion, and carrion, in fact, of all sorts. This ant, to which has been given the official title of "emerald-coloured leaf dweller", constructs a pocket with leaves of living trees (and, very rarely, of the blades of living grass), and dwelling therein establishes populous colonies. The queen or mother ant sets up her separate establishment by curling a small leaf or the corner of a large one, joining the edges with a white cottony fabric, and forthwith begins to raise a family. She is a portly creature—unlike her slim, semi-transparent workers and warriors—and most prolific, and her family increases marvellously. As it multiplies, ingenious additions of living leaves are made to the pocket or purse, until it may assume the size of a football and be the home of millions of alert, pugnacious, inquisitive, foraging insects, whose bites are dreaded by individuals whose skin is extra sensitive.

Is it not astonishing that insects, possessing even in combination such trivial muscular power as the green tree-ant, should be able to cause leaves twelve inches long by eight inches wide to curl up so that the apex shall almost touch the base, or that the parallel borders shall be brought together with the nicest apposition? The astonishment increases when it is recognized that at the founding of a colony there are but few workers to co-operate in the undertaking.

The minute caterpillar of a certain species of moth mines leaves, and eating away the cellular structures, causes them to twist irregularly, and eventually spins on the spot a cocoon of green silk in which it undergoes metamorphosis. A local caterpillar, too, converts the tough harsh leaves of a fig-tree (*Ficus fasciculata*) into a close and perfect scroll by an elaborate system of haulage, spinning silken strands as required, having primarily rendered the leaf the more easy to manipulate by nibbling away a portion of the mid-rib. In this scroll the insect dozes until in process of time it is transformed, and emerges a bright but short-lived butterfly.

But, as far as my personal observation goes, the green tree-ants do not effect any alteration in the superficial appearance, nor destroy the structure of leaves, nor employ any physical power at the first stages of the construction of a habitation. The process by which a leaf is curled extends over several days, and but few take part in it. Half a dozen ants may be seen perpetually engaged in, apparently, an unmethodical but extremely minute and critical inspection of the rhachis and the nerves or ribs of the leaf. Days pass. The ants are there all the time, examining the leaf and communicating with each other whensoever they meet. Imperceptibly the leaf begins to curl. The ants continue to make mesmeric passes over the nerves with ever-waving antennae.

In accordance with the will and the design of the architects, who merely stand by and gesticulate, the opposite margins approach, or the apex curls towards the base, or towards one of the sides to form a miniature funnel. When the extremities are so close that the intervening space may be spanned, threads of white gossamer are laced across, and the slack being taken up by degrees, in a few days a cosy pocket with closely-fitted seams is completed.

How is this folding of the leaf accomplished? A theory which presents itself is that the ants eject some active chemical principle into certain of the cells of the leaf tissue, and that the stimulus is transmitted by excitation from cell to cell, bringing about a general and uniform contraction without destroying the vitality of the leaf. Further, by the application of the injection to specific cells the ants convey impulses to specific nerves, causing the leaf to curl longitudinally or laterally, or at any angle they design. The poison that a single ant injects into the neck of a brawny man so affects his nervous system that he twists and writhes and stamps his feet with energy sufficient to destroy millions of the species. Maybe a slightly different compound is reserved for vegetable substances, which can offer only a flabby sort of remonstrance. If this theory be supported on investigation, surely the green tree-ant will deserve to be catalogued among creatures who have solved labour-saving problems—who employ consciousness, if not rational thought, to compensate for physical frailty. This theory is applicable to the manipulation of a single leaf only, and of a leaf of considerable size. Yet these feeble folk more frequently take up their quarters in trees bearing small leaves, of which scores are embodied in a mansion.

Immense and concentrated exertion is necessary to draw far-flung branchlets and leaves together, and the feverish host accomplishes a seemingly impossible feat by an organized combination of engineering with co-operative labour. Spaces between leaves and twigs four and five inches wide are bridged by chains of ants—each individual clasping with its mandibles above the abdominal segment its immediate companion; occasionally the ant grips its fellow by the posterior legs, and is so held by the next in order. In the construction of these chains ants hastily mass at each side of the gulf to be spanned, and crawling, or rather running over each other, form pendant strands, each ant a living link.

The chains sway until the terminal links engage, when they are immediately shortened up. Several of these chains are swung across parallel to each other with astonishing rapidity; and in addition to the constant strain of the hauling workers at each end they are used as bridges by innumerable other workers and fussy superintendents, the traffic on them being almost as voluminous and bustling as that of a Thames thoroughfare. Gradually the most obstinate branchlet with its spray of leaves is drawn into juxtaposition with the main part of the mansion. Then the living spans become more numerous, presenting the appearance of great stitches. As the edges of the leaves are brought together they are fastened with white gossamer while the tireless workers strain themselves, heroically holding the edges in apposition. The gossamer seems to be obtained in part from the pupae, which, borne in the mandibles of workers, are passed to and fro as weavers' shuttles. As a rule, insects which house themselves in leaves are vegetarian, but the green ant is demonstratively carnivorous, using leaves solely for shelter.

An aboriginal—to repeat perhaps a needless observation—regards most of things of this earth from a dietetic standpoint. He does not so regard the green tree-ant in vain. He knows when the pocket is packed with white larvae and white helpless infant ants, or with helpless green ones big of abdomen, and consenting to the assaults of the adults, cuts away the supporting branch and shakes off the furious citizens, or expels them with the smoke and fire of paper-bark torches, or, maybe, casts the pocket into water so that the adult ants may swim ashore, abandoning those that cannot, on account of immaturity or incompetence, to their fate.

Eaten raw, the larvae are pungent morsels, or macerated in water in company with relatives distended to the degree of helplessness, form a cordial that is sharp to the palate, scarifying to the throat, and consoling to the stomach replete with the cold and sodden foods with which blacks often have to be content.

Tetchy and quarrelsome, staccato in action, the warriors of a colony bury their forceps in the skin and stand upon their heads to give all their weight to the attack; but each individual retains its grip until squashed and crumpled up, and the human being who has suffered the assault comments on it in language corresponding with the sensitiveness or otherwise of his skin. Consequently the green tree-ant is not as a rule regarded with any tenderness or consideration, and there never existed a green ant which hesitated to attack the greatest man. He is quite as heroic as a bee—though armed much less efficiently—and far more resentful.

A brilliant black ant imitates its green cousin in the construction of a leafy dwelling, somewhat similar in design but on a smaller scale, and having no apparent weapon of defence, save odour—and not very much of that—adopts a novel plan of protecting its refuge against assaults. However gently the leafy house is touched the denizens set up a violent agitation, the simultaneous efforts of hundreds making a sound quite loud enough to scare away intruders whose senses are attuned to the silence and rustlings of the jungle. The noise, which resembles that which results from the easy agitation of coarse sand in a crisp paper envelope, seems to be caused by the ants kicking or drumming on the sides and partitions of the house, the partitions being composed of a light brown fabric, tense, tough, and resonant.

WOOING WITH WINGS

Among the many engaging scenes and frolics that are ever taking place along the flounces of the jungle, where the serrated leaves of the fern of God make living lacework up and among the tangle of foliage, none is prettier than the love flight of the green and gold bird-winged butterfly (*Ornithoptera cassandra*). Human beings, who in their marriage ceremonies array themselves to the best advantage and assume their most charming traits, can hardly withhold attention from other and more ethereal creatures when they become subject to the divine passion. All have their moments of bliss, and the butterfly—"the embodiment of pure felicity—happy in what it has and happier still in searching for something else"—reveals its "lovesickness and pain" as the bloom of its gay and sportful existence.

In the courtship of this particular species the male exercises a singular fascination, while the female gracefully and without hesitation submits to the spell. He has flitted airily in the sunshine, glorying in a livery of green and gold and black, has daintily sipped nectar from the scarlet hibiscus flowers, has soared over the highest bloodwood in wild but idle impulse, and in a flash, is fervently in love. Judged by appearance alone he has chosen quite an unworthy bride. She is much the larger, darker and heavier, and has little of the colouring of her passionate wooer on her wings, though her body is decorated with unexpected red. Her flight, ordinarily, is cumbersome and slow, and her demeanour pensive —almost prim. She seems to be of a steady, matronly disposition, whereas the shape of the wings of her mate alone denotes quite a different ideal of life. He is all alert, charged to the full with nervous energy—free, careless, inconsequent, but absolutely irresistible.

When the pair meet, what time the fancies of butterflies lightly turn to thoughts of love, he swoops impetuously towards her and rises in a graceful curve, seemingly to enchant her with the display of his colours. She forthwith amends her staid behaviour, and begins a quivering, fluttering flight, rising and falling with gentle, rhythmical grace. He, hovering about with rapid wing movements harmoniously responds to her undulations. Still maintaining her coy contours she floats over the tree-tops, or descends among the ferns or bushes, past the blue berries of the native ginger, while with quaint courtliness he pays his compliments and bewilders by his audacity. As the amorous dalliance proceeds, he flits in brilliant spirals round and before her, and again resumes his tremulous flight, consonant with her emotional flutterings. However intricate, however long the dance she leads, he follows, blithesomeness and confidence in all his poses. Exhausting work this aerial flirtation. The bride alights among the red knobs of the umbrella-tree for refreshment. Her wings quiver as she sips, while her admirer poises a yard in the air above her, flashes hither and thither, briefly steadying his flight in positions whence all his loveliness may be advantageously revealed; poises again a yard above her; gyrates with the air of a dandy of over-weening assurance, vanity, and pride; swoops until his wings in their down-strokes salute her; and then the dainty pair dance into the sunless mazes of the jungle.

A SWALLOWING FEAT

Everyone knows that small snakes are capable of swallowing comparatively large eggs. But is the way in which the feat is accomplished generally understood? That is the question. No doubt a big snake glides jauntily to a moderately-sized egg, grips it with its incurved teeth, the jaws loosen and begin their alternating movement, and unhook themselves at the bases to permit of the eggs passing down the throat. That is easy. But how does a small snake, the neck of which is an inch and a half in circumference, swallow whole an egg five inches and more in circumference? Actual observation enables me to explain.

If the snake were to begin the act straightforwardly, the egg, presenting but little resistance, would be continuously pushed away. The snake slides its head and neck over the egg, and pressing downward upon it with that part of its body which for the present purpose may be termed the bosom, prevents it moving. The head turns over as if the snake was preparing for a somersault; the jaws fit over the end of the egg, the upper below and the lower above, and begin to work. Presently the upper and lower jaws become entirely disassociated, the egg is encompassed and forced down into the throat. The process seems a most distressing one to the snake, for so great is the distension of the flesh tissues and the skin that they become semi-transparent, revealing the colour of the egg. When the egg is safe in the stomach, the shell submits to the action of the gastric juices, and the meal is digested. That is if it is a hen's egg. A porcelain counterfeit, which the most subtle snake cannot distinguish from a natural egg, passes on its way unblemished.

PART TWO

STONE AGE FOLKS

CHAPTER I

PASSING AWAY

SOME investigators tell us that the aborigines of Australia came out of Egypt carrying with them their ancient signs and totemic ceremonies; others, that they are representatives of the Neolithic Age; others assert that Australia is the cradle of the human race, the primitive inhabitants the stock whence all sprung.

Without pausing to hazard an opinion upon any of these theories, it may be said that stone axes, shell knives, and fish-hooks of pearl and tortoiseshell now in use are among the credentials of a people whose attributes and conditions are in line with those who, in other parts of the world, had their day and fulfilled their destiny ages upon ages ago, leaving as history etchings on ivory of the mammoth and the bone of the reindeer. Implements similar to those which are relics of a remote past elsewhere are here of everyday use and application. The Stone Age still exists.

To speculate upon those phases of aboriginal life and character which go to establish the antiquity of the race and its profound unprogressiveness, is no part of the present purpose, which is merely to relate commonplace incidents and the humours of to-day. Much of that which follows is necessarily matter of common knowledge among those who have studied the blacks of the coast.

There is nothing obscure, and but little that concerns even the immediate past, in the philosophy of those natives of North Queensland with whom I am in touch. With the black, to-day is —"to be, contents his natural desire". The past is not worth thinking about, if not entirely forgotten; the future unembarrassed by problems. Crafts and artifices, common enough a few years ago, are fast passing away. New acquirements are generally saddening proofs of the unfitness of the aboriginal for the battle of life when once his primitive condition is disturbed by the wonder-working whites. Bent wire represents a cheap and effective substitute for fish-hooks of pearl-shell, which cost so much in skill and time, and ever so shabby and worn a blanket more comfortable and to the purpose that the finest beaten out of the bark of a fig-tree.

Many of the wants of the race are supplied through the agency of the whites, and there are so many new tasks and occupations and novelties generally to occupy attention, that the decent and often ingenious handicrafts lapse and are lost. Our blacks still decorate rocks and the bark of trees with rude charcoal drawings; but the art of making stone axes is lost, though trees yet exhibit marks of those handled by the fathers of the present generation.

TURTLE AND SUCKERS

Generally unprogressive and uninventive, the aboriginals of the coast of North Queensland apply practically the result of the observation of a certain fact in the life-history of a fish in obtaining food. By them the sucker (remora) is not regarded as an interesting example of a fish which depends largely upon turtle, dugong, sharks and porpoises for locomotion, but as a ready means of effecting the capture of the two first-mentioned animals, always eagerly hunted for their flesh.

In the days of antiquity it was believed that this strange fish was wont to affix itself to the bottom of a ship, and was able of its malice to hold it stationary in a stiff breeze though all sails were set. According to the legend (a popular method by means of which the descendants of great men explained away their faults and blunders), at the famous sea-fight at Actium, Mark Antony's ship was held back by a remora in spite of the efforts of hundreds of willing galley-slaves. Shakespeare may say that Cleopatra's "fearful sails" were the cause of Anthony's fatal indecision and flight, and a lesser poet may cast the blame upon her "timid tear"; but the tribute to the remora's interference with the fate of nations was accepted in good faith at the time, and was, moreover, supported and confirmed by the inglorious experience of other great men who hung back when they should have sailed boldly on to victory or noble disaster.

Vulgarly known nowadays as "the sucker", and to science as the *Echeneis remora* and *Echeneis naucrates*, and to the blacks as "Cum-mai", the fish upon which such grave responsibility was thrown by the ancients monopolizes the sub-order of *Acanthoptaygii* (*discocephali*). Its distinguishing feature is a shield or disc extending from the tip of the upper jaw to a point behind the shoulders, and said to be a modification of the spurious dorsal fin. This structure consists of a mid-rib and a number of transverse flat ridges capable of being raised or depressed. The disc has a membranous continuous edge or margin. When the fish presses the soft edge of the disc against any smooth surface and depresses the ridges and the intervening spaces, a vacuum is formed, giving it enormous holding power. Other countries have sucker fish of different form; but it remained for the benighted Australian blacks, among a few other savage races, to make practical use of the creature, which, as a means of locomotion, forms strong attachments to the dugong, turtle, shark and porpoise. It can hardly be called domesticated, yet it is employed after the manner of the falcon in hawking, save that the sucker is fastened to a light line when the game is revealed.

Some assert that the sucker swims on its back when not adhering to its host, but my observation denounces that theory. Becalmed among the islands, where the water is transparently clear, I have seen the sucker swim cautiously to the boat, apparently reconnoitring. Shy and easily startled, a wave of the hand over the gunwale is sufficient to scare it away; but it comes again, keeping pace as the boat drifts, and liking to remain in its shadow. Then it is easily seen that it swims with the sucker uppermost.

Occasionally when the blacks harpoon a turtle or a dugong a sucker is secured. They declare that it stays in one locality until a suitable host happens along, and then forms a life-long attachment.

If one is seen among the rocks the blacks are at pains to catch it, and as it is shark-like in its nervousness, the sport demands considerable skill and patience. "Feed 'em plenty" is the ruling principle. Delectable morsels of fresh fish are tendered abundantly until the sucker abandons his usual caution, and then when he is feeding freely a hook temptingly baited is let down casually among the other dainties, and if the fish has been liberally and yet not over fed, it will probably accept the line, and after protesting and holding back to the best of its ability, find itself flapping in the bark canoe. Should it get away—"Well! Plenty more alonga salt water. Catch 'em to-morrow." When determined to secure a sucker whose haunt they have discovered, the blacks will feed it at intervals for a day or two to overcome its nervous apprehension. In other localities along the coast the fish is plentiful and by no means shy, taking bait ravenously.

Having secured the sucker, the blacks farm it in their haphazard fashion. They fasten a line above the forked tail so securely that it cannot slip, nor be likely to readily cut through the skin, and tether it in shallow water, when it usually attaches itself to the bottom of the canoe. When, as a result of frequent use and heavy strain, the tail of the sucker is so deeply cut by the line that it is in danger of being completely severed, a hole is callously bored right through the body beside the backbone, and the line passed through it for additional security.

Turtle being wanted, the blacks voyage out each in a bark canoe, which weighs about forty pounds, is eight feet long, two feet beam and one foot deep amidships, where the sides are much depressed, leaving little more than an inch of freeboard. There is a good sheer forward and a slight tilt at the stern, while the bottom is level. Occasionally two men fit themselves into a canoe of the dimensions given.

Naked and unashamed, the blacks are well equipped for sport. They may have three or four harpoons of their own manufacture, besides a live fire-stick lying on a piece of bark sprinkled with sand, or they may carry a couple of dry sticks for raising a fire by friction. The haft of the harpoon is probably red or orange mangrove (*Bruguiera rheedi*), heavy and tough. It has been duly seasoned and straightened by immersion in running water and exposure to fire. At the heavy end it is hollowed out to a depth of four inches. The point is preferably of one of the black palms, and a barb is strapped to it with the fibre of the "Man-djar" (*Hibiscus tiliaceus*) and cemented with "Toon-coo".

In sight of the game the sucker which has been adhering to the bottom of the canoe is tugged off and thrown in its direction. As a preliminary the disc and shoulders of the sucker are vigorously scrubbed with dry sand or the palm of the hand, to remove the slime and to excite the ruling passion of the fish. It makes a dash for a more congenial companionship than an insipid canoe. The line by which it is secured is made from the bark of the "Boo-bah" (*Ficus fasciculata*) and is of two strands, so light as not to seriously encumber the sucker, and yet strong enough to withstand a considerable strain. Two small loops are made in the line about an interval of two fathoms from the sucker, to act as indicators.

As soon as the sucker has attached itself to the turtle, a slight pull is given and the startled turtle makes a rush, the line being eased out smartly. Then sport of the kind that a salmon-fisher enjoys when he has hooked a forty-pounder begins. The turtle goes as he pleases; but when he begins to tire, he finds that there is a certain check upon him—slow, steady, never-ceasing. After ten minutes or so a critical phase of the sport occurs. The turtle bobs up to the surface for a gulp of air, and should he catch sight of the occupants of the canoe, his start and sudden descent may result in such a severe tug that the sucker is divorced. But the blacks watch, and in their experience judge to a nicety when and where the turtle may rise; telegrams along the line from the sucker give precise information. They crouch low on their knees in the canoe as the game emerges with half-shut eyes and dives again without having ascertained the cause of the trifling annoyance to which he is being subjected. The line is shortened up. Perhaps the turtle sulks among the rocks and coral, and endeavours to free himself from the sucker by rubbing against the boulders. Knowing all the wiles and manoeuvres, the blacks play the game accordingly, and hour after hour may pass, they giving and taking line with fine skill and the utmost patience. The turtle has become accustomed to the encumbrance, and visits the surface oftener for air. One of the harpoons is raised, and as the turtle gleams grey, a couple of fathoms or so under the water, the canoe is smartly paddled towards the spot whence it will emerge, and before it can get a mouthful of air the barbed point, with a strong line attached, is sticking a couple of inches deep in its shoulder.

There is a mad splash—a little maelstrom of foam and ripples, the line runs out to its full length, and the canoe careers about, accurately steered by the aft man, in the erratic course of the wounded creature. As it tires, the heavy haft of the harpoon secured by the half hitches round the thin end being a considerable drag, the line is shortened up, but too much trust is not placed on a single line; some time may pass before the canoe is brought within striking distance again. When that moment arrives, a second harpoon is sent into the flesh below the edge of the carapace at the rear. Unable to break away, the turtle is hauled close alongside the canoe, secured by the flippers and towed ashore. I have known blacks, after harpooning a turtle, to be towed six miles out to sea before it came their turn to do the towing.

How they accomplish the feat of securing a turtle that may weigh a couple of hundredweight from a frail bark canoe, in which a white man can scarcely sit and preserve his balance, is astonishing. In a lively sea the blacks sit back, tilting up the stem to meet the coming wave, and then put their weight forward to ease it down, paddling, manoeuvring with the line and baling all the time. The mere paddling about in the canoe is a feat beyond the dexterity of an ordinary man.

In passing, on the point of the turtle endeavouring to rid itself of the sucker, a European pearl-sheller told me of a unique experience that befell him in Torres Strait. Groping along the bottom, pushing his way against an impetuous current, he was almost knocked down by a move-on sort of shove. Instinctively his hand clutched the life-line, when he was again pushed disrespectfully, and in the greenish light saw that a monstrous turtle was using him as the afflicted Scotch were said to use the stones set up by the humane and sympathetic Duke of Argyle, and without so much as invoking a blessing.

A "KUMMAORIE"

Having caught their turtle and brought it ashore, and having seen the extent to which the tail of the sucker (which has been faithful to its host to the death) has been cut by the line, and having decided that it will do one time more and put it back in the water tethered, or "that fella no good now", and cast it callously on the sand, to writhe about until dead, the blacks proceed to the cooking. Possibly the camp decides upon a "Kummaorie".

A big fire is made and a dozen or so smooth stones about the size of saucers put on the embers to get red hot. In the meantime the turtle is killed, the head, neck, and sometimes the two fore flippers, removed. The entrails and stomach are taken out, and after being roughly cleansed are put back into the cavity. A hole is scraped in the sand, and the turtle stuck tail-first into it, the sand being banked up so that it remains upright. Then the red-hot stones are lifted with sticks and dropped into the turtle, hissing and spluttering, and stirred about with a stout stick. Another hole has been scooped in the sand and paved with stones, upon which a roaring fire is made. When the stones are hot through, the fire is scraped away, and the steaming turtle eased down from its upright position, care being taken not to allow any of the gravy to waste, and carefully deposited on the hot stones—carapace down. Quickly, so that none of the "smell" escapes, the whole is covered with leaves—native banana, native ginger, palms, etc., and over all is raised a mound of sand. In the morning the flesh is thoroughly cooked. The plastron (lower shell) is lifted off, and in the carapace is a rich, thick soup. No blood or any of the juices of the meat have gone to waste—the finest of meat extracts, the very quintessence of turtle, remains.

What would your gourmands give for a plate of this genuine article? Who may say he has tasted turtle soup—pure and unadulterated—unless he has "Kummaoried" his turtle to obtain it? With balls of grass the blacks sop up the brown oily soup, loudly smacking and sucking their lips to emphasize appreciation. Then there are the white flesh and the glutin, the best of all fattening foods. Having eaten to repletion for a couple of days, the diet palls, and they begin to speak in shockingly disrespectful terms of turtle.

WEATHER DISTURBERS

In the arid parts of Australia, where rain rarely occurs, the blacks have acquired much out-of-the-way knowledge on the means of obtaining water. White men, unable to read the secret signs of its existence, have perished in all the agonies of thirst in country in which water, from a blackfellow's point of view, was plentiful and comparatively easy to reach. Here there is never any anxiety on the subject. The minds of the blacks turn rather upon attempts to account for the rain, at times excessive and discomforting. Bad weather, in common with other untoward circumstances, is frequently ascribed to the machinations of evilly disposed boys. A boy may accept the credit or have the greatness thrust upon him of the manufacture of a gale which has brought about general discomfort, and to spite him, regardless of consequence to others, another boy will promise a still more destructive breeze next year. And so the game of wanton interference with the meteorological conditions of the continent proceeds, each successive infliction being arranged to serve out the author of the one preceding. It may be that the instigator of a gale lives far away, at the Palm Islands, or on Hinchinbrook, or at Mourilyan. Those who are terrified or inconvenienced agree to ascribe it to him, and having done so there is nothing of the mysterious to explain away. Usually the boy upon whom the responsibility is fixed is not available for cross-examination; but that renders the fact all the more conclusive. Here is the storm. Peter of the Palms must have made it.

An old gin known as Kitty, and who lived on Hinchinbrook Island, was famed on account of her successful manipulation of the weather. She was a grim personage—held in respect, if not awe, because of the peculiar distinctions ascribed to her. She could command not only the wind and the rain, but the thunder and lightning also, and to offend her was to run the risk of bringing about a terrifying storm. Years after her death blacks had faith in her potency for ill. One of the few white men who have attempted to climb the highest peaks of the island mountain, informed me that when he reached a certain elevation, the boys who accompanied him never spoke above an awe-struck whisper, and solemnly reproved him whensoever he uttered an unguarded exclamation. They were afraid that the "debil-debil" might be aroused; that Kitty would resent the intrusion of her haunt. At last they refused to go higher, and the ascent up in the dreaded regions was continued alone, while they abandoned themselves to sinister prognostics. One lonely night was spent high up on the mountain, and when the adventurer came back on his tracks in the morning, the boys were surprised to find that no harm had befallen him. To go into the very stronghold of mischievous and vindictive spirits, and to come away again, was to them almost beyond comprehension, and because no hurricane swooped down upon them, as they hurried to the lower and safer levels, nothing short of the marvellous.

However fantastic this supposition of human influence on the weather, there is an inclination to treat it with a semblance of respect when it is borne in mind that up to a comparatively recent date a similar belief prevailed even in enlightened England. Addison has a sarcastic reference to the superstition in one of his delightful essays. Detailing the news brought from his country seat by Sir Roger de Coverley, he says that the good knight informed him that Moll White was dead, and that about a month after her death, the wind was so very high that it blew down the end of one of his barns. "But for my own part," says Sir Roger, "I do not think that the old woman had any hand in it." In this particular, blacks are not so very far in the wake of races quite respectable in other points of civilization.

Among other causes to which bad weather is ascribed is the eating by the young men of the "porcupine" (Echidna), a dainty reserved for the wise, conservative old men. If young men should eat of the forbidden flesh, a terrible calamity will befall—the clouds will "come down altogether". One day Tom picked up a young porcupine before it had time to dig a refuge in the soil, and took it to his camp alive. That afternoon a south-east gale sprang up, masses of rainclouds driving tumultously to the mountains of the mainland, but Tom was still youthful, and we felt fairly safe in respect of the stability of the dull, heavy, and windswept firmament. As we watched, a cloud settled on the summit of Clump Point Mountain, assuming shape as fancy pictures the Banshee—drooping head and shoulders, and arms with pendant drapery uplifted as in imprecation. The boys, in awe-struck attitude, pointed to the vapoury spectre, and prognosticated fearsome rain and wind. It all came during the night. Next morning one of the boys was eager to declare that the nocturnal tempest was due to Tom, who had eaten the porcupine. We had seen his weird mother-in-law, aged and decrepit, preparing it for supper. When Tom appeared, he was duly denounced and challenged with the responsibility of the storm. "No!" he cried with scorn. "Me no eat 'em that fella porcupine; chuck 'em away." He had intended to, but the thought of the apparition on Clump Point Mountain, and of the awful responsibility of causing the collapse of the clouds had taken away his inclination.

But the other boy was not to have his theories as to the weather brushed aside lightly. It was "that fella along a mountain", who caused the trouble, or else "another boy alonga Hinchinbrook!" Having thus completely and satisfactorily settled the point, his face assumed a slow, wise smile, and his agitated mind rested. Was it not all another palpable proof, a precedent to be cited, of the manner in which a no-good boy wantonly brought about a big wind?

Most of the dainties are forbidden the young members of the camp. Bony bream and bony herring will be passed on to the boys and girls, and, so too, the rough parts of turtle; but the sweet fish and flesh are retained by the old and lusty men, who proclaim that they alone may eat of such things with impunity. No youngster will dare to partake of echidna ("coom-be-yan") at the risk of the prescribed consequences; and to the old men the fiction stands in the place (as was recently pointed out) of an annuity or old age pension.

To fare sumptuously every day was not the lot of the natives of Dunk Island. In excessively rainy weather they were often glad of the coarsest and hardest of foods. Certain sharks are eaten with avidity whenever they are secured; but some species are too rank and tough to be endurable under any but extraordinary circumstances. Oysters were always plentiful, but a diet restricted to the most delicate of molluscs palls on the palate even of a blackfellow. Ordinarily, food was abundant. For the most part it had only to be picked up and cooked. Frequently it was eaten on the spot, fresh from bountiful nature's hands; but blacks appreciate changes of diet—even when the change is retrogressive —from the well-cooked, clean food of a white household to that of the sodden and strong stuffs common to the camp. When, as sometimes happened, the desire for novelty came, the whole population would paddle away to the mainland or to one or other of the adjacent islands, voyages being undertaken as far away as distant Hinchinbrook. Turtle do not favour the beaches and sandbanks of Dunk Island generally as safe depositories for their innumerable eggs, and when the longing came for these delicacies the inhabitants would with one accord travel to those islands in the security of which turtle still exhibit faith. The drift of the population hither and thither was not due to the scarcity of food but to a wayward impulse. As a rule there was little for the population to do save to eat, drink, laze away the hotter hours of the day, and "corroboree" at night.

Astonishment can scarcely be withheld when an attempt is made to catalogue the available foods of the island, the variety and quantity. No effort was made at cultivation. Blacks took no heed of the morrow, but accepted the fruits of the earth without thought of inciting nature to produce better or more abundantly, and yet how plenteous were her gifts!

Permitting imagination to soar away into regions of romance, one might picture a dinner-party of the bygone days, the lap of Mother Earth furnished with edibles and dainties, and the hungry and expectant members of the camp squatted round in anticipation of the various courses. Such a scene would be worthy of being classed among the most improbable; but as it would not be absolutely impossible, may not an attempt be made to treat it as a reality?

The repast might be initiated with a few oysters on the shells (with a choice of three or four varieties); a selection of many fish would be succeeded by real turtle ("padg-e-gal") soup (in the original shell), and made as before described; the joint, a huge piece of dugong ("pal-an-gul") kummaoried, rich and excellent, with *entrées* of turtle cutlets and baked grubs ("tam-boon"), ivory white with yellow heads, as neat and pretty a dish as could be seen, and rather rare and novel too. When the beetles into which these stolid grubs and fidgety nymphs develop, are chopped out of decaying wood, they have the odour of truffles, and emit two distinct squeaky notes from the throat and the abdominal segments respectively. Each maintains a duet with itself until the hot embers impose silence and convert them into dainty nutty morsels. Roast scrub fowl eggs would be no novelty, and baked crayfish ("too-lac"), bluey-white and leathery—"such stuff as dreams are made on"—might lend a decorative effect. Raw *Echinus* ("kier-bang"), saline and tonic, would clear the palate for succeeding delicacies.

The tough sweet yam ("pun-dinoo"), the heart of the Alexandra palm ("koobin-karra"), the hard rhizome of *Bowenia spectabilis* ("moo-nah") after being allowed weeks to decompose, the core of the tree fern ("kalo-joo"), the long root-stock of *Curculigo ensifolia* ("harpee"), crisp and slightly bitter, the broad beans of the white mangrove ("kum-moo-roo"), would stand as vegetables.

Sweets would be the weakest part of the menu. One pudding might certainly be included, vermicelli (shredded bean-tree nuts —"tinda-burra") with honey and orange-coloured balsamic custard, scraped from the outside of the drupes of the *Pandanus odoratissimus* ("pim-nar").

Dessert, on the other hand, might be plentiful and varied. "Bed-yew-rie" (*Ximenia americana*), thirst-allaying and palate-sharpening; "Top-kie" (Herbert River cherry, *Antedisma Dallachyanum*), resembling red currants in flavour; "Pool-boo-nong" (finger cherry, *Rhodomyrtus macrocarpa*), sweet, soft and appeasing; "Panga-panga", raspberry (*Rubus rosaefolius*); "Koo-badg-aroo" (Leichhardt-tree, *Sarcocephalus cordatus*), resembling a strawberry in shape, but brown, spicy and hot; "Murl-kue-kee" (snow-white berries of *Eugenia suborbicularis*), vapid, and as insipid as an immature medlar; "Raroo" (*Careya australis*), mealy and biting. Various figs, ranging in size from a large red currant to a tennis-ball, and in colour from white through all the tints from pale yellow and green to red, purple and black, sweet and generally mawkish. The banana would be there in the *Musa Banksia* ("boo-gar-oo"), although "close up all bone"; but the Davidsonian plum, plentiful on the mainland, would be absent. The scrape of the *Elettaria Scottiana*, oozing viscid nectar, might stand as a sweetmeat.

Then, dallying with tomahawks and flat stones with the tough nuts of the "Moo-jee" (*Terminalia melanocarpa*), and the drupes of the "Can-kee" (*Pandanus aquaticus*) to extract the narrow sweet kernels, and sipping the while cordial compounded of the larvae of green tree-ants ("book-gruin"), acidulous and nippy, the men might indulge in after-dinner stories and reminiscences, as the gins and piccaninnies drink heartily of water sweetened with sugar-bag (honey-comb), and chew the seeds contained in the china-blue pericarp of the native ginger—"Oool-pun" (*Alpinia caerula*).

Many vegetable foods would still be unenumerated, and there would be numerous shell-fish—periwinkles, cockles, muscles, scallops, dolphins, besides crabs. On rare occasions a scrub fowl (the blacks had no reliable means of capturing that wary bird, and when fortune favoured, it was an instance of bad luck on its part), with pigeons, carpet snakes, and sea-birds' eggs might make high tea.

BLACK ART

Time and diligent search revealed the location on the island of two art galleries, or rather independent studios, where there are exhibited works of distinct character. Tradition points to the existence of a third, the discovery of which gives zest to each exploratory expedition. Possibly it may also display original exploits in the realms of fancy, and so confirm the opinion that the black artists were not mere copyists of each other, but belonged to different schools, each having his own method and allowing his talent free and untrammelled development.

What may be designated the Lower Studio is on the eastern slope, and is only to be approached from the sea in calm weather, the alternative route being a tiresome climb, a long and tormenting struggle through the jungle, and a descent among a confusion of rocks and boulders. It is situated about a couple of hundred feet above sea-level, quite hidden in the leafy wilderness which covers that aspect of the island from high-water mark to the summit of the ridge. Unless the spot was indicated, one might search for it for years in vain, and though I had made frequent inquiries, its existence was made known only by chance, its importance being considered insignificant compared with the other studio, the glories of which had frequently been descanted upon. Taking the sea-route, there is a natural harbour available, just capacious enough for a small dinghy, and up above the rocks, swept bare by the surges, a dense and tangled scrub "whereto the climber upwards turns his face", and taking advantage of such aids as aerial roots, slim saplings, and the reed-like growths of the so-called native ginger, begins the steep ascent. Where the rock does not emerge from the surface, the black soil is loose and kept in perpetual cultivation by scrub fowl, the wonder being that earth reposes at such an angle. But for interlacing and matted roots all must slide down to the sea.

A few minutes' exertion lands one at the portal of the studio, which is of the lean-to order of architecture, a granite boulder having one fairly vertical face being over-shadowed by a much higher rock having a dip of about sixty degrees.

Here originally there were five exhibits. Two have weathered away almost to nothingness, some faint streaks and blotches of red earth, in which medium all the pictures have been executed, alone remaining. Those subjects that are readily decipherable are muti-lated after the style of certain much-prized antiques.

Of those which have successfully withstood the ravages of time, two apparently represent lizards, and the third seems to portray a monstrosity—a human being with a rudimentary tail. A Ger-man philosopher might possibly build upon this embryonic tail a theory to prove that the Australian aboriginal is indeed and in fact the missing link, and thereby excel in ethnological venture those who merely recognize in him the relic from a prehistoric age of man. Could it not be argued that the picture reveals an act of unconscious cerebration—an instinctive knowledge of ancestors with tails?

However that may be, the unconscious artist took further artless liberties with the human form divine. He had been at pains, too, to smooth down the face of the rock for the reception of the unshaded daubs of terra-cotta, using peradventure the flat stone upon which he was wont to bruise the hot and biting roots of the aroid (*Colocasia macrorrhiza*) which formed part of his diet. The utensil lies there at the entrance where he left it; the plants grow in profusion close by among the rocks; but of the artist there is no record, save the crude and grotesque figures in fading red on the grey granite.

Most of the central figure is clearly discernible; but parts of the outline have become blurred and irregular. Tradition says that all the figures once had black heads—the only attempts at the introduction of a second colour—but no traces of the black heads are now visible. They must have succumbed to the tender but irresistible assaults of Time long ago. In one case, fact seems to belie tradition, for there exist faint suggestions of a red head—and a red-headed black is as rare as a black with a tail; but the traces are so extremely vague and indeterminate as to render any attempt at restoration hopeless. But does not this obscurity and partial dismemberment lend an air of antiquity, much prized elsewhere, to these savage frescoes?

Of quite a different order are the works in the Upper Studio at the sign of the White Stripe. This lies close to the backbone of the island, in the heart of a bewildering jumble of immense rocks overgrown with jungle. Circumstantial accounts of the treasures there to be seen had determined me to persevere in attempts to discover it; but though the traditions of the blacks were strengthened by a mild sort of enthusiasm, and the exhibition of no little pride, they did but slight service towards revealing the precise locality. None of the living remnants of the race had seen the paintings. All trusted to the saying of "old men" and had faith. Experience had taught me to accept with caution and reserve legends founded on the unverified testimony of "old men" which had passed down to the present generation; but being much interested, and having become elated with the hope of discovering that which had not been seen by white folk, nor, indeed, by any living person, I trusted and persevered.

From ships that pass to the East may be seen a bold white streak on the face of a huge rock, so sharply defined and accurate in alignment that it might be mistaken for a guide to mariners, or rather a warning, for the floor of the ocean is strewn with patches of coral, and the rocks are singularly forbidding, save on calm days. Opinion current among the blacks asserted that the paintings were on a rock below the disjointed precipice on the top of the ridge made conspicuous by the broad white band. The sign was found to be due to the bleaching of the rock face by the drainage from a mass of stag's horn fern. Possessed of this information, which proved in the long run to be trustworthy, several exploratory trips were undertaken. To reach the locality from Brammo Bay, one must cross the middle of the backbone of the island, and descend some little distance on the Pacific slope.

I scaled and scrambled over and crawled upon huge rocks, peered into gloomy crevices with daylight edges fringed with ferns and orchids, squeezed through narrow tunnels, and groped in dark recesses without finding any evidence of prehistoric art. Blacks do not care to venture into places where twilight always reigns, though they are curious to learn the experiences and sensations of other explorers of the gloom. At last, however, patience was rewarded, and beneath a great granite rock, which on three previous excursions had been overlooked, the paintings were discovered. In their execution the artist must have lain on his back, for the "cave" does not permit one to sit upright in it, except towards the wide and expansive front, and the subjects are on the ceiling, which is fairly flat. The floor, thick with a fine brown dust mingled with shining specks of decomposed granite, and dimpled with hundreds of pitfalls of the ant-lion, slopes upward. It is cool, and a dry, secure spot. Not even the torrential rains of many decades of wet seasons have damped the floor. One feels as though he were disturbing the dust of ages; when sitting back to admire the decorated ceiling, he necessarily imprints patterns which are the replicas of those made by flesh and bone long since numbered among the anonymous dead.

The sea leaves the hot rocks six hundred feet below, and booms and gobbles in the cool crevices; but up here the outlook is obscured by rocks and giant trees, and an artistic soul, longing for some method of expression, might serenely gratify itself in accordance with its lights—crude though they were. Here, at the entrance, lie a couple of charred sticks, significant of the last fire of the artist, which smouldered out perhaps half a century ago. On the very door-step is a disc of pearl-shell, the discarded beginning of a fish-hook. These relics give to the scene a pathetic interest. As I looked at them ponderingly, a frog in the back of the cave gave a discordant, echoing croak, which startled the sulky and suspicious black boy who attended me into an abrupt exclamation of semi-fright; while a scrub fowl, scratching for its living overhead, dislodged a chip of granite which went clicking down the rocks. "Tom", at the instant, felt that the spirit of the departed was manifesting, in the hollow tones of a frog and the activity of a bird, resentment at the intrusion of his haunts, and was warning us to begone. But we had come far on a toilsome errand, and were not to be scared away by trifles, though a transient feeling of reluctance to disturb the solemnity of the studio could not be with-held.

Remembering the fervid praises of the treasures by those who had not seen them, a sense of disappointment when they came to be examined was inevitable. They are not to be classed in any standard beyond that displayed on early school-slates; but imperfect as they are, they possess a certain symmetry and proportion, and the facts that they are where they are, and that the artist—dead and forgotten—had no light or leading, and was in other respects probably one of the most rude, most uncouth of human beings, are sufficient to lend to the drawings an interest as absorbing (though of a nature quite apart) as that with which the average individual contemplates the stiff works of masters of Continental fame.

One able critic of aboriginal art refers to similar rock paintings as frescoes, for lack of a significant title. Apparently the rock surface was slightly smoothed where inequalities existed—in one case the design follows the ridges and hollows—the subjects being worked in in dry earth of a chalky nature, dull red in colour. Animated nature and still life have been studied and reproduced. The turtle is true, and the most conspicuous and sharply-defined study the least convincing. It resembles those fantastic inter-woven shapes that some men in fits of abstraction or idleness sketch on their own blotting-pads, and which signify nothing.

Comparing the works of the two studios, there is little doubt that there were at least two artists native of Dunk Island in times past, and in that respect the island was infinitely superior to its present state. Each appears to have effected a different kind of work—one devoting himself to realistic reptiles and the human form debased, and the other almost solely to the creation of conventional designs, and the representation of the animals and of weapons of his age. One illustrated man, and even gave to one of his reptiles a semi-human shape; the other exercised an exuberant fancy for ornamentation. Each bequeathed to the present day and generation works that are at least free from the subtleties of art.

Most of us have had moments of rapture before the glowing embodiment of the inspiration of some great artist, whose gifts have been developed to maturity by enthusiastic and patient striving for perfection. Do not these clumsy drawings, too, reveal that which, considering their environment, is talent—original and unacademic? Here is the sheer beginning, the spontaneous germ of art, the labouring of a savage soul controlled by wilful aesthetic emotions. For these pictures are not figurative, not mere signs and symbols capable of elucidation, but the earliest and only efforts of an illiterate race, a race in intellectual infancy, towards the ideal—a forlorn but none the less sincere attempt to reach the "light that quickens dreams to deeds".

A POISONOUS FOOD

One of the chief vegetable foods of the blacks is the fruit of "tinda-burra" (Moreton Bay chestnut—*Castanospermum australe*). The plentiful pea-shaped flowers range in colour from apple-green, pale yellow, orange to scarlet, and contain large quantities of nectar, which attracts multitudes of birds and insects. Blacks regard this tree with special favour and consideration. A casual remark, as I observed the industry of insects about the flowers, that the bean-tree was good for bees, elicited the scornful response, "Good for man!" The tree is of graceful shape, the bole often pillar-like in its symmetry, the wood is hard and durable and of pleasing colour, and so beautifully grained that it is fast becoming popular for furniture and cabinet-making. It bears a prolific crop of large beans, from two to five in each of its squat pods, but they are, as Mr Standfast found the waters of Jordan, "to the palate bitter, and to the stomach cold", and require special treatment in order to eliminate a poisonous principle. Many chemists analysed the beans (one finding that they may be converted into excellent starch) without discovering any noxious element; but as horses, cattle, and pigs die if they eat the raw bean, and a mere fragment is sufficient to give human beings great pain, followed by most unpleasant consequences, the research was continued, until within quite a recent date the presence of saponin was detected.

Before science made its discovery, the blacks were very positive on the point of the poisonous qualities of the bean, and took measures to eliminate it. In some parts of the State the beans, after being steeped in water for several days, are dried in the sun, roasted in hot ashes, and pounded between stones into a coarse kind of meal, which may be kept for an indefinite period. When required for use the meal is mixed with water, made into a thin cake or damper, and baked in the ashes. Prepared in this way the cake resembles a coarse ship's biscuit. In other parts, the beans are scraped by means of mussel-shells into a vermicelli-like substance, prior to soaking in water. Our blacks have a more ingenious method of preparation, and employ a specially formed culinary implement, which is used for no other purpose. They take the commonest of the land-shells—"kurra-dju" (*Xanthomelon pachystyla*)—and breaking away the apex grind down the back on a stone until but little more than half its bulk remains. The upper edges being carefully worked to a fine edge, the only housewifery implement that the blacks possess is perfect. With the implement in the right hand, between the thumb and the second finger—the sharp edge resting on the thumb-nail—the beans are planed, the operator being able to regulate the thickness of the shaving to a nicety.

It is women's work to collect the beans, make the shell-planes, and do the shredding. In the first place the beans are cooked, the oven consisting of hot stones covered with leaves. In three or four hours they are taken out and planed, a dilly-bag (basket made of narrow strips of lawyer-cane or grass) full of the shavings is immersed in running water for two or three days, the food being then ready for consumption without further preparation. In appearance it resembles coarse tapioca, and it has no particular flavour. To give it zest, some have a shell containing sea-water beside them when they dine, into which each portion of the mess is dipped. As saponin is very soluble in water, by soaking the shredded beans for a few days the blacks resort to an absolutely perfect method of converting a poisonous substance into a valuable and sustaining, if tasteless, food. No doubt, made up into a pudding with eggs, milk, sugar and flavouring, shredded beans would pass without comment as a substitute for tapioca.

There came to our beach one afternoon some poor exiles from Princess Charlotte Bay—three hundred miles to the north. Exiled they felt themselves to be, and were longing to return to their own country, although their engagement for a six months' cruise in quest of the passive bêche-de-mer had just begun. One boy stepped along with an air of pride and importance. His companions were deferential to a certain extent, but they, too, exhibited an unusual demeanour. Some of the glory and honour that shone in Mattie's face was reflected in theirs. With the assurance of an ambassador bearing high credentials he saluted me—

"Hello, mister! Good day."

"Good day," I responded. "You come from that cutter?"

Mattie—"Yes, mister. Mickie sit down here, now? Me got 'em letter. Brother belonga gin, belonga Mickie; him gib it!"

"No; Mickie sit down alonga Palm Islands. Come back, bi'-mby."

Mattie (with a downcast air)—"My word! Bo'sun (the brother-in-law) gib it letter belonga Mickie."

"Where letter?" I asked.

Mattie—"Me got 'em." And, drawing out a very soiled little parcel, he proudly exposed a piece of greyish wood, about the size and shape of a lead pencil, on which had been cut two continuous intersecting grooves. "Me giv' 'em Mickie; Bo'sun alonga Cooktown. He want to come up this way now."

The letter was a mere token of material expression of the fact that the sender was in the land of the living, and of his faith in the bearer, who was charged with all the personal messages and news. It was a sad rebuff to Mattie, elated with responsibility and eager to unburden himself of the latest domestic intelligence, to find that Mickie was not on the spot to receive it all. And, after fondling the wooden document for a while, he wrapped it up and carefully bestowed it within the bosom of his shirt. The disappointment was general. The gleam faded from the faces of the boys. For several days, first one and then another was entrusted with the honourable custody of the "missive". Whoever possessed it for the time being was the most favoured individual. His worthiness for the office he acknowledged with an amusing air of self-consciousness and pride. The transmission of a "letter" is not an ordinary occurrence, and though there is an entire absence of form and ceremony in its delivery, the rarity of the event lends to it novelty and importance.

Aboriginal letters are of great variety, and some there are who profess to interpret them. The dispatches are, however, invariably, in my experience, transmitted from hand to hand, the news of the day being recapitulated at the same time. It is not essential that the unstudied cuts and scratches on wood should have any significance or be capable of intelligible rendering. Though blacks profess to be able to send messages by means of sticks alone, the pretension is not recognized by those who have crucially investigated it.

On a certain station a youthful son of the proprietor was accidentally drowned in a creek not far from the homestead. The grief of the parents was participated in by all engaged on the station, for the boy, full of promise, had been a general favourite. None seemed more sorrowful and gloomy than the blacks camped in the neighbourhood, and when the first shock of sorrow was of the past, they were eager to send the news to distant friends. A letter was laboriously composed. It was a short piece of wood, narrow and flat; an undulating groove ran from end to end on one side; midway was an intersecting notch. These were the principal characteristics, but there were other small marks and scratches. Bearing this as his credentials, a messenger departed, and in a week or so members of camps hundreds of miles away had seen the letter and were in possession of all the details of the sad event, the messenger in the meantime having returned. The letter was duly credited with having conveyed the particulars. Is it not obvious, however, that the news had been transmitted orally, and that the crude carvings on the stick merely indicated an attempt to give verisimilitude to the intelligence—the wavy line indicating the creek, and the notch the fatal waterhole? If not, then a black's message-stick is a model of literary condensation, their characters marvels of comprehensiveness and exactitude.

Another letter is before me—one of the best specimens with regard to workmanship I have ever seen. Upon one edge of a piece of brown wood six inches long, one inch broad, flat and rounded off at the edges and ends, there are five notches, and on the opposite edge a single notch. Close to the end is a faint, crude representation of a broad arrow, below which is a confusion of small cuts, in a variety of angles, none quite vertical, some quite horizontal. On the reverse is a single—almost perpendicular—cut, and a bold X, and near the point, two shallow, indistinct diverging cuts. So far no one to whom the letter has been submitted has given a satisfactory reading. Blacks frankly admit that they do not understand it. They examine it curiously, and almost invariably remark—"Some fella mak' 'em." No attempt to decipher it is undertaken, because no doubt it was never intended to be read. Yet a plausible elucidation is at hand. The single notch, let it be said, represents a black who wishes to let five white fellows (who have made inquiries in that direction) know that a corroboree is to begin before sundown, the setting sun being the end of the stick. The guests are expected to bring rum to produce a bewildering, unsteady effect upon the whole camp—none, big or little, but will stagger about in all directions and finally lie down. On the other hand the guests are not to bring "one fella" policeman with handcuffs (the cross), otherwise all will decamp —the two last are seen vanishing into space. By a rare coincidence this very free interpretation could be made to apply to an actuality at the time the "letter" was received, but as a matter of fact it came from quite a different source to the blackfellow who had engaged to let some students of the aboriginal character know when the next corroboree would take place. It still remains undecipherable. My investigations do not support the theory that the blacks are capable of recording the simplest event by means of a system of so-called picture-writing, but rather that message-sticks have no meaning apart from verbal explanations. Blacks profess to be able to send messages which another may understand, but the tests applied locally invariably break down.

Another message-stick was made on the premises by George, but not to order. A genuine, unprompted natural effort, it is merely a slip of pine, four inches long, a quarter of an inch broad and flat, upon which are cut spiral intersecting grooves. George's birthplace is Cooktown, and his message-stick resembles in design that brought by Mattie from Bo'sun of Cooktown for Mickie of the Palms. Now, George professes to be able to write English, but he is so shy and diffident over the accomplishment that neither persuasion nor offer of reward induces him to practise it. When he produced the "letter", more than usual interest was taken in it, for it seemed to offer an exceptional opportunity for

ascertaining the extent of his literary pretensions. I asked him—
"Who this for, George?" George looked at the stick long and
curiously with a puzzled, concentrated expression, as one might
assume when examining a novel and interesting problem demanding prompt solution. With an enlightening smile he in time
replied, "This for Charlie".

"Charlie" is the name of a boy who recently visited the island,
but who hitherto had not been known by George.

"Well, what this letter talk about?" A very long pause ensued,
during which George appeared to be putting his imaginative
powers to frightful over-exertion. His forehead wrinkled, his lips
twitched, his head moved this way and that, once or twice a
gleam of inspiration passed over his face, and then the expression
of the deep and puzzled thinker came on again. Finally he said,
"Y-e-e-s. Me tell 'em, sometimes me see Toby".

Toby is the tallest of the survivors of Dunk Island, another
acquaintance of George's, who refers to him as a hard case, for it
is said Toby's affections are very fitful and uncertain.

"Then that letter tell 'em something more?" The strenuous
pause, the desperate plunge into thought again, and George
continued, "This for Johnny Tritton, before alonga Cooktown;
now walk about somewhere down here. Might be catch 'em
alonga mainland".

This message-stick was freshly made, and its meaning, had it
possessed any, might have been repeated pat. But it was evident
that the boy was putting a devastating strain upon a tardy wit
when he endeavoured to ascribe to it a literary rendering. His
hesitancy and contradictions were at least amusingly ingenuous.

Exceptional opportunities were available in this neighbourhood
recently for the formation of an opinion upon the value of message-
sticks for the transmission of intelligence. The bushman who on
horseback carried his Majesty's mails inland among the settlers
and to distant stations, was frequently also entrusted with the
delivery of message-sticks by blacks along the route. Invariably
the stick was accompanied by a verbal communication—a request
for some article (a pipe, a knife, looking-glass, handkerchief) or
an inquiry as to the whereabouts or welfare of some relative or
friend. The mailman quickly found that the often elaborately
graven stick was to no purpose whatever without the verbal message. Frequently the sticks would become far more hopelessly

mixed up than the babes in *Pinafore*; but as long as he recollected the message aright, not the slightest concern or dissatisfaction was manifested.

In this neighbourhood the making of pearl-shell fishhooks is one of the lost arts. The old men may tell how they used to be made, but are not able to afford any satisfactory practical demonstration. Therefore, to obtain absolutely authentic examples, it was necessary to indulge in the unwonted pastime of antiquarian research. During an unsympathetic, unmethodical overhauling of the shell heap of an extensive kitchen midden—to apply a dignified title to a long deserted camp—interesting testimony to the diligence and patience of the deceased occupants was obtained. It was evident that the sea had been largely drawn upon for supplies, if only on account of the many abortive and abandoned attempts at fish-hooks in more or less advanced stages of completion. The brittle-ness of the fabric and the crudeness of the tools employed had evidently put the patience of the makers to severe task; for one satisfactory hook they must have contemplated many disappointments. The art must be judged as critically by the exhibition of its failures as by its perfections, as Beau Nash did the tying of his cravats. "Those are our failures," the spirits of the departed, brooding over the site of the camp, might have sighed, as we sorted out crude and unfashioned fragments. Presently the discovery of a small specimen established the standard of perfection —a crescent of pearl, which alone was ample recompense for the afternoon's research. Smaller than the average hook, it represented an excellent object-lesson in patience and skill. Many other examples, some complete, have since been found, and have been arranged for illustration to exhibit the process of construction in several stages. Do they not confirm the opinion that the maker of pearl-shell fish-hooks suffered many mishaps and disappointments, and that he had high courage in discarding any that evidenced a fault?

The method of manufacture was to reduce by chipping with a sharp-edged piece of quartz a portion of a black-lip mother-of-pearl shell to a disc. A central hole was then chipped—not bored or drilled—with another tool of quartz. The hole was gradually enlarged by the use of a terminal of one of the staghorn corals

(*Madepora laxa*) until a ring had been formed. Then a segment was cut away, leaving a rough crescent, which was ground down with coral files, and the ends sharpened by rubbing on smooth slate.

Discs were also cut out of gold-lip mother-of-pearl shell, but by what means there is no evidence to tell. When such a prize as a gold-lip shell was found, it was used to the last possible fragment. Most frequently the black-lip mother-of-pearl was the material whence the hooks were fashioned, and, when no other was available, the hammer oyster. In one case an unsuccessful endeavour had been made to fashion a hook from a piece of plate-glass, obtained, no doubt, from the wreck of some long-forgotten ship. The fractured disc lying among other relics of the handicraft spoke for itself.

Not only have many samples of partially-made hooks been found, but also the tools employed in the process. The sharp-edged fragment of quartz used to chip away the shell, the anvil of soft slate upon which the shell rested during the operation, the quartz chisel for chipping the central hole, the coral terminals, resembling rat-tail files, and the smooth stone upon which the rough edges of the hook were ground down and finished.

Hooks without barbs and manufactured of such materials as pearl-shell and tortoiseshell may throw light upon the Homeric quotation—"caught fish with the horn of the ox". In those far-off days, bronze wire rope, similar in design to the steel rope which is of common use in the present time, was employed. Ancient Greeks, though they anticipated one of the necessities of trade nowadays, depended upon fish-hooks resembling those just being abandoned by the Australian blacks. Fish are guileless creatures. They are captured to-day with hooks of the style upon which fishermen of the Homeric age depended.

From the appearance of the camps, and the age of the islander who took part in the various searches, and who was ready to admit that though pearl-shell hooks were used when he was a piccaninny he had never seen one made, I judge the age of these relics of a prehistoric art to be between thirty and forty years.

This boy has supplied samples of hooks made by himself with the aid of files, etc., in imitation of the old style, being careful to explain that the old men made them much better than anyone could in these degenerate days of steel. Two of these modern hooks bound to bark lines are illustrated. What was the origin of the peculiar pattern of the pearl-shell fish-hooks? To this question, those who maintain that no handiwork of man exists which does not borrow from nature, or from something precedent to itself, may find a satisfactory answer offhand. As it weathers on the beach, the basal valve of the commonest of the oysters of these waters occasionally assumes a crude crescent. Indeed, several of these fragments have at odd times attracted attention, for they have so closely resembled pearl-shell hooks in the rough that second glances have been necessary to dispose of the illusion that they were actually rejects from some old-time camp. Is it not reasonable to suppose that the original design was copied from this elemental model, as in like manner the boomerang is traceable to a leaf? The pattern is so profoundly persistent in the minds of the blacks of to-day, that in fashioning a hook from a piece of straight wire they invariably form a crescent, though the superiority of the shape approved by civilization must have been exemplified to them times out of number. In this particular the blacks seem unconsciously to follow the idea of their ancestors as birds obey instinct in the building of nests and in migratory flights.

Piccaninnies at this date remind us of the genesis of the boomerang as they sport with the sickle-shaped leaves (or rather *phyllodia*) of the *Acacia holcocarpa* as with miniature boomerangs. The piccaninny of the remote past chuckled gleefully as the jerked leaf returned to it. As a boy he fashioned a larger and permanent toy, surreptitiously using his father's stone tomahawk and shell knife, while the old man was after wallaby with a waddy. As a young man, hunting or fighting, he found his boyish toy a very effective missile. Even for a straight shot it had a longer range and far higher velocity, with less strength expenditure, than the waddy or nulla-nulla; and its homing flight had practical if not frequent uses. In his childhood, adolescence and maturity the black of to-day so graphically summarizes a chapter in the history of his race that he who runs may read.

In the origin of the boomerang and the shell fish-hook we have instances, hardly to be doubted, of direct inspirations from nature, proofs of the art and the infinite patience with which she sets her copies and expounds her texts.

All the blacks of my acquaintance have had the rough edges of savagedom worn down. Consequently I lay no claim to original research or to the possession of any but common knowledge of the race at large. Learned societies and learned men have done and are doing all that is possible to acquire and accumulate information of the fast vanishing race. I merely record odd incidents, which may or may not prove useful and of interest. An occasional gleam of satisfaction is vouchsafed even to casual and superficial students of human nature.

The supply of bait ran out one day when we were fishing off the rocks with throw-lines. Mickie said—"We catch 'em plenty little fella fish with wild dynamite." I asked him what he know about dynamite. "Not white fella's dynamite. Wild dynamite— I show you."

Growing on the blistering rocks, with roots down in the crevices, was a lowly vine, or rather a diffuse creeping shrub with myrtle-like leaves and racemes of white flowers. "That fella wild dynamite," said Mickie, as he tore up several strands of the plant and bunched them, leaves and all, in his hand. He made a small bundle, and, going to an isolated pool in the rocks in which were small fish he beat the leaves with a nulla-nulla, dipping the bruised mass frequently in the water. In a few minutes the fish were darting about erratically, apparently making frantic efforts to get out of the water. One by one they became stupefied and helpless, floating belly up. Mickie filled his hat with them, and as the soporific effects of the juice of the leaves passed off, the remaining fish recovered and were soon swimming about again as if nothing had happened. Mickie had seen dynamite used to kill fish wholesale, hence his adaptation of the name of the plant known to him as "Pagg-arra", and to botanists as *Derris scandens*.

Another method by which the blacks secure fish in pools left by the receding tide is to scrape off the inner bark of the "Koie-yan" (*Faradaya splendida*) with a shell and spread it evenly on the bottom of a shallow pit in the sand, and place thereon stones made hot in the fire, or they may rub the powdered bark on hot stones. While still warm the stones are thrown into the water, upon which the fish become helpless. They die if left in water so impregnated, whereas the effects of the *Derris scandens* is merely temporarily soporific. How blacks became acquainted with this process of speedily extracting the toxic principle of the *Faradaya*, and as speedily dissipating it, is unknown. One generation passes on the knowledge to the other without explanation, and it is accepted as a matter of course, without comment or inquiry.

A CAVERN AND ITS LEGEND

Caves and caverns in the rocks and the tops of the mountains are not favourite resorts of blacks. According to them nearly every mountain has its mysterious lagoon, which none but old men have visited, but which teems with fish and waterfowl. When direct inquiries are made as to the precise locality of any particular lagoon, invariably inconclusive evidence is tendered. "Old man, he bin see 'em"; and the old man is never forthcoming for cross-examination. The origin of the romance, no doubt, is to be attributed to the desire of the blacks to account to themselves for the water which glitters on the face of the rocks far up the mountains. One boy gave an exceptionally graphic description of a lagoon on the top of one of the highest peaks of Hinchinbrook Island, in which all manner of sea fish revelled. When doubt was expressed as to the possibility of sea-water and sea-fish getting up so far "on top" and it was suggested—"What you think, that old man humbug you?" "Yes," was the ready response; "me think that old fella no tell true. Him humbug." Some blacks possess something wiser than knowledge.

On the northern aspect of Dunk Island, where the sea swirls about the buttresses of the hills, there is a cavern only approachable by boat. The mouth is overhung by vines and ferns, and through the moss which covers the lintel water trickles and splashes with pleasant sound. When the bronze orchid lavishly decorates the rocks with its crinkled flowers of dull gold, the entrance has a specific character; and quite another when the glossy leaves of the umbrella-tree form the relief and its long radiating spikes of dull red, bead-like flowers attract the brilliant sun-bird, and big blue and green and red butterflies. Even when the sea is lustrous the cavern, with all the artfulness and grace of the decorations of its portals, is a black blotch—the entrance to something un-knowable and unknown—at least to the blacks. None had ever ventured near it and none ever will. They tell you how it came to be made—how a long, long time ago, a big man, "all a same debil-debil", took out with his mighty fingers a plug of rock and put it "on top alonga Hinchinbrook". Now, the particular decapitated pinnacle of Hinchinbrook is twenty miles away, and out of all proportion. But these facts do not affect the legitimacy of the legend. There is the hole, and there on the top of the far-away mountain the prodigious plug demonstrative evidence too obvious to be set aside on any such plea as the eternal fitness of things. Is not the blue point of the mountain a defiantly triumphant fact? Is not the legend authenticated by tradition and confirmed by topography? Why, therefore, doubt it for a moment?

And the hole—it goes a long, long way under the mountain. It is a bad place, a very bad place. No one has ever been there. Suppose any fella go inside, bi'mby that fella sick, bi'mby that fella die.

Braving all the honest traditions, one fine day I took a lantern in the boat and induced the boys to row to the entrance of the cave. Neither would venture in; indeed, they did all they could to dissuade me, protesting that evil was sure to befall. A minute's exploration showed that the cave did not extend thirty feet, and that it was dry, and resonant with "the whispering sound of the cool colonnade", with no suggestion of unwholesomeness or weirdness. But the blacks still pass it by. The legend is indestructible. Although the boys persist in their account of the origin of the cave, it is known to them as "Coo-bee co-tan-you", which signifies "that hole made by the meteor", or, literally, "falling-star hole"'.

Romance, too, follows the Hinchinbrook pinnacle. Some local blacks regard it with awe, believing that it covers a deep hole in the mountain in which the winds and rain are pent up. When a malignant "debil-debil" lifts the peak away the elements escape, roaring and hissing with anger and mischief. When tired, they retire sulkily to the hole, which the "debil-debil" blocks with the monstrous rock. Fine weather then prevails, and the rock, which has been hidden away among the mists by the fiend, becomes visible once more.

A SOULFUL DANCE

Of the many corroborees that I have witnessed, the most novel in conception was performed on Dunk Island by blacks who came from the neighbourhood of Princess Charlotte Bay, some two hundred miles to the north.

The imitation of the frolicsome skip and wing movements of the native companions is one of the typical dances of the aboriginals frequenting open plains where the great birds assemble. In its performance the men—decorated with streaks and daubs of white and pink clay, and wearing in their hair down and feathers—form a circle, and, bowing their bodies towards the centre, chuckle in undertones to the pianissimo tapping of boomerangs and the beating of resonant logs. In strict time, to a crescendo accompaniment, the performers throw out their arms, extend their necks downward and upward, simultaneously utter squawks in imitation of the bird, and finally whirl about, flapping their arms, ceasing instantly, by a common impulse. The ballet is modelled in accordance with a study of nature.

The corroboree of the Princess Charlotte Bay boys also owes its origin to nature, but nature in one of her most unpoetical moods—a mood as typical of Constantinople as of their native shores, for its motif is nothing more than an everyday dog-fight.

Shall the uncultured blacks not have their own way when they seek entertainment, holding "as it were the mirror up to nature", and finding that it reflects the commonest of all themes? They among all the nations of the world alone have discovered what to them is music and the poetry of motion in an occurrence that has no geographical limitations, is not restricted by language, and is not to be withered by age.

While the orchestra taps its boomerangs and claps its hands and grunts, two boys in mere nature progress towards the fire in a series of stiff, stilty jumps, the legs from the hips to the ankles being rigid; then the knees shake in a rapid succession of spasmodic jerks; the actors emit sounds resembling the preliminary growling and snarling of a couple of angry dogs. Action and utterance develop in speed and time as the fight begins in earnest, and the art of the performance consists in its duration—the powers of sustained effort, the accuracy of time maintained between the orchestra and the actors, and the fidelity to nature of the vocal effects. A singularly uncouth subject for an opera or even a ballet—the snarling, scuffling and snapping of quarrelsome dogs whose fury is working up to a climax, and it soon becomes as monotonous to unaccustomed ears as the masterpieces of some German composers to those whose musical education is below the required standard; but the boys will spend the best part of the long night in its unvarying repetition.

187

Once a variation did take place. "Yellowbelly" (pronounced decently "Yellowby") danced first in the company of giggling "Peter"; and then fat "Charley" and big "Johnny", shy "Mammeroo" and little deaf "Antony", in turns, his body glistened with perspiration, and his eyes sparkled with the joy of a phenomenal accomplishment. All beholders were filled with wonder and gratification. It was Yellowby's night out. The spirit of Terpsichore was upon him. His enthusiasm amounted to exultation. He was astonishing not only the silent and subdued natives of Dunk Island, but even his own familiar friends. Never had any seen such a classic interpretation of the theme, such brilliant leg movement, nor heard such realistic growling and snapping and intermittent yelps, such muffled, sob-like inspirations. Yellowby danced as dances the artist, so graphically interpreting the subject that the bewildered orchestra forgot itself. All were borne away in spirit to the scene of some far-off, familiar camp, where the scents of decayed fish and turtle-bones, and of a multitude of uncleanly dogs commingled with the bitter smoke of mangrove wood fires, where amid the yells of gins and the screeches of piccaninnies and the walloping of men, two mangy curs noisily wrestled. It brought home sweet home to each of the exiles, so vividly that all sat still and transfixed; and as the last chord of the orchestra "trembled away into silence", Yellowby, panting and sweating, gasped as he fell flat on the sand—"No good you fella corroboree like that fella, belonga me fella." But for the collapse of the orchestra, due to his own inimitable art, he would have danced till dawn.

A SONG WITHOUT WORDS

Mickie is a famous vocalist, although his repertoire is limited. He sings lustily and with no little art, putting considerable expression into his phrases, and ever and anon taking a sharp but studied rest to increase his emphasis, when he will burst forth again with full-throated ease. His masterpiece is not original. Indeed, he claims no title to the gifts of a composer. "Jacky", a Mackay boy, taught Mickie his favourite romance, and it came to Jacky in a dream. Mickie explains—"Cousin alonga that fella die. Jacky go to sleep. That fella dead man all a same like debil-debil—come close up and tell 'em corroboree close up ear belonga Jacky."

"What that debil-debil say?"

Mickie—"No talk—that fella. Just tell 'em corroboree. No talk."

It was just a song without words—the final phrases being three gutteral gasps, diluendo, which Mickie says represent the wail of the "debil-debil" as he retires into the obscurity of spirit-land.

Mickie sings this song of inspiration most vigorously when Jinny, his portly spouse, comes to "wash 'em plate" in the evening, and she explains with a fat chuckle—"Mickie corroboree loud fella. He fright. He think subpose he corroboree blenty debil-debil no come up!"

ORIGIN OF THE SOUTHERN CROSS

Blacks are students of natural events. The winds have their specific titles, they catalogue all the brighter and more conspicuous stars and planets, and their astronomical legends are quaint and entertaining.

According to Mickie, the Southern Cross is of earthly origin. He thus "repeats the story of its birth":

"You see that fella. That one me call 'em dooey-dooey—all a same shubel-nose shark, like that fella you bin shoot longa lagoon. Two fella, more big, come close up behind dooey-dooey, two fella black boy. Black boys bin fishing alonga reef close up alonga where red mark, alonga Cape Marlow—you know. They bin sit down alonga canoe. Bi'mby spear 'em that dooey-dooey—beeg fella, my word! That dooey-dooey when catch 'em spear he go down quick, come up under canoe capsize 'em. Two fella boy swim about long time by that reef; no catch 'em that canoe. Swim; swim l-o-n-g way; no catch 'em beach; go outside; follow canoe all time. One fella say—'Brother, where we now?' 'Long way yet. Swim more far, brother.' Bi'mby two fella talk—'Where now, brother?' 'Long way outside. Magnetic close up now. We two fella swim more long way.' Bi'mby catch 'em Barrier. One fella catch 'em hand—'Come along, brother, youn-me go outside.'

"Two fella boy swim-swim-swim. Go outside altogether; leave 'em Barrier behind. Swim; finish; good-bye; no come back! Swim where cloud catch 'em sea. Swim up-up-long way up! You see now. Sit down up there altogether. Dooey-dooey first time; two fella boy come behind!"

Does not this stand comparison with that referred to by the *Scientific American* in answering the question, "Why do you refer to the Great Bear as feminine?" We must go back into the age of classical mythology for the reason. It was known to the Egyptians, who called it hippopotamus. The people of southern Europe saw in the same stars the more familiar figure of a bear, and the legends which grew up around it were finally given permanent shape by Ovid in his *Metamorphoses*. As he tells the story, Callisto, an Arcadian nymph, was beloved by Jupiter. Juno, in fierce anger, turned her into a bear, depriving her of speech that she might not appeal to Jupiter. Her son, Arcas, while hunting, came upon her, and failing to recognize her in her metamorphosed form, raised his bow to shoot. Jupiter, moved by pity, prevented the matricide by transforming the son into a bear, and took them both up to the heavens, where they were placed among the con-stellations.

SUICIDE BY CROCODILE

It has been said that Australian blacks never commit suicide. An instance which goes in proof of the contrary occurred not many months ago. All the creeks and rivers flowing from the coastal range to the sea are more or less infested with crocodiles. In crossing creeks, blacks take every precaution against surprise, rafts of buoyant logs strapped together with lawyer-vine being used. These rafts are continually drifting across to the island, proving how general is their use. Maria Creek (about a dozen miles or so up the coast) is well known to be a popular resort of the crocodile, and at the mouth, where the blacks wade at low-water, an un-usually big fellow had his headquearters. A member of the Clump Point tribe, painfully afflicted with a vexatious skin disease, was fishing at the mouth of the creek when his hook fouled. To a com-panion he said he would dive to get it clear. His friend endeavoured to dissuade him, reminding him of the crocodile which they had seen but a short time before. But the boy, worn with pain and weary with never-ending irritation, said if he was taken—"No matter. Good job. Me finished then." He dived, and there was a commotion in the water. The boy appeared on the surface, making frantic appeals for help, while the crocodile worried him. He escaped for a moment, and his friend clutched his hand and drew him to the bank, only to have him torn from his grasp. The blacks believe the crocodile took the fish bait in the first instance, and lured the boy to dive. The boy certainly knew the risk he ran when he did so.

A new, if not altogether agreeable, sensation is added to the gentle art if it is realized that a cruel and stealthy beast is engaged in a similar pastime, with the fisherman as the object of its sport.

DISAPPEARANCE OF BLACKS

The rapid disappearance of blacks from localities which held a considerable population causes wonder. In the early days—less than a couple of decades past—they swarmed on the mainland opposite Dunk Island. Now the numbers are few. Within sight of Brammo Bay is the scene of an official "dispersal" of those alleged to have been responsible for the murder of some of the crew of a wrecked vessel, who had drifted ashore on a raft. One boy bears to this day the mark of a bullet on his cheek, received when his mother fled for her life, and vainly, with him an infant perched on her shoulders.

In those days "troublesome" blacks were disposed of with scant ceremony. An incident has been repeated to me several times. A mob of "myalls" (wild blacks)—they were all myalls then—was employed by a selector to clear the jungle from his land. They worked, but did not get the anticipated recompense, and thereupon helped themselves, spearing and eating a bullock, and disappeared. After a time the selector professed forgiveness, and, the fears of the blacks of punishment having been allayed, set them to work again. One day a bucket of milk was brought to the camp at diner-time and served out with pannikins. The milk had been poisoned.

"One fella feel 'em here," said my informant, clasping his stomach. "Run away; tumble down; finish. 'Nother boy run away; finish. Just now plenty dead everywhere. Some fella sing out all a same bullocky."

Possibly this may be greeted as another version of the familiar story of poisoned flour or damper. It is mentioned here as an instance from the bad old days when both blacks and whites were offhand in their relations with each other. Such episodes are of the past. The present is the age of official protection, with perhaps a trifle too much interference and meddlesomeness.

Two blacks of the district confessed upon their trial that they had killed their master for so slight an offence as refusal to give them part of his own dinner of meat. On the other hand, an instance of a callousness of the white man may be cited. In a fit of the sulks one of the boys of the camp threw down some blankets he was carrying, and made off into the scrub. It was considered necessary to impress the others, and unhappy chance gave the opportunity. A strange and perfectly innocent boy appeared on the opposite bank of the creek. The "boss" was a noted shot, and as the boy sauntered along he deliberately fired at him. The body fell into the water and drifted down stream. One of the boys for whose discipline the wanton murder was committed related the incident to me.

CHAPTER II

GEORGE: A MIXED CHARACTER

GEORGE, who considered himself as accomplished and as cultivated as a white man, was assisting his master in the building of a dinghy. Contemplating the work of his unaccustomed hands in a rueful frame of mind, the boss recited, "Thou fatal and perfidious barque, built in eclipse and rigged with curses dark!" "Ah," said he, "you bin hear that before, George?" "No," replied the boy; "I no bin hear 'em. What that? Irish talk?"

A few days after, George peered into one of the rooms of the house, the walls of which were decorated with prints, among them some studies of the nude. He sniggered. "What you laugh at, George?" "Me laugh along that picture—naked. That French woman, I think, Boss!" He was evidently of opinion that all true and patriotic Irishmen talk in verse, and in throaty tones, and that the customary habit of French ladies is "the altogether".

Proud of his personal appearance, George shaved regularly once a week, borrowing a mirror to assist in the operation. He was wont to apply the lather from pungent kerosene soap with a discarded tooth-brush which he had picked up. Long use had thinned the bristles, woefully, but the brush was used faithfully and with grave deliberation. One morning he came and said—"Boss, you got any more brush belonga shaving? This fella close up lose 'em whisker altogether."

The sensational episodes of his trooper days provided George with unending themes. He gave an account to a friend of the suppression of a black rogue, a faithful report of which is presented as an example of unbowdlerized pidgin-English.

George—"You bin hear about Mr Limsee have fight? My word, he fight proper; close up killed. We three fella ride about. Cap'n —big strong boy that—me and Mr Limsee. Wild boy—boy from outside; myall—beggar that fella—longa gully. Hit Mr Limsee. He bin have long fella stick, like that one Tom take a longa fight —short handle. Heavy fella that—carn lif'em easy, one hand. Mr Limsee tumble down. Get up. That boy kill 'em one time more hard. My word, strong fella boy that. Catch 'em Mr Limsee—tchuk longa ground, hard fella—like that. Me and Cap'n come. Mr Limsee alonga ground yet—'Hello! Mr Limsee, you bin hurt?' 'Yes, my boy! hurt plenty. Not much; only little bit. That fella hit me alonga sword. You catch that fella. Hold 'em.' Me and Cap'n say—'You no run away, you boy.' 'Me no fright.' He have 'em spear. Me tell 'em—'You no run away. Me catch you.' He say —'Me no fright, you fella.' Me say—'You no run away. I shoot you.' He say all a time—'Me no fright. Me fight you.' Me say— 'You fool, you carn fight alonga this fella bullet. He catch you blurry quick.' That fella stop one place. We two fella go up alongside. Cap'n he say—'Hold up your hand. Le' me look your hand?' He hold up hand. Quick we put 'em han'cup. That fella no savee han'cup before. He bin sing out loud—loud like anything. We two fella laugh plenty. Mr Limsee tie 'em up hand longa tree, and belt him proper. Belt him plenty longa whip. My word, that fella sing out—sing out—sing out. Mr Limsee belt him more. All time he sing out. Bi'mby let 'em go. He bad fella boy that alto-gether. We fella—go home along camp. Mr Limsee feel 'em sore tchoulder. Nex' day that boy—very tchausey fella—come up along camp. He say—'Me want fight that fella Cap'n.' Cap'n come up. That fella catch 'em. Cap'n tchuk him hard alonga ground. Get up; tchuk him two time. Head go close up alonga stone. Two fella wrastle all about long time. Cap'n strong fella. That boy more strong. Knock 'em about like anything. Bi'mby come back he have spear—three wire spear—long handle. Tchuk 'em spear. Catch 'em Cap'n longa side, Cap'n 'e hurt longa inside, hurt bad. Cap'n 'e carn stay—tumble down. Good boy that; my mate long time. Some fella go alonga house tell 'em Mr Limsee—'That boy bin kill you, fight long a camp. Cap'n catch 'em spear longa inside.' Mr Limsee come down. He say—'Cap'n, my boy, I think you finish now; me very sorry for you.' Bad place for spear longa side. Hollow inside. Suppose spear go along a leg and arm, no matter. Suppose go inside, hollow place inside, you finish quick. Plenty times me bin see 'em man finish that way. Mr Limsee he very sorry. We catch that boy. Put han'cup behind, lika that way. My word he carn run away now. Chain alonga leg. Mr Limsee bi'mby send 'em down Cooktown. That fella no more come back. He go along Sen'eleena (St Helena penal establishment). Me bin think he bin get two years. Cap'n he carn stay. Two days that fella dead.

He bin good mate, me sorry. Mr. Limsee he very sorry. Good fella longa boy."

Once George illuminated his conversation with an aphorism. Describing a battle between the Tully River blacks and those of Clump Point, in which his mate, Tom of Dunk Island (leader of the Clump Point party), had been severely wounded, he said—
" 'Nother fella boy, from outside, come up behind Tom. He no look out that way. That boy tchuk 'em boomerang. Boomerang stick in leg belonga Tom. Tom no feel 'em first time. He stan' up yet. Bi'mby when want walk about, tumble down. Look out. Hello! see 'em boomerang alonga leg. He no more can walk about."

The boss remarked—"Might be long time, Tom feel 'em leg sore."

George—"Ah! me like see 'em kill alonga head. Finish 'em one time. Danger nebber dead." Whether George wished to enforce the opinion that in battle nothing short of death was glorious, or that Tom though wounded was still valorous and would live to fight again, was not clear, but "Danger nebber dead", probably represents the only aboriginal aphorism extant.

George is not in the least superstitious. He takes everything for granted. Rain, in his opinion, comes from a big tank up above somewhere. Asked as to his belief in the personal "debil-debil", of whom the mainland boys have such dread that few will stir out after dark, he said with a guffaw—

"Me nebber bin see one yet. Suppose me see 'em, me run 'em!"

George is, therefore, as yet unable to give a description of the fiend; but from hearsay authority declares that it possesses three eyes, two in the ordinary position, and one at the back of the head. It is believed that the third eye insures the "debil-debil" against all possible surprises, thus preserving the mystery of identity.

Though he has not a shadow of respect for the "debil-debil", George has a firm faith in the existence in the neighbourhood of Cooktown of a camp of what he calls "groun' gins". His experience with these mysterious subterranean sirens he thus describes—

"Little bit outside Cooktown camp belonga groun' gins. Me and Sargen' go look big corroboree; my word. Some gins come out alonga groun' from hole. When go down, groun' close up himself, like winda. My word, me fright. Me shake. One good fella nicc gin come up. Sargen' says—'You go corroboree dance along that fella.' Me say—'We go home now, me fright. We want go alonga town. This no good place.' Sargen' laugh little bit. He say—'No, my boy, you no fright. All right here. You dance alonga that fella gin—good nice gin.' Me go up. Me feel 'em fright. Feel 'em cold inside. Too much fright. My word; han' belonga that fella gin—cold like anything. That gin say—'Where you from?' Me say—'Me come from alonga town.' That gin say —'What you look out?' Me say—'Me look out bullocky, musser 'em cattle. Tail 'em up. Look out weaner alonga paddick. Plenty hard work.' Me dance little bit alonga that gin. Not much. Too fright. Bi'mby that gin go down below. Groun' shut 'em up. All day down below. Come up night time. Carn come up alonga sun. Soft fella that. Suppose come up alonga sun, sun kill 'em. Too soft altogether."

George was not pressed to display his accomplishments. He chose during many months to hold himself in reserve, and to live up to the reputation of being quite a scholar, as far as scholarship goes among blacks. But in accordance with expectations, his pride and enthusiasm got the better of him. He produced two scraps of paper, on each of which was a number of sinuous lines and scrawls, saying—

"You write all asame this kind?"

"No," I said, "I no write like that."

"This easy fella? All the time me write this kind."

"Well, what you write?"

George's attention at once became concentrated, and gazing steadfastly on the paper for a minute or so for the marshalling of his wits, he said—

"This fella say Coleman Riber, Coen Riber? Horse Dead Creek, Massac (Massacre) Riber, Big Morehead, Kennedy Riber, Laura Riber."

These are the names of some of the streams north from Cooktown, George's country. On the other scrap of paper, according to him, the names of some of the islands in this neighbourhood were written. Though the papers were transposed and turned upside down, George could read them with equal facility. The list of rivers would be read for the islands, and the islands for the rivers, quite indifferently, and with entertaining naivete. But he treasured the papers, and continued to delude his fellows with the display of what they considered to be wonderful cleverness.

YAB-OO-RAGOO, OTHERWISE "MICKIE"

He said that his name was Mickie, and that he was an Irishman, and a native of the great Palm Island—forty miles south. He hath no personal comeliness—his face is his great misfortune. Though he asserts with pride his nationality, he admits that his mother, now among the stars, "sat down alonga 'nother side", and his complexion, or rather what is seen of it through an artless layer of charcoal and grease, applied out of respect to the memory of his deceased brother-in-law, shows no Celtic trace. Yet he has a keen appreciation of fun, has ready wit, and, according to his own showing, is not averse to a shindy, so that, perhaps his given name is at least characteristic of his assumed race.

A flat overhanging forehead, keen black eyes, a broad-rooted, unobtrusive nose, a most capacious mouth, beard and whiskers thin and unkempt, and a fierce-looking moustache, a head of hair which in boyhood days had probably been a mass of crisp curls, but now shaggy tufts, matted and uneven, altogether a shockingly repulsive physiognomy, and yet an "honest Injin" in every respect, and one who would always look on the happy side of life, but for twinges of neuralgia—"monda" he calls it—which rack his head and face with pain.

Mickie is very proud of his well-conditioned spouse, "Jinny"— "Missus Michael", as Mickie calls her when in the sportive vein— and Jinny, or "Penti-byer", her maiden name, reciprocates the regard, and sees that the dilly-bag, which does duty for the larder, is supplied with yams, nuts, roots and shell-fish, Mickie being responsible for the fish—speared in the lagoon at low tide—and the scrub-fowl eggs, and the ivory white grubs, etc., upon which they live when there is no "white fella" sitting down. When providence sends a "white fella", they appreciate flour, tea, sugar, potatoes, meat, and all sorts of game, from cockatoos to flying-foxes.

Once Mickie was asked how he managed to win the favour of such a fine gin. "Unkl belonga her giv 'em me," he replied. There was no marriage ceremony. There was no knocking out of a tooth, or the administration of a stunning blow on the head with a nulla-nulla, no eating of maize-pudding from the same plate, no drinking brandy together, no "hand fasting", nor boring of the bride's ears by the bridegroom, no tying of hands, nor smearing with each other's blood, nor binding together with ropes of grass; simply, "Unkl belonga her giv 'em me".

Once in possession, however, Mickie proceeded to set his mark on his bride, so that should any dispute arise as to identity, he at least would have authentic brands. With an apparently studied array of cicatrices, each three inches long and half an inch wide, on her arms and shoulders, Mickie marked Jinny for his own.

The couple have one girl—Mickie prefers to use the word "daw-tah"—and his child had been but lately received into the bosom of the family, after several years' exile among the whites. It is somewhat of a trouble that Minnie had almost forgotten her native tongue, and that her parents have to yabber to her in English. According to them it will be a year before Minnie regains lingual facility. In the meantime great pains are being taken with her education, and her accomplishments promise to be varied, though entirely unornamental. She will in time be able to recognize at a glance the particular kind of decayed timber in which the delicious white grub resides, will know that the nut of the cycad has to be immersed in a running stream before it is "good fella", and how to grind the kernel into flour, and how to mould the dough into a German sausage-shaped damper; she will be able to walk about the reef, picking up black-lip oysters and clams, without lacerating the soles of her feet, and to make a dilly-bag, and, finally, to enjoy a smoke.

Mickie appreciates a joke. When Jinny complained that the scrub had caught her brand-new pipe and broken it short off, Mickie, with an extravagant grimace, softly urged her to go along Townsville and buy another.

He is also superstitious. After dark he will not move a yard from his camp without a flaring torch of paper bark, a fiery aspersorium for the scaring of the "debil-debil". His opinions on the supernatural are unsatisfactory. He does not know what the "debil-debil" is like, or what form the ill-will of that mystic being would take—nothing but "that fella sit down alonga scrub", and that he has "long fella needle alonga hand"; and so he carries and waves about his paperbark torch to scare this viewless and dreaded enemy.

Mickie's views as to the future are not quite explicit. "Suppose me go bung, me go alonga sky. Bi'mby jump up 'nother fella." He is not at all certain whether the transformation would be into a white man or not; in fact, he appears absolutely indifferent. Another time he will say: "Suppose me go bung. Good-bye, finish; no come back. Plenty fella alonga Palm Island go bung. He no come back."

Daylight disperses all his fears. In point of fact he has nothing to fear. His foes are dead, and there is no poisonous snake or offensive animal on the Palms. Once he sprang suddenly and excitedly into the air as we tramped through the long grass on the edge of the sweetly-smelling jungle, with the exclamation, "Little fella snake!" Being reminded that he had boldly asserted that there was no bad snake on the island, Mickie replied: "That fella no bad. Only mak'em foot big!" He never missed a chance of securing a hatful of grubs, which, together with the chrysalids and the full-grown beetle (brown and glossy) were devoured after being warmed through on the ashes. When the tomahawk in the process of cutting out damaged a grub, Mickie with a leer of satisfaction would eat the wriggling insect with a feigned apology, "Me bin cut that fella". Baked in the ashes the chrysalids have a wholesome, clean appearance, with a flavour of coconut, and the "white fella" always came in for his share.

Mickie's bush-craft, his knowledge of the habits of birds and insects and the ways of fish, is enviable. Signs and sounds quite indeterminate to "white fellas" are full of meaning to him. Of course, by failure to comprehend such things, no doubt he has many a time gone hungry, and the keenness of his appetite has so sharpened his perceptions that he is seldom at fault now. The scratching of a scrub fowl among decayed leaves is heard in the jungle at an extraordinary distance, and a splash or ripple far out on the edge of the reef tells him that a shark or kingfish is driving the mullet into the lagoon, where he may easily spear them. He can tell to a quarter of an hour when the fish will leave off biting; he hears the scamper of the iguana in the grass when the "white fella" fails to catch a sound, and knows when the giant crabs will be "walking about" in the mangroves. He is trustworthy and obliging, and ready to impart all the lore he possesses, an expert boomerang thrower, a dead shot with a nulla-nulla, and an eater of everything that comes in his way except "pigee-pigee".

Having long had the pleasure of his acquaintance, I can cordially wish him a never-failing supply of "patter" and tobacco, and surcease of "monda"; and what more can the heart of a blackfellow desire—save rum?

Tom has been thrice married—at least he has possessed three wives. For a few months he had two at a time, and placidly endured the consequences.

Of the bride of his youth history has no word—for Tom is the only historian of that period, and he ever bears sorrows in silence.

Nelly, whose country borders the beach of the mainland opposite, could not speak his language when he fought for her fairly and honourably, and won her from her first man. Though reared but a little over two miles apart, these twain have totally different words for the same objects. During married life each has added to the vocabulary of the other.

When we took possession of the island, Nelly would glide into the jungle like a frightened snake and hide for days. She was wild, suspicious, uncleanly, uncouth—a combination of all the shortcomings of the savage. Now she lights the fire every morning, kneads the bread, makes the porridge and the coffee, feeds the fowls, washes plates and clothes, scrubs floors, and generally does the work of a domestic. She is cheerfully industrious, emphatic in her admiration of pictures, and smokes continuously, preferring a pipe ornamented with "lead", for she has all the woman's love of show. From the most quarrelsome and vixenish gin of the camp she has been transformed into a decent-minded peacemaker— always ready to atone for the misbehaviour of others, and to display without a trace of self-glorification the virtue of self-sacrifice. Nelly is never happier than when working about the house, except when she saunters off on a Sunday morning, in the glare of a new dress, and with the smoke curling from her ornamented pipe, beneath a hat which, in variety of tints, shames the sunset sky.

Students of ethnology who may scan these lines may find food for reflection in the fact that Tom and Nelly offer exceptions to the rules that the totems of Australian blacks generally refer to food, and that those whose totems are alike do not marry. Tom's totemic title, "Kitalbarra", is derived from a splitter of a rock off an islet to the south-east of Dunk Island. "Ooongle-bi", Nelly's affinity, is a rock on the summit of a hill on the mainland, not far from her birthplace. The plea of the rocks was not raised as any just cause or impediment to the match when Tom by force of arms espoused Nelly. "Jimmy", Tom and Nelly's son, born in civilization, bears a second name, that of a deceased uncle, "Toola-un-guy", the totemic rendering of which is now unknown. Another "Jimmy", a native of Hinchinbrook, is differentiated by "Yaeki-muggie", the title of the sand-spit of one of the Brook Islands.

The confusion of tongues between Tom and Nelly may be briefly illustrated:

	TOM ("Kitalbarra")	NELLY ("Ooongle-bi")
Sun	Wee-yee	Car-rie
Moon	Yil-can	Car-cal-oon
Sky	Aln-pun	Moogah-car-boon
Mainland	Yungl-man	Mung-un
Island	Cul-qua-yah	Moan-mitte
Sea	Mutta	Yoo-moo
Fire	Wam-pui	Poon-nee
Water	Cam-moo	Pan-nahr
Rain	Yukan	Yukan
Man	Mah-al	Yer-rah
Woman	Rit-tee	Ee-bee
Baby	Eee-bee	Koo-jal
Head	Poo-you	Oom-poo
Foot	Pin-kin	Chin-nah
Leg	Waka	Too-joo
Hand	Man-dee	Mul-lah
Fish	Tar-boo	Kooyah
Bird	Poong-an	Toon-doo

The big-eyed walking fish of the mangroves, which the learned have named *Periophthalmus koelreuteri*, Tom knows as "manning-tsang", and Nelly as "mourn".

During one of his bachelordom interludes a smart young gin known as "Dolly" attracted Tom's fancy. He had just "signed on" for a six-months' cruise with the master of a bêche-de-mer schooner. Dolly smiled so sweetly upon Tom that Charley, her boy, raged furiously. Tom—never demonstrative, always cool and deep —obtaining an advance from his captain, bought, among a few other attractive trifles, an extremely gaudy dress, and having art-lessly displayed the finery, took it all on board the schooner, which was to sail the following morning at daylight.

During the evening Dolly strolled casually from the camp and the society of the fuming Charley, and disappeared. Tom had quite a trousseau, new and bright, for his sweetheart, when she clambered on board, naked, wet, and with shining eyes. Next morning Charley tracked her along the beach. An old and soiled dress—his gift—on a little promontory of rocks about a mile from the anchorage of the schooner completed the love-story.

This intrigue took place many years ago, but Charley was so deeply mortified that he hates Tom to this day—and Tom is an uncomfortable fellow for anyone disposed to resentfulness.

We know, because he says so, that Tom fought for her, and that Nelly gladly accepted the protection of the staunchest man of the district. Tom, in his surly moments, is exquisitely cruel; but Nelly's devotion is unaffected. Her vanity led her to flaunt her gaudy hat in the hut. Tom reproved such flashness—he invariably selects the gayest shirts himself—by burning the hat and all the newly-acquired finery. Nelly struck back, and Tom, as her eyes were big and ablaze with fury, threw—at the cost of burnt fingers —a handful of hot sand and ashes into her face. From Tom's point of view it was a splendid feat—one of those bold and effective master-strokes that only a ready and determined sportsman could conceive and on the instant carry into effect. Nelly's eyes were closed for weeks—wellnigh for ever—and the skin peeled off her face; but she consented to the cruel punishment without a murmur after the first shriek of agony, and won Tom to good temper and tolerance of her vanity by all sorts of happy concessions.

How many such tiffs—tough and smart—has poor Nelly borne? Her grief has been so sore that she has torn her hair out by the roots in frenzy and stamped upon it; but Tom, surly and impassive Tom, is her lord as well as her most exacting master, and in their own way they are devoted to one another.

The roughest cross Nelly was called upon to bear was the presence of Tom's third wife—"Little Jinny"—the manner of whose wooing and home-coming is to be told.

News came from Lucinda Point to Clump Point—passed from one to another—that Tom's half-brother (a purely fictional relationship) had died, leaving a young widow. According to Tom's rendering of the matrimonial laws, he was the rightful heir. The widow was all that his half-brother had left that was of the slightest consequence.

Tom, telling the circumstances, asked for a holiday that he might personally lay claim to his inheritance. Reminded that he had one wife, he frankly declared in Nelly's presence, and she seemed to acquiesce, that she was no good; but that the other one was a "good fella" in every respect, even to washing plates and scrubbing floors.

His holiday was granted. He went away with money in his pockets, blankets, several changes of raiment—among them Nelly's best dress and hat, dilly-bags brightly coloured, and weapons—boomerang, two black palm spears, a great wooden sword, a shield decorated with a complicated pattern in red and white earth, and a flashing new tomahawk.

So he departed, with Nelly's best wishes, and full of hope and expectation, promising to return in two weeks.

Two months slipped past, and one evening a forlorn, ragged, lean scarecrow of a black boy—without a hat, unshaven, without a blanket, and even destitute of a pipe, clambered over the side of the steamer, and dropped into the boat without a word. It was Tom!

In shreds and patches the history of his experience was related. He had arrived at Lucinda, had charmed Little Jinny with his manly presence and spruceness and the amount of his personal property, supplemented by the display and free bestowal of Nelly's choicest finery, and had, as a matter of course, been compelled to fight for her. He had been beaten, terribly beaten. One ear had been viciously "marked", a triangular slice being missing (a subsequent combat removed all trace of this mark), and he showed the meritorious scar of a spear-wound on the arm.

Having failed in the stand-up fight, he had resorted to stratagem, had been foiled, and was forced to flee, abandoning everything, even to that last vestige of independence—his pipe.

We knew that he had been hard pressed, for on going gaily away he had volunteered to bring a fat young pig from one of the wild herds of Hinchinbrook, and he came back empty-handed. He talks of the pig—how fat and very young it was—even to this day. He came with his life—that was all, and a threadbare sort of life it was at that.

Several months went by—a black boy recovers condition in a day or two as does a starved dog—and Tom had saved money. He never forgets, never swerves from a purpose. He is as determined as a dung-beetle.

Another leave of absence was granted. A second raid was made upon Nelly's wardrobe—two big bailer shells. Elated, freshly shaved and smiling, he was a different sort from the individual who had shame-facedly slipped over the side of the steamer, bereft of everything but life.

He said he would be back in two weeks, and to the day he appeared. His youthful third wife he handed down into the boat, and the boat was full of their luggage. Ah, that desolated camp at Lucinda! The young lady's trousseau was complete even to lingerie. He had won the fight, and the bride and the spoils were his.

Poor Nelly. She welcomed Little Jinny effusively, and Little Jinny gave her a dress and a second-best hat. Life for a couple of days at the camp was idyllic. Then they took back the gifts of clothing, and turned Nelly out of the hut. She built a separate establishment—a dome of dried grass on bent sticks, and in it she wept and upbraided, and fired up frequently under the torments of jealousy.

Shrill squabbles were of daily occurrence, until the great Peacemaker removed Tom's favourite wife. And who more sorely grieved than Nelly!

Will the title bear a few words as to Tom the hunter? Was ever a keener, a more patient, a more self-possessed, and consequently a more successful, sportsman? He it was who, from a cranky punt (no white man would venture out to sea in such a craft), at three o'clock one windy afternoon, harpooned an immense bull-turtle, which towed him towards the Barrier Reef, into the track of the big steamers four miles to the east. He battled with the game all the afternoon and evening, overcame it at "the dead waste and middle of the night", and towed it back to the beach, landing after thirteen hours' continuous work. Tom accomplished the feat in a strong breeze and with a turtle diving and tugging, when he might have cut the line at any moment and paddled home comfortably.

He is as much at home on the top of a bloodwood tree, hanging round a swaying limb while cutting out a "bee nest", as in a frail bark canoe among the sharks on the skirts of a shoal of bonito.

As we neared the beach one day a big sea-mullet came into view. Without a moment's hesitation, and as it flashed past the boat, Tom, using the oar as a spear, hit the slippery fish with such precision and force as to impale it. He will harpoon a turtle as it rushes away from the boat, five feet beneath the surface, with the coolness of a billiard-player, and with unerring accuracy "taking off" for the speed of the boat and the refraction of the water. All the ways and habits of fish, and their favourite feeding-grounds, are to him as pages of an open book.

A groper, more voracious and bolder than usual, followed a safely-hooked perch from the dim coral garden, worrying it like a bull-dog. As the struggling fish splashed on the surface the groper, abandoning its illegitimate prey, swerved swiftly downwards. The retreat was a second too late, for Tom had seized the harpoon lying athwart the boat, and though the fish appeared through a fathom and a half of water, a vague, fleeting, contorted shadow, he reached it. The barbed point passed through it, carrying a foot or two of the line, and a thirty-pounder was added to our catch at one stroke and without a tremor of excitement on Tom's part.

He sailed his punt—twelve feet long and four feet wide—six miles, loaded with eight adults, eight piccaninnies, five dogs, a cat, blankets for the crowd, and all the frowsy miscellanea of a black's camp. It was not a boatload that landed on the beach; it was a procession. But Tom would go to sea on a chip. His skill as a sailor of small boats is largely a manifestation of characteristic caution, his precept being—"Suppose big seas come one, one—all right. Subpose come two, two—look out!"

"LITTLE JINNY": IN LIFE AND IN DEATH

She was called "Little Jinny" to distinguish her from another of the blacks about the place—a great, good-natured, giggling creature who laughs perpetually and grows ever fatter. There was nothing in common between the two. Indeed they frequently had differences, for Jinny proper is industrious, obliging, cheerful, and full of fun, while she, Little Jinny, was silent, sulky, and ever averse from toil.

Tom, her man, alternately petted and beat her. She, no doubt, deserved both, for she was proud and haughty for a black gin, and as venomous at times as a scorpion. His hand is heavy, and when he lifted it in anger poor Little Jinny suffered—but suffered in silence. Her chastisements were not frequent, but they seemed to increase her loyalty towards her lord and master.

From a European standpoint, Little Jinny had little of which to be vain. She had a fuzzy head of hair. Some, like fur, crept down across her brows, giving her face a singularly unbecoming cast. I did not notice this peculiar uncomeliness until she was dying, and I felt then more than ever that she was not to be judged in accordance with our standard of beauty—though she had many of our little weaknesses. Her ignorance of civilized ways was pathetic, yet she was vain and coquettish as the fairest of her sex. And her besetting vanity was endeavouring to be a "lady". Work was sordid, for she wore garments which made her the leader of fashion. She possessed a pair of—well, a bifurcated garment—and her whole life was spent in trying to live up to it—or them. She succeeded to a certain extent. Her ways were mincing and precise, and she lazed away her days quite artistically. A can of water was too heavy for her to carry, less than two hours "spell" at a time quite an offence to her ideal of the amount of repose that a lady wearing the bifurcated garment should permit herself. She was wont to sit in the shade of the mango-tree and pretend to do a little gardening. It was all pretence. What she really loved to do was to wander among the bloodwoods—with Tom, of course—with next to nothing on, the next to nothing being the drawers. There, you have them. Then you saw her at her best—or rather worst, for she was a thin sapling of a girl, of a dull coppery colour, and the garment was not always snowy-white.

Hers, after all, was an ideal existence. She had plenty to eat, as much tobacco as was good for her, and outer raiment that in gaudiness outrivalled the flame-tree and the yellow hibiscus. She was the favourite of two consorts, and only when her pride and scorpion-like attributes got the better of her was she corrected.

Just the other morning, Tom announced that Little Jinny was sick "along a bingey" (stomach), and suggested that salt medicine might do her good. It was quite a common occurrence for her to be sick. It was such an easy and excellent excuse for a day's holiday, when she would bask on the soft grey sand and smoke, gazing across the placid bay and waiting for meal-times. So no one took her sickness seriously. Subsequent inquiries, however, elicited the fact that Little Jinny had eaten little or no tucker the day prior to Tom's application for medicine on her behalf, and that she was really entitled to sympathy of the most practical kind. But no one had the least suspicion of the fact. Dinner-time came and she did not appear, though she was strolling about the flat below the house, apparently only a "little bit sick", as Tom reported when he came up to his work.

"That one all right to-morrow," was the reply to an inquiry.

But at five o'clock Tom visited his hut, and hurried back for medicine. Little Jinny was bad. We went down with remedies that seemed fit from his diagnosis of the case and description of the symptoms, and there lay Little Jinny, obviously dying. She had never complained nor whimpered when Tom's heavy hand had corrected her, though the dried trickle of blood had been seen on her forehead, and now that she lay a-dying, with her figure strangely swollen, she moaned only when Tom, with his heavy hand, sought to squeeze out the dead man, "all the same like debil-debil", who was, according to him, the cause of the trouble.

But it was all too implacable and crafty a "debil-debil" for Tom to cast out. We did our best with brandy and steaming flannels; but it was all so useless, for none understood the sickness, or how to prescribe a remedy that might be effective. Our helplessness was grievous. We could only repeat the sips of brandy and water, and endeavour to warm the chilly little body with steamy flannels.

All did something. Even Nelly, the second best wife, who had had to play a very subordinate part in the camp, and whom Little Jinny had slapped and had abused with all the volubility of spite and temper, crouched beside her dying rival, chafing her cold hands and warming her cheeks.

And here was the most touching incident of the pathetic scene. We had brandy and blankets and flannels wherewith to endeavour to afford relief. Poor Nelly had nothing. Her poverty was grim, but she had some resource. She had no means of alleviating the suffering save those which spendthrift nature provided—the smooth oily leaf of the "Raroo". She used these aromatic leaves, all that she had, with no little art and tenderness. Warming them over the fire until the oil exuded, she would apply them to the hairy jowl of the girl, and anon to her furry forehead and cheeks.

While there is life there is hope is evidently Nelly's creed, and so she crunched and warmed the pungently odorous leaves, and rubbed the hands that had often smitten her in anger. Poor Nelly sighed piteously as she continued her work, while Tom massaged the body of the girl, hoping to expel the "debil-debil". His theory was, and is, that some man whom Little Jinny had known down about Hinchinbrook had died, and his "debil-debil all the same like dead man", had "sat down" in "Little Jinny's bingey"—hence her distended condition.

His efforts to cast out this personal "debil" were futile, and as the poor creature lapsed into unconsciousness he would blow gusty breaths upon her big black eyes. It was his method of revivification. In my ignorance I knew none more to the purpose. But it was all in vain. The great eyes of this specimen of uncivilized humanity clouded over, and then brightened. She moaned in response to Tom's well-intended but too forcible massaging. Nelly applied without ceasing the one means of relief that she possessed, the heated raroo leaf, to cheek and forehead, while we exhausted our woefully meagre stock of knowledge in endeavouring to ease the last moments of the dying.

But poor Little Jinny's creditor was not to be denied. He was exacting, cruelly exacting, imperious, implacable. He would have the uttermost farthing's worth of her poor, crude life.

Nelly might sigh and use the whole armful of raroo leaves; Tom might massage, and the others do their best, which was pitiably poor, and their uttermost, which was ever so mean and little, the Conquering Worm would have its victim. And so with a few long-drawn, gulping sighs, each at a longer interval than the last, until the final one, Little Jinny passed away as the sun touched the dark blue barrier of mountains across the channel to the west.

Then Nelly's sighs changed into a wail, in which the other members of the camp joined, a penetrating falsetto cry which continued for two days, mingled with the strong man's expression of woe, a low, weird yet not inharmonious hum. For two days they chanted the virtues of the dead, told of her likes and dislikes, and of their grief, crouching beside the blanket-covered form. Then they buried her in the smoky hut in which she lived, digging a shallow grave in the black sand, and there she rests with them.

Tom has put on the mourning of his tribe, and will not for several years eat of a certain fish associated with Little Jinny's original name. Nor can he bear to be reminded of her. The day after she was buried he spent the hours between daylight and sunset wandering about wherever Little Jinny had been wont, obliterating the tracks made by her feet. With the keenest of sight, which is one of the superior qualifications of the race, he discerned the tracks on the sandy, forest-clad flat, and rubbed them out with his foot.

When I ponder upon Nelly's raroo leaves and Tom's terrible and precise earnestness in blotting out the memory of the past, I am convinced that this race, despised and neglected of men, can be as devoted to one another as truly as we who are so superior to them in many attributes.

LAST OF THE LINE

The last King of Dunk Island—known to the whites as "Jimmy"—was a tall, lanky man, irreclaimably truculent, incapable of recognizing the dominance of those who bestowed his Christian name. Long after most of his fellows had submitted in a more or less kindly spirit to the o'ermastering race, Jimmy held aloof, and in his savage, self-reliant way, deemed himself a worthy foe of the best of them. Often he endeavoured to persuade his companions to join him in a policy of active resentment. Once, when remonstrated with on account of some offence against the rights of property, he assumed a hostile disposition, and calling upon others, took up a spear, determined if possible to rouse a revolt. Few in number, the whites could not permit their authority to be questioned, and a demonstration with a rifle silenced all show of opposition. Jimmy, disgusted with the docility of his fellows, departed, uttering wrath and threatenings, and was no more seen in the vicinity. This incident took place nearly twenty years ago on the mainland. "King Jimmy, the Irreconcilable", died a natural death. He does not sleep with his fathers on his native soil, but at Tam o' Shanter Point; nor are any of his acts and deeds remembered, save that which illustrates his hatred of the whites, and his bold and truculent spirit.

None of those who remain is equal to the last of the royal line in stature. Toby stands five feet seven and a half inches. Tom, five feet seven inches. Brow, five feet two and three-quarter inches, and Willie, five feet two inches. Tom's expanded chest measures thirty-six and a half inches, and Toby's thirty-six; Brow's, thirty-four and a half inches, and Willie's, thirty-four inches.

CHAPTER III

BLACKS possess acquirements which white people cannot success-fully imitate, are industrious in fashioning weapons and in the invention and practice of primitive forms of amusement, and are in many respects entertaining subjects to those who apply them-selves, though superficially, to the study of their habits and cus-toms. On the impulse of the moment, they are generous or cruel, erratic, purposeless, unstable as water.

A few anecdotes may perhaps throw unaccustomed light upon attributes not generally understood, and show that the Australian aboriginal, uncouth savage as he is, is not altogether devoid of smartness and good humour.

THE RAINBOW

One of childhood's most fascinating fables was, that at the places where the rainbow touched the earth would be found a bag of gold and glittering gems. Among some North Queensland blacks almost exactly the same fairy tale is current. "Muhr-amalee", remarked a boy, pointing to a rainbow which seemed to spring from the Island of Bedarra. "That fella no good. Hot, burning. Alonga my country too many. Come out alonga ground, bend over, go down. Subpose me go close up kill 'em along spear, run away and plant. Bi'mby come back, find plenty red stone, yalla stone. Fill 'em up dilly-bag. Old man bin tell 'em. Me no go close up along Muhr-amalee. Too fright!"

SWIMMING FEATS

In their endurance as long-distance swimmers, and in the ease with which they perform various incompatible operations in the water, there are few to equal the coastal blacks of North Queens-land. For a trifling consideration they will successfully undertake feats which prove that they are almost as much at home in deep water as upon land, and when put to the test their strength and hardihood are extraordinary.

During the Princess Charlotte Bay cyclone one of the survivors, after an absence of nearly twenty-four hours, came ashore. He explained that the boat of which he had been one of the crew was "drowned finish", and that the sea had taken him out towards the Barrier. He swam for a long time, and at last got tired and went to sleep, and for the best part of that frantic night he slept as he swam. Then the wind changed, and he came in with it, landing very little the worse. Others, on the same occasion, swam for fifteen and twenty hours; but Dick was the only one who went far out to sea, had a night's rest, landed fairly fresh, and seemed to accept the experience as a matter of course.

Again, three boys and a gin—Charley, Belle Vue, Tom and Mary—were sailing out to a reef in a little dinghy, when they sighted a turtle basking on the surface. Charley and Belle Vue jumped overboard and seized the turtle. It was a monster, and so strong that they called for help, and Tom plunged in to their assistance. Mary, frightened of being alone in the boat, also sprang overboard, taking her blanket with her, and the boat speedily sailed and drifted beyond reach. Charley and Belle Vue at once swam to a beacon marking a submerged reef about a mile away, but Tom and Mary, being caught in the current, were swept past the only available resting-place. They were eight miles from shore. Tom soon began to flounder, but Mary, keeping her heart and her precious blanket, cheered him on, and, changing her course, took a "fair wind down", as she afterwards said, towards a distant point of the mainland. Lifting the giant despair from her boy's shoulders with encouraging words, holding him up occasionally when he got tired, and clinging all the time to the only piece of personal property she possessed, Mary eventually landed in a quiet bay. Tom was so exhausted that she had to drag him up on the sand, and having made him comfortable with her safe but sodden blanket, she hurried into town to report the circumstances to the police. A boat was sent to the rescue of Charley and Belle Vue, still clinging to the beacon, and the derelict dinghy was picked up. Nothing was lost but the turtle.

THUNDER FACTORY

A boy who had visited towns, listening intently to a reverberating peal of thunder asked—"How make 'em that row, boss? He got big wheel?"

Home-keeping blacks have homely wits. Having no experience

of the rumble and rattle of traffic they ascribe to thunder a mysterious origin, and indicate, though with reserve, the very place where it is made. The swirl of a creek in the mainland has excavated a circular waterhole in a soft rock, brick red in colour. This hole is the local thunder factory, and the blacks were wont to hang fish-hooks across it from pieces of lawyer-cane, with the idea of ensnaring the young thunder before it had the chance of becoming big and formidable.

THE ORACLE

Divination by means of the intestines of animals is practised by the blacks in some parts of North Queensland. A young gin died suddenly on the lower Johnstone River. Immediately after, the young men of the camp went out hunting, bringing back a wallaby. The entrails were removed, and an old woman—the Atropos of the camp—stretched them between her fingers in half-yard lengths, simultaneously pronouncing the title of a tribe in the district. The tribe, the name of which was being uttered as the gut parted, was denounced as the source of the witchcraft which had occasioned the untimely death of the gin. Vengeance followed as a matter of course.

A REAL LETTER

Sam, a boy living in the Russell River scrub, spoke thus to his master—

"One fella boy, Dick, he come up fight along me four days."

"How you know, Sam?" asked the boss.

"Dick, he bin make 'em this one letter," replied Sam, picking up a palm-leaf from which all the leaflets save seven had been torn. Three of the seven had been turned down at the terminal point, and Sam continued his explanation. "He no come Monday, he no come Tuesday, he no come Wednesday, he come Thursday," indicating the first upright leaflet.

Sam said that he had an outstanding quarrel with Dick and had expected the challenge conveyed by the letter he had picked up on the track that morning.

When Thursday came Dick appeared well armed, and the two had an earnest, honourable and exhilarating combat and parted good friends.

EVERYTHING FOR A NAME

To the blacks of North Queensland there is a great deal in a name.

When a piccaninny is born, the first request is—"You put 'em (or make 'em) name belonga that fella!" When a strange boy, a myall, "comes in" he wants a name, and until he gets it he is as forlorn as an ownerless dog. Anything does, from "Adam" to "Yellow-belly" or "Belle Vue". He seems as proud of the new possession as a white boy of his first pair of trousers, and soon forgets his original name. "What name belonga you, your country?" I asked an alert boy. "I bin lose 'em; I no find 'em. Boss, he catch 'em alonga paper!"

HONOUR AND GLORY

As we sat enjoying the cool moonlight, Mickie announced that Jinny desired an interview.

"All right, Mickie, tell her come along."

"No, bi'mby. When finish wash 'em plate."

That duty disposed of, Mickie—"Now, boss?"

"Well, come along, Jinny. What you want?"

"No, boss; I no want talk alonga you; Mickie humbug you. What for you humbug boss, Mickie?"

Jinny was bashful, for the subject was momentous, touched her pride, and had been depressing her gaiety for many weeks. Presently she came and with emphatic deliberation said—"Boss—no—good—missis—call—out—Jinny! Jinny! when want wash 'em plate. More better you hammer 'em that fella, all asame Essie!"

Jinny did not wish that the missis should be chastised, but that she should be summoned to the plate-washing with the pomp and ceremony of a dinner-gong, as the maid used to do in a more civilized home.

AWKWARD CROSS-EXAMINATION

Mickie and Jinny being privileged became familiar, and spoke all sorts of confidences in the ears of their mistress. Visitors came, an old friend and her daughters, a blonde and a brunette. The contrast in the types of the girls puzzled Mickie. He took an early opportunity to cross-examine one from whom he thought he could obtain confidential information.

"What Gwen sister belonga Glad?" he asked.

"Yes, Mickie."

"Same mother?" queried Mickie.

"Yes, of course."

Then came without hesitation or reserve the dumb-founding question: "Same father?"

Some may sneer when absolute originality is claimed for the following little anecdote, for almost a facsimile of it happens to be among the most time-honoured of jests. Rounding Clump Point in a light centre-board cutter, the boss, who was steering, asked Willie, whose local knowledge was being relied on: "Any stone here, Willie?"

"Yes," was the response, "one fella."

The words were yet on the lips of the boy when the centre-board jumped with a clang.

"Why you no tell me before?" angrily remonstrated the boss.

Willie—"No more. Only one fella. You catch 'em!"

SAW THE JOKE

Our blacks saw "friends" on the mainland beach, and lit two signal fires. Mickie said, "Me tell 'em that fella bring basket." Cross-examined, he had to admit that the two fires merely signified a general invitation to his mainland friends to come across. Then—"That fella got 'em basket, me get 'em."

A friend doubted the range of the black's vision, which was truly telescopic, as we frequently verified with a pair of powerful fieldglasses, but not to be thought inferior in this respect, he solemnly declared that he saw Jinny's cousin on the beach strike a light for his pipe. At first the irony of the remark was not appreciated, then Jinny (after vainly peering across the sea), saw the joke and gave a wild exhilarating exhibition of amusement. She sat down and rolled about shouting and screeching, hardly able to tell Mickie the fun, and when he was let into it the pantomime was the more extravagant. The outburst continued throughout the day at intervals, Jinny apologizing for her boisterousness with reiterations—"Misser Johnssing say he been see 'em cousin belonga me light 'em pipe!" Jinny still rehearses the story at frequent intervals, and with hysterical outbursts.

ROYAL BLANKETS

Nelly was extravagantly fond of pictures; anything, from an illustrated advertisement up, pleased her, and when the subject was not very obvious to her she would indifferently gaze lovingly upon it upside down. A pair of fine photographs of King Edward and Queen Alexandra in all the sumptuousness of their coronation robes was shown to her, and she was told that "fella King belonga white man. That fella Queen wife, you know." Putting her democratic forefinger on each alternately, Nelly said: "That fella man; that fella missis! My word! Got 'nother kind blanket!"

AN APT RETORT

A meeting between a steamer smartly captained and a sailing boat steered by a smart black boy familiar with the rules of the road at sea was taking place. The steamer having too much way on, the boat narrowly escaped being run down.

"Why didn't you keep out of the road?" yelled the captain. "Why do you let the nigger steer?"

Tom in reply, "Why you no luff up? You got blurry steamer, I no got 'em!"

MAGIC THAT DID NOT WORK

Under the spell of the first sensations of Christianity, Lucy found and took unauthorized possession of a gold cross. Retiring to a secluded spot on the bank of the river, she hung the cross to a string round her neck, imagining it to be a charm, by the magic of which she would become a white girl. Twenty-four hours of patient expectancy passed without any change in Lucy's complexion, so she lost faith in the golden symbol, and bartered it to a Malay pieman for cakes. Then good Christian folks charged her with the theft of the cross, and the pieman with receiving it, knowing it to have been stolen. Lucy was pardoned, but the pagan went to prison.

ANTI-CLIMAX

A boy was asked if he thought Jimmy Governor (a notorious desperado who had given the New South Wales police much trouble) ought to be hanged. "Baal. No fear hang 'em; too good."

"What you do then?"

"Me! me punch 'em nose!"

A FATEFUL BARGAIN

A squatter, travelling on foot with his black boy, came to a river almost a "banker", and there was no recourse but to swim. After

Charcoal had taken a couple of trips with the clothes, the Boss told the boy to swim alongside him, in case of emergency. Halfway across, just as the boss was feeling that there was some risk in swimming a flooded river in which were many snags, Charcoal cheerily observed—

"Suppose you drowned finish, boss, you gib me you pipe?"

Summing up all the possibilities in a second, the boss gasped out —"No; you bin get pipe when I'm across!"

The boy's aid was prompt and effective.

EXCUSABLE BIAS

Two of the beachcombing class resumed an oft-recurring discussion on the seaworthiness of their respective dinghies. Tom, the silent black boy, a more experienced boatman than either, listened as he watched his own frail bark canoe dancing like a feather in response to every ripple.

"Tom!" shouted one of the disputants, "suppose you want to go out in big wind and big sea, which boat you take? This one belonga me, or that one belonga your boss?"

Tom glanced at the boats with the eye of an expert, paused in the exercise of his judgment, and said with emphasis—"Me take 'em my boat!"

THE TRIAL SCENE

"Boiling Down", a boy with a not very reputable past, had once stood his trial for a serious offence. On returning to his free hills, he was wont to describe with rare art the trial scene.

Clearing a patch of ground, he would place one chip to represent the judge—"big fella master"; a small chip would be His Honour's associate; twelve chips were the jurymen; three were the lawyers; a big chip between two others was Boiling Down with attendant policemen, and many scattered about stood for the audience.

Having arranged his properties, the boy would proceed.

"Big fella master, he bin say—'Boinin' Down, you hear me? You guinty—you not guinty?' Me bin say 'Guinty!'"

At this point Boiling Down invariably broke into such paroxysms of laughter that further utterance was impossible. Often as he attempted it, his narrative of the proceedings ended in such violent mirth that his hearers could not restrain themselves from joining in. They were obliged to acknowledge that he looked upon the affair as the funniest incident of his life.

Mickie is apt at repeating the sayings of others. Often his rendering of a commonplace becomes humorous by reason of a slight verbal twist. As the boys toiled to supplant a glorious strip of primeval jungle by a few formal rows of bananas, the boss, glancing over the ruined vegetation, remarked in encouraging tones—

"Well, we are getting on fine! Getting on like a house on fire!"

For half an hour or so the boys hacked and chopped away at the vines and trees, and then Mickie swept the scene with a comprehensive glance, saying—"We getting on good fella now. All a same burning down house."

"AND YOU, TOO"

Two ladies, who were wont to meet at infrequent intervals, spent the delightful morning in the settlement of arrears of gossip, while two black gins sat in the shade of a mango-tree, smoked incessantly and did nothing placidly. At dinner-time the latter began to chatter volubly, and the mistress of the house, in an outburst of vicarious energy, called from the veranda—"Come, Topsy—Come, Rosey. You do nothing all day. You two fella talk all the time."

Rosey—"Yes: me fella yabber, yabber, plenty—all asame white woman."

PARADISE

The beliefs of blacks on the subject of "the other-where" seem to be varied and adjustable to individual likes and predilections. Some have no faith whatever in statements as to existence following upon death. Others assert that a delightful country is reached after a long and pleasant journey, that there reunion with relatives and friends takes place, and happiness is in store for all, good and bad alike.

An intelligent boy was asked if after death all went along the same road to the aboriginal paradise. He was reminded that he was a good fellow, and that one of the members of the camp was notoriously a rogue.

"Mootee go along a you, all asame place? That fella no good. You good fella."

"Yes," he answered. "All one track me fella go. Good track—blenty tchugar-bag, plenty hegg, plenty wallaby, close up. You no wan' run about. Catch 'em blenty close up. Bi'mby me go long way. Me come more better country—blenty everything. Father belonga me sit down. He got two good young fella gins. My word, good one gins. He say—'Hello! you come up? You sit down here altogether. Two fella good gins belonga you!'"

This was paradise!

CHAPTER IV

AND THIS OUR LIFE

I would admonish the world that all persons, indifferently, are not fit for this sort of diversion.

WHEREAS the average town-dweller could not endure the commonplaces of nature which entertain me, rouse my wonder, enliven my imagination, and gratify my inmost thoughts, so his pursuits are to me devoid of purpose, insipid, dismally unsatisfactory. To one whose everyday admission (apology if you like) is that he is not as other men are—fond of society and of society's occupations, pastimes, refinements, and illusions—the unsoiled jungle is more desirable than all the prim parks and clipped gardens; all this amplitude of time and space than the one "crowded hour".

Here I came to my birthright—a heritage of nothing save the most glorious of all possessions: freedom—freedom beyond the dreams of most men in its comprehensiveness and exactitude. These haphazard notes refer to the exercise of rare independence. They reveal my puny efforts to be none other than myself. So tranquil, so uniform are our days, that but for the diary—the civilized substitute for the notched stick—count of them might be lost. And this extorts yet another confession. One year, Good Friday passed, and Easter-time had progressed to the joyful Monday, ere cognizance of the season came. Speedy is the descent to the automaton. A mechanical mis-entry in the diary threw all the orderly days of the week into a whirling jumble. We knew not Wednesday from Thursday, nor Thursday from Friday, though we calculated and checked notes of the transactions and traits of successive days.

To what purpose was the effort to memorize one day from another when all were precisely alike in colour and uneventfulness? Each day had been blue—radiantly blue—nothing more. And the entries in the diary set at naught dogmatic assertions of disproof. But the steamer cuts a deep weekly notch. We jolted into it and became harmonized once more with the rigid calendar of the workaday world.

Thus we keep the noiseless tenor of our way, finding in life if not great and gaudy pleasures, at least content and relief from many of the vexations that gnaw away the lives of the multitude. Though it was acknowledged a long time ago to be an abominable thing for a man to commend his ways; though his mode of living may not commend itself to others; though it may seem blank and colourless, thin and watery, devoid of expectation, and the hope of fame, name, and that kind of success which comes of the acquirement of riches, yet—and in a spirit of thankfulness be it said—the obscure and minor part the writer plays in the tragic-comedy of life affords gratification. He does what he likes to do. He frankly confesses that he sought isolation because of the lack of those qualities which make for dutiful citizenship, because of indifference to the ordinary enchantments of the kaleidoscopic world, not because of any lack of appreciation of the wisdom of the majority. He has dared to be what he is, rather than submit to be pulled this way and that on the rack of fashion and custom.

Remember that "the measure of choosing well is whether a man likes what he has chosen". Other men have other ranks to take, other fates to command. Do not politicians and publicists; professional men and princes of trade; those who toil for others, with brain or hands; the charitable and the miserly; those who pine if removed from the noise and breath of the crowd; those who spend their days in meditation and study; those who live conscientiously every moment in "the gateway of the life eternal"; those who are at enmity to law and order; the honest toiler and the imposter, the thief and the rogue, each respectively find pleasure in the particular walk of life he elects to take? "Each to the favourite happiness attends." When God gave manna to His people, every Israelite found in it what best pleased him. "The young tasted bread, the old honey, and the children oil." No doubt an expert burglar feels as keen a sense of joy in the planning and execution of a deed of darkness demanding originality, skill, daring and resourcefulness, as does the humane surgeon in the performance of an operation for the salvation of a valuable life, or as does his lordship the bishop in the delivery of a homily overflowing with persuasive eloquence. The burglar has his appreciation of pleasure, and the others theirs; and so long as the pleasures of the individual are not immoral and dishonourable, do not trespass upon the rights and liberties of others, let each pursue that which allures.

In the long run he will find himself responsible to himself; and if his days have been ill spent, and his opportunities slighted, his the punishment and the remorse. But—

If the day and the night are such that you greet them with joy, and life emits a fragrance like flowers and sweet-scented herbs, is more elastic, more starry, more immortal—that is your success.